Commercial Crime Insurance and Financial Institution Bonds

Commercial Crime Insurance and Financial Institution Bonds

Arthur L. Flitner, CPCU, ARM, AIC
Assistant Vice President
American Institute for CPCU/Insurance Institute of America

Jerome Trupin, CPCU, CLU, ChFC
Partner
Trupin Insurance Services

Carol B. Szender, CPCU
President
Szender & Associates

Second Edition • Seventh Printing

American Institute for Chartered Property Casualty
Underwriters/Insurance Institute of America
720 Providence Road, Suite 100
Malvern, Pennsylvania 19355-3433

© 2002
American Institute for Chartered Property Casualty Underwriters/Insurance Institute of America

All rights reserved. This book or any part thereof may not be reproduced without the written permission of the copyright holder.

Unless otherwise apparent, examples used in AICPCU/IIA materials related to this course are based on hypothetical situations and are for educational purposes only. The characters, persons, products, services, and organizations described in these examples are fictional. Any similarity or resemblance to any other character, person, product, services, or organization is merely coincidental. AICPCU/IIA is not responsible for such coincidental or accidental resemblances.

This material may contain Internet Web site links external to AICPCU/IIA. AICPCU/IIA neither approves nor endorses any information, products, or services to which any external Web sites refer. Nor does AICPCU/IIA control these Web sites' content or the procedures for Web site content development.

AICPCU/IIA specifically disclaims any implied warranties of merchantability or fitness for a particular purpose. No warranty may be created or extended by sales representatives or written sales materials.

AICPCU/IIA materials related to this course are provided with the understanding that AICPCU/IIA is not engaged in rendering legal, accounting, or other professional service. Nor is AICPCU/IIA explicitly or implicitly stating that any of the processes, procedures, or policies described in the materials are the only appropriate ones to use. The advice and strategies contained herein may not be suitable for every situation.

Second Edition • Seventh Printing • September 2007

Library of Congress Control Number: 2001098670
ISBN 978-0-89462-155-0

Foreword

The American Institute for Chartered Property Casualty Underwriters and the Insurance Institute of America (the Institutes) are independent, not-for-profit organizations committed to expanding the knowledge of professionals in risk management, insurance, financial services, and related fields through education and research.

In accordance with our belief that professionalism is grounded in education, experience, and ethical behavior, the Institutes provide a wide range of educational programs designed to meet the needs of individuals working in risk management and property-casualty insurance. The American Institute offers the Chartered Property Casualty Underwriter (CPCU®) professional designation, designed to provide a broad understanding of the property-casualty insurance industry. CPCU students may select either a commercial or a personal risk management and insurance focus, depending on their professional needs.

The Insurance Institute of America (IIA) offers designations and certificate programs in a variety of disciplines, including the following:

- Claims
- Commercial underwriting
- Fidelity and surety bonding
- General insurance
- Insurance accounting and finance
- Insurance information technology
- Insurance production and agency management
- Insurance regulation and compliance
- Management
- Marine insurance
- Personal insurance
- Premium auditing
- Quality insurance services
- Reinsurance
- Risk management
- Surplus lines

You may choose to take a single course to fill a knowledge gap, complete a program leading to a designation, or take multiple courses and programs throughout your career. No matter which approach you choose, you will gain practical knowledge and skills that will contribute to your professional growth and enhance your education and qualifications in the expanding insurance market. In addition, many CPCU and IIA courses qualify for credits toward certain associate, bachelor's, and master's degrees at several prestigious colleges and universities, and all CPCU and IIA courses carry college credit recommendations from the American Council on Education.

The American Institute for CPCU was founded in 1942 through a collaborative effort between industry professionals and academics, led by faculty members at The Wharton School of the University of Pennsylvania. In 1953, the American Institute for CPCU merged with the Insurance Institute of America, which was founded in 1909 and which remains the oldest continuously functioning national organization offering educational programs for the property-casualty insurance business.

The Insurance Research Council (IRC), founded in 1977, helps the Institutes fulfill the research aspect of their mission. A division of the Institutes, the IRC is supported by industry members. This not-for-profit research organization examines public policy issues of interest to property-casualty insurers, insurance customers, and the general public. IRC research reports are distributed widely to insurance-related organizations, public policy authorities, and the media.

The Institutes strive to provide current, relevant educational programs in formats and delivery methods that meet the needs of insurance professionals and the organizations that employ them. Institute textbooks are an essential component of the education we provide. Each book is designed to clearly and concisely provide the practical knowledge and skills you need to enhance your job performance and career. The content is developed by the Institutes in collaboration with risk management and insurance professionals and members of the academic community. We welcome comments from our students and course leaders; your feedback helps us continue to improve the quality of our study materials.

Peter L. Miller, CPCU
President and CEO
American Institute for CPCU
Insurance Institute of America

Preface

Commercial Crime Insurance and Financial Institution Bonds covers many practical topics necessary to understand crime insurance. It includes information about ISO/SAA crime coverage, underwriting and loss control, and claims. This text is required reading to prepare for the AFSB 153 examination, one of five examinations for the Associate in Fidelity and Surety Bonding (AFSB) designation, which is administered and awarded by the American Institute for CPCU/Insurance Institute of America. A course guide accompanies this text.

Each chapter covers a separate topic and should be studied for approximately three hours when preparing for the exam. Some chapters are longer than others or cover complex material, so you might want to adjust your study time, depending on your background and familiarity with each topic.

Educational objectives, which describe what you are expected to be able to do after studying each chapter, are contained in the course guide that accompanies this text. The course guide also includes exercises for each chapter and a practice examination.

Words and phrases that are key to your understanding of the material appear in boldface type. A definition or an explanation accompanies each boldfaced key word or phrase.

Exhibits and other items appear throughout the text. You should study all exhibits to gain a complete understanding of the material.

We are grateful to the people and organizations that assisted in planning, writing and compiling, and reviewing material for this text. Members of the Publications and Curriculum Departments of the AICPCU/IIA were tireless in their efforts to produce this text.

The members of the AFSB Advisory Committee served as curriculum advisers, technical reviewers, and cheerleaders in completing the first edition of this text. Those members are:

John P. Coonan
David L. Hixenbaugh, CPCU, AFSB
William H. Kelley, Jr.
Ronald M. Metcho, CPCU, ARM, AAI
Karen Mummert, AAI
Robert Olausen
Ralph V. Pulver, AFSB
Jane E. Sjoman, CPCU, AFSB, ARe

Special recognition goes to the following people:

- Arthur L. Flitner, CPCU, ARM, AIC, who coauthored Chapters 1, 2, and 3 of this text, reviewed the entire text, and provided valuable recommendations to improve the design and content of the material. He also took the initiative to provide the changes in the second edition as a result of changes in the ISO forms.
- Jerome Trupin, CPCU, CLU, ChFC, who coauthored Chapters 1, 2, and 3 of this text.

Several chapters of this text describe standard policy forms and endorsements that were developed and filed on behalf of their member insurers by either Insurance Services Office (ISO) or the Surety Association of America (SAA). Both of these organizations generously provided information describing their products.

In addition, the following individuals reviewed manuscripts or provided technical expertise to develop the first edition of the text:

J. Julia Awad	Lisa Kelly
Steve Balmer	David Lewis
Joseph Burke	Eugene M. Mazzilli
John Furletti	Debbie McManigle
Robert Gallagher	Dolores A. Parr
John Hawley	Melinda Price
Jeff Hodges	Rich Thomas
James R. Jones	Rob Weldy

Their comments provided continuity among the chapters, and their experience contributed greatly to the content.

Thanks go to Audrey R. Rhodes, CPCU, ARe, AIS, who updated the ISO Crime Endorsements Appendix and was helpful in proofing the entire manuscript in preparation for the publication of the second edition.

A good textbook requires that material be continually updated and enhanced. We monitor and evaluate developments that affect the surety business and incorporate those developments into future editions. We would also like to gather information from you. We welcome your opinions and suggestions.

For more information about the Institutes' programs, please call our Customer Support Department at (800) 644-2101, e-mail us at customersupport@cpcuiia.org, or visit our Web site at www.aicpcu.org.

Lowell S. Young

Contributing Authors

The American Institute for CPCU and the Insurance Institute of America acknowledge with deep appreciation the work of the following contributing authors:

Doris Hoopes, CPCU, AIC, ARe
Project Manager
WR Berkley Corporation

Pamela A. Lyons, AIIC, FIIC, CRM
Consultant

Contents

1 Commercial Crime Insurance — 1.1
- Overview of Commercial Crime Insurance — 1.1
- Basic Crime Insuring Agreements — 1.3
- Exclusions — 1.22
- Summary — 1.29

2 Commercial Crime Insurance, Continued — 2.1
- Optional Crime Insuring Agreements — 2.1
- Crime Policy Conditions — 2.11
- Employee Dishonesty Coverage — 2.20
- Summary — 2.23
- Appendix: Summary of Selected ISO Crime Endorsements — 2.25

3 Financial Institution Bonds — 3.1
- Form 24 for Banks and Savings Institutions — 3.2
- Bonds for Other Financial Institutions — 3.9
- Other Financial Institution Bonds and Policies — 3.13
- Summary — 3.15
- Appendix: Summary of Riders for SAA Financial Institution Bonds and Policies — 3.17

4 Underwriting and Loss Control — 4.1
- Sources of Underwriting Information — 4.1
- Underwriting Considerations — 4.12
- Additional Underwriting Considerations for Financial Institutions — 4.15
- Employee Theft/Dishonesty Exposures — 4.26
- Employee Theft/Dishonesty Loss Control — 4.28
- Summary — 4.37

5 Underwriting and Loss Control, Continued — 5.1
- Physical Security Considerations — 5.1
- Computer Fraud Considerations — 5.18
- Extortion Considerations — 5.22
- Pricing — 5.25
- Summary — 5.28

6 Claim Handling — 6.1
- Claim Management — 6.1
- Unfair Claim Settlement Practices Acts — 6.3
- Claim Process — 6.4
- Rights of Recovery — 6.22
- Summary — 6.24

Index — 1

Chapter 1

Commercial Crime Insurance, Part I

This text describes the various kinds of commercial crime insurance that are commonly available in the United States, including financial institution bonds. Financial institution bonds are crime insurance policies designed to meet the specific needs of banks, savings and loan associations, securities dealers, insurance companies, and other types of financial institutions.

Crime insurance encompasses many different coverages, but the most significant crime coverage for most policyholders is employee theft (or employee dishonesty) insurance, which protects organizations against theft (or other dishonest acts) committed by their employees. Employee theft (or dishonesty) insurance evolved from fidelity bonds, which were a branch of suretyship. The traditional connection of employee theft or dishonesty insurance to fidelity bonds is evident in financial institution bonds, which are still called "bonds" and still use the term "fidelity."

The contents of this text can be summarized as follows:

- Chapter 1 of this text describes the employee theft coverage provided by the commercial crime insurance forms of Insurance Services Office, as well as six additional crime insuring agreements contained in those forms.
- Chapter 2 continues the discussion of commercial crime insurance by examining several optional insuring agreements that can be added to the commercial crime forms by endorsement.
- Chapter 3 discusses financial institution bonds.
- Chapters 4 and 5 describe underwriting and loss control considerations.
- Chapter 6 addresses the handling of crime insurance claims.

Because of the predominance of employee theft (or dishonesty) insurance, the emphasis of discussion in most of these chapters is often on that coverage.

OVERVIEW OF COMMERCIAL CRIME INSURANCE

In the United States, crime causes more property loss, in total, than any other insurable peril. The exact total is unknown and perhaps unknowable, but several years ago the United States Chamber of Commerce estimated the total of losses caused by employee dishonesty alone at $40 billion a year and growing.[1] Fire losses in the United States for 1998, in contrast, totaled $12.3 billion.[2]

Crime insurance is not the only source of insurance for crime losses. Motor vehicle theft, a widespread crime exposure, is insured under automobile policies. Cargo theft, another significant crime exposure, is insured under inland and ocean marine policies. Theft losses to other property can be insured by the Causes of Loss—Special Form, by various inland marine forms, and by the Businessowners Special Property Coverage Form.

However, most commercial property and inland marine policies exclude loss of money and securities entirely or provide only nominal amounts of coverage for those items. And few policies, other than crime insurance, provide any coverage for theft committed by employees. In addition, theft is not a covered peril under the Causes of Loss—Basic Form or the Causes of Loss—Broad Form and is sometimes excluded by endorsement from the Causes of Loss—Special Form. To fill these gaps, crime insurance can be used to cover money, securities, and other property against various crime perils, such as theft, premises burglary, safe burglary, robbery, computer fraud, and extortion. Crime insurance can also be used to cover money and securities against noncriminal causes of loss.

This chapter examines the crime insurance forms that Insurance Services Office (ISO) introduced in the year 2000. These forms can be used for insuring most types of organizations other than financial institutions such as banks, stockbrokers, and insurance companies.

FOR FURTHER THOUGHT

Crime Risk Control

Risk control measures play an important role in treating crime loss exposures, regardless of whether an organization insures its crime exposures. An organization that chooses not to insure its crime loss exposures has a direct incentive to exercise risk control. An organization that insures its crime exposures also has incentives to exercise crime control measures because insurers often grant premium discounts if the insured implements certain crime control measures. In some cases, an insurer will not provide crime insurance *unless* the insured exercises certain crime loss control measures.

Some crime loss exposures are not insurable. In such cases, risk control takes on added importance. For example, product forgery—the unauthorized use of a firm's logos or trademarks—is estimated to cost American businesses as much as $200 billion a year. Not only does the victimized firm lose sales, but its reputation for quality may be tarnished by low-quality knockoffs.* Although the product forgery exposure is outside the scope of commercial crime insurance, it can be treated by noninsurance risk management techniques.

*David Stipp, "Farewell, My Logo," *Fortune Magazine*, May 27, 1996, pp. 128–135.

The ISO commercial crime program includes ten basic crime coverage forms and policies, shown in Exhibit 1-1, plus numerous endorsements. The coverage forms are designed to be added to a commercial package policy, whereas the policies are designed to stand alone as monoline crime policies. The principal difference between the coverage forms and the policies is that the policies include the six conditions of the Common Policy Conditions form (IL 00 17) that is attached to commercial package policies.

Each coverage form or policy comes in two versions: a "discovery form" and a "loss sustained form." Basically, a discovery form covers losses that are discovered during the policy period (even though they may have occurred earlier), and a loss sustained form covers losses that are actually sustained during the policy period and discovered no later than one year after the policy expires. The "discovery" and "loss sustained" coverage triggers are described in more detail later in this chapter.

EXHIBIT 1-1

ISO Crime Forms and Policies

Commercial Crime Coverage Form (Discovery Form) CR 00 20
Commercial Crime Coverage Form (Loss Sustained Form) CR 00 21
Commercial Crime Policy (Discovery Form) CR 00 22
Commercial Crime Policy (Loss Sustained Form) CR 00 23

Government Crime Coverage Form (Discovery Form) CR 00 24
Government Crime Coverage Form (Loss Sustained Form) CR 00 25
Government Crime Policy (Discovery Form) CR 00 26
Government Crime Policy (Loss Sustained Form) CR 00 27

Employee Theft and Forgery Policy (Discovery Form) CR 00 28
Employee Theft and Forgery Policy (Loss Sustained Form) CR 00 29

The first four coverage forms and policies listed in Exhibit 1-1 are designed for insuring any type of nongovernmental commercial or nonprofit entity other than financial institutions such as banks, savings and loan associations, credit unions, securities dealers, investment bankers, and insurance companies. The next four coverage forms and policies listed in Exhibit 1-1 are designed for insuring governmental entities, such as states, counties, public utilities, fire districts, transit authorities, state universities, school districts, and boards of education. The last two policies listed in Exhibit 1-1 are designed for insureds that wish to buy only (1) employee theft coverage and (2) forgery or alteration coverage.

BASIC CRIME INSURING AGREEMENTS

The commercial crime forms and policies listed in Exhibit 1-1 each contain the following insuring agreements:

1. Employee Theft
2. Forgery or Alteration
3. Inside the Premises—Theft of Money and Securities
4. Inside the Premises—Robbery or Safe Burglary of Other Property

5. Outside the Premises
6. Computer Fraud
7. Money Orders and Counterfeit Paper Currency

The four government crime forms and policies contain the same insuring agreements listed above except that the government forms and policies contain two employee theft agreements: one applies on a per loss basis and the other applies on a per employee basis. The last two policies listed in Exhibit 1-1, as their names imply, contain only insuring agreements 1 and 2 listed above.

The sections that follow describe the seven basic crime insuring agreements found in the commercial crime forms and policies, along with the policy provisions that are primarily or exclusively applicable to each particular insuring agreement. Significant differences in the government crime forms are described in text boxes that supplement the main discussion.

Employee Theft

Loosely speaking, the **employee theft** insuring agreement covers theft from an employer by its own employees. Exhibit 1-2 summarizes the key elements of employee theft coverage, and the discussion that follows provides a more complete description of the coverage.

EXHIBIT 1-2

Summary of Employee Theft Coverage

Cause of Loss	"Theft" committed by any "employee"
Property Covered	"Money," "securities," and "other property"
Where Coverage Applies	U.S. (including its territories and possessions), Puerto Rico, and Canada, plus ninety-day worldwide travel extension *

* In the government crime forms, the policy territory for employee theft coverage does not include Canada except when the ninety-day worldwide travel extension applies.

Covered Cause of Loss

The covered cause of loss is *"theft" committed by an "employee."* The policy definitions of "theft" and "employee" are therefore instrumental in defining the scope of employee theft coverage.

"Theft"

The policy defines **theft** as follows:

> "Theft" means the unlawful taking of "money", "securities" or "other property" to the deprivation of the Insured.

The crime coverage forms of the prior commercial crime program jointly developed by ISO and the Surety Association of America (SAA) covered employee *dishonesty* instead of employee *theft*. The current Crime Protection Policy filed by the SAA (which will be discussed in Chapter 2) and some independently filed crime policies still use the employee dishonesty approach. In most cases, losses that would have been covered as employee dishonesty are also covered as employee theft. However, the two terms are not completely equivalent. The present discussion will focus on employee theft, and Chapter 2 will examine employee dishonesty coverage and compare it with employee theft coverage.

A common misconception about the definition of employee theft is that proof of unlawful taking requires conviction of the employee. In reality, the ISO forms do not even require that employee theft claims be reported to the police. The act must be unlawful, but the proof does not have to meet the requirement that would be needed to obtain a criminal conviction. Rather, the standard of a preponderance of the evidence would apply, as in most civil cases. *Black's Law Dictionary* does not define "unlawful taking," but it defines "unlawful act" as "[c]onduct that is not authorized by law; a violation of a civil or criminal law."[3]

> **FOR FURTHER THOUGHT**
>
> **Employee Theft Coverage That Requires Criminal Conviction**
>
> Unlike standard employee theft forms, some independently developed forms require conviction of the dishonest employee to trigger coverage. These limited forms are usually purchased by insureds that are unable to obtain standard employee theft or dishonesty coverage.
>
> Such a form, for example, might provide coverage for "any act of larceny or embezzlement established by criminal prosecution and conviction." This is much narrower coverage than standard employee theft coverage. Convictions are hard to obtain. Even when clear evidence of wrongdoing exists, public prosecutors are often unwilling to spend their limited resources on what they regard as minor crimes. Furthermore, a plea bargain to a lesser felony may not satisfy the requirement of conviction for embezzlement or larceny.

"Employee"

The policy definition of "employee" is much longer than the definition of "theft" and therefore is only summarized here. According to the definition, a person must meet all three of the following criteria in order to be considered an employee:

1. The person must be currently employed by the insured or an ex-employee who was terminated in the past thirty days.
2. The person must be compensated by the insured in salary, wages, or commissions.
3. The person must be subject to the control and direction of the insured.

Temporary Employees The definition explicitly *includes* personnel furnished temporarily to the insured by employment contractors either to substitute for permanent employees who are on leave or to meet seasonal or short-term workload conditions. Such temporary employees are included as employees while performing services for the insured and are subject to the insured's direction and control. However, such temporary personnel are *excluded* while having care and custody of property outside the insured's premises.

Persons Excluded   The definition of employee specifically excludes "any agent, broker, person leased to you [the named insured] by a labor leasing firm, factor, commission merchant, consignee, independent contractor or representative of the same general character." In addition to eliminating leased employees (regular workers who are nominally employed by a labor-leasing firm but subject to day-to-day control by the insured firm that leases the workers), this clause eliminates various persons who fit the description of agent or independent contractor. Such persons could include brokers, factors, commission merchants, and similar representatives of the insured who perform duties similar to those often performed by employees and who may present a serious theft exposure.

Standard endorsements are available to broaden the definition of employee to include various individuals, such as leased employees, agents and their employees, noncompensated officers, students, volunteer workers, and the spouse and children of building managers. Including such individuals as employees can be very important for some firms. For example, loss caused by a real estate manager who misappropriates rent collections would not be covered if the real estate manager was an independent contractor—unless the manager or the real estate management firm was included in the definition of employee by endorsement. Two other endorsements are available to add any other person or entity: CR 25 02 (Include Designated Agents as Employees) and CR 25 41 (Include Designated Persons or Classes of Persons as Employees). Both endorsements contain blank spaces that can be filled in with whatever names the insured and the insurer agree to include.

Directors and Officers   The definition of employee excludes the insured's directors or trustees except while performing duties usual to an employee. Corporate officers are covered because they are also employees.

A question arises in connection with closely held corporations where some corporate officers are also the controlling stockholders of the corporation. Because the definition of employee requires that an employee be subject to the insured's control, insurers frequently take the position that controlling stockholders do not meet the definition of employee even if they are corporate officers and actively involved in the business. The reasoning is that an insured corporation cannot be said to control stockholders/officers who themselves, by virtue of their stock ownership, control the corporation.

In one case, two corporate officers who were the sole officers, directors, and stockholders of the corporation had engaged in dishonest acts that had caused losses to the corporation and personal gain to the officers. The court upheld the insurer's contention that, as the alter egos of the corporation, the two stockholders were not subject to the corporation's control and were therefore not covered employees.[4] Not all other courts have followed this decision, reasoning that the insurer could have specifically excluded controlling stockholders if it had wished to do so.[5]

The dishonest acts of controlling stockholders can be excluded by endorsement when a policy is issued on corporations with controlling stockholders. The endorsement, titled Exclude Designated Persons or Classes of Persons or Employees (CR 25 01), can also be used to eliminate coverage for other employees or classes of employees.

Blanket Versus Schedule Coverage   The employee theft insuring agreement in the ISO commercial crime forms covers theft committed by any person who meets the definition of employee. Thus, the employee theft insuring agreement provides what has traditionally been called "blanket" coverage, in contrast with "schedule" coverage, which limits coverage to theft committed by employees whose name or position is listed in the policy. As will be discussed in Chapter 2, the ISO crime program includes an optional insuring agreement for employee theft coverage on a name schedule basis or a position schedule basis. Virtually all employers prefer the blanket approach.

Covered Property

The employee theft insuring agreement covers loss of or damage to "money," "securities," and "other property." The policy definitions of these terms are paraphrased below.

- **Money** is defined as currency, coins, and bank notes in current use and having a face value; and travelers checks, register checks, and money orders held for sale to the public.
- **Securities** are defined as negotiable and nonnegotiable instruments or contracts representing either "money" or other property. Examples of securities include tokens, tickets, revenue stamps and other stamps in current use (including unused value in a postage meter), and evidences of debt issued in connection with charge or credit cards other than cards issued by the insured.
- **Other property** is defined as all tangible property other than money and securities that has intrinsic value and that the coverage form or policy does not exclude. "Tangible" is an important qualification. Dictionaries define tangible to mean "possible to touch." Copyrights, patents, intellectual property, and other valuable intangible items are all "property," but they are not *tangible* property.

Limit of Insurance

The most that the insurer will pay under the employee theft insuring agreement depends on the Limit of Insurance provision and the policy definition of "occurrence." For purposes of employee theft coverage, the definition of occurrence is "all loss caused by, or involving, one or more 'employees', whether the result of a single act or series of acts." According to the Limit of Insurance provision, the most that the insurer will pay for loss in any one occurrence is the limit of insurance shown in the declarations for employee theft. Thus, if the applicable limit of insurance is $100,000, the most the insurer would be required to pay for one embezzlement—regardless of how many employees might have been involved in the crime—is $100,000.

Note that the limit of liability applies to a single act or a series of acts. In one case, the bookkeeper of a small insurance agency embezzled $190,000 by pocketing cash receipts and inserting her name as payee on customers' checks in over 100 separate incidents. The agency had employee theft coverage with a limit of only $10,000. It claimed that the limit should be applied to each act, which would have enabled the agency to collect the full loss because no one incident involved more than $1,000. The insurer contended that it was all one series of acts and that the $10,000 limit was the most the insurer was liable to pay. The court sided with the insurer.[6]

> **GOVERNMENT CRIME FORMS**
>
> ### "Per Loss" Versus "Per Employee" Coverage
>
> Each government crime form contains two employee theft insuring agreements. One of these insuring agreements provides "per loss coverage," and the other provides "per employee coverage." With **per loss coverage**, the applicable limit of insurance applies *per loss*; with **per employee coverage**, the limit applies *per employee*.
>
> For example, assume that five employees colluded to steal funds from the insured employer, and it could be proven that each had stolen $25,000 for a total of $125,000. Per loss coverage with a $25,000 limit would pay only $25,000 for the entire loss, whereas per employee coverage with a $25,000 limit would pay $125,000.
>
> The above analysis is based on the assumption that the amount stolen by each employee could be proven. If only the involvement of one or more employees and the amount of the loss, $125,000, could be proven, but not the amount stolen by each employee, neither form would pay more than $25,000. Because (1) it is rare that many employees are involved in a loss (in one study only 11 percent of the losses involved collusion)[*] and (2) establishing the amount stolen by each employee is usually difficult, per loss coverage with an adequate limit is generally preferable to per employee coverage.
>
> [*] John P. Guerico, E. Barry Rice, and Martin F. Sherman, "Old Fashioned Fraud by Employees Is Alive and Well: Results of a Survey of CPAs," *The CPA Journal,* September 1988, p. 75.

Special Conditions

Two of the many conditions contained in the commercial crime forms are chiefly (if not exclusively) applicable to the employee theft insuring agreement. These two conditions are titled Cancellation as to Any Employee and Employee Benefit Plan(s). The commercial crime forms and policies also contain a Territory condition that applies only to the employee theft insuring agreement. These three conditions are described below.

Cancellation as to Any Employee

This condition contains two distinct parts. The first part addresses *automatic* cancellation of coverage with respect to employees who have committed dishonest acts. The second part addresses how the insurer can cancel coverage with respect to any employee by providing notice to the insured.

Automatic Cancellation When the named insured or any of various other individuals—consisting of any partner, officer, director, or, if the named insured is a limited liability company (LLC), any member or manager of the LLC—learns that an employee has committed theft or any other dishonest act, coverage ceases automatically with respect to future acts by that employee. This provision applies whether the dishonest act occurred in connection with present employment or otherwise. For example, if the named insured discovered that an employee had embezzled funds from her church, coverage would cease with regard to that employee. This provision does not apply to knowledge possessed by partners, officers, directors, or LLC members or managers who are in collusion with the dishonest employee.

> **GOVERNMENT CRIME FORMS**
>
> **Cancellation as to Any Employee**
>
> The condition dealing with cancellation as to any employee is modified in the government forms. In those forms, insurance for any employee who has committed theft or any other dishonest act is canceled immediately upon discovery of the theft or other dishonest act by the insured *or any official or employee authorized to manage, govern, or control the insured's employees.* Under the commercial forms, discovery by the insured *or any partner, officer, or director* causes cancellation.
>
> The government forms thus encompass a broader group of employees whose knowledge is imputed to the insured. For example, knowledge by a supervisor who is not an officer would not trigger automatic cancellation for the employee under the commercial forms but would do so under the government forms.

The automatic cancellation provision can present a difficult problem for an employer, because the employer may hesitate to discharge a valuable employee even though the employee has been discovered to have acted dishonestly. Some employers overlook minor instances of employee theft or dishonesty as long as the employee is a valuable asset to the organization. Other employers believe that the employee will not repeat the dishonesty or are hesitant to confront an employee if the amount stolen is small. In contrast, insurers believe that the likelihood that dishonest employees will commit additional crimes is too high for an insurance company to continue coverage on an employee who has already been discovered in a dishonest act.

Cancellation by Insurer In addition to the automatic cancellation provision described above, the Cancellation as to Any Employee condition permits the insurer to cancel coverage as to any employee by giving the named insured at least thirty days' written notice. An insurer might exercise this option if it learns that one of the insured's employees has committed theft or another dishonest act of which the insured may be unaware.

> **FOR FURTHER THOUGHT**
>
> ### ERISA Fidelity Bonding Requirements
>
> The Employee Retirement Income Security Act of 1974 (ERISA) requires each fiduciary of a qualifying employee benefit plan and each person who handles plan assets to be bonded. (A fiduciary, as defined by ERISA, includes practically anyone whose role in employee benefits involves discretionary control or judgment in the design, administration, funding, or management of a benefit plan.) The type of bond required is a fidelity bond, which is now better known as employee theft or employee dishonesty insurance. Several types of organizations, including financial institutions and governmental entities, are granted regulatory exemption from the fidelity bond requirement of ERISA.
>
> ERISA bonding can be provided by naming the particular plan or plans as insureds for the employee theft agreement of the ISO commercial crime forms under discussion. When outside agents (nonemployees of the plan sponsor) are used as plan administrators or investment advisers, they can, if the insurer is willing, be defined as employees by endorsement, thus covering the plan against loss resulting from their dishonest acts. ERISA requires the bond amount to be at least 10 percent of the amount of each plan's assets handled, not to exceed $500,000 for each covered plan (unless the Secretary of Labor requires a higher amount).
>
> Because ERISA requires bonding coverage for "fraudulent or dishonest acts," the Employee Benefit Plan(s) condition uses the same wording (instead of the employee theft wording) with regard to the coverage provided to ERISA plans. Even when a business firm and its employee benefit plans are covered by one policy, the firm has only employee theft coverage; only the benefit plans are covered for fraudulent or dishonest acts. In addition, any deductible that may apply to employee theft is not applicable to ERISA bonding coverage.
>
> Coverage for employee benefit plans under the government crime forms is different. ERISA does not apply to government plans, so coverage remains as employee theft and is not modified to employee dishonesty.

Employee Benefit Plan(s)

The Employee Benefit Plan(s) condition explains how employee theft coverage will apply when the policy includes one or more employee benefit plans as insureds under the employee theft insuring agreement. The condition eliminates the need for attaching an ERISA compliance endorsement to the policy when the policy is being used to satisfy the fidelity bonding requirement of ERISA. The ERISA fidelity bonding requirement is discussed in the accompanying text box.

Territory

The employee theft insuring agreement is subject to a special extension of the coverage territory. This extension provides coverage for loss caused by any employee while temporarily outside the regular policy territory for a period of not more than ninety days. The regular policy territory for the commercial crime forms limits coverage to acts committed or events occurring within the United States (including its territories and possessions), Puerto Rico, and Canada. The many firms that have operations in other parts of the world must make special arrangements to obtain coverage, using either standard endorsement CR 20 09 (Amend Territorial Limits) or a nonstandard policy that provides the desired coverage territory.

Enhancements to Employee Theft Coverage

Some insurers, including those that write the largest premium volume of employee theft coverage, offer a number of independently filed enhancements of employee theft coverage. Examples are as follows:

1. ERISA welfare and employee benefit plans maintained by the insured are automatically included as named insureds.
2. The policy territory is amended to include locations anywhere in the world. (Although the standard Amend Territorial Limits Endorsement can be used to provide worldwide coverage, an underwriter may be unwilling to provide worldwide coverage.)
3. Coverage on an employee is not terminated because of prior fraudulent or dishonest acts if the act involved $10,000 or less.
4. Knowledge of prior fraudulent or dishonest acts is limited to knowledge by the insured's risk manager.
5. Coverage for terminated employees is increased to sixty or ninety days instead of thirty days.
6. Ninety-day notice of consolidation/merger/new acquisition is waived provided the total assets of the insured do not increase by more than 25 percent.
7. The definition of employee is extended to include persons who might not be covered under the standard coverage forms and endorsements.

Not all insurers offer these enhancements, and the exact provisions differ by insurer. These enhancements highlight some problem areas that all insureds and their advisers should consider.

GOVERNMENT CRIME FORMS

Coverage Territory

The general territory condition in the government crime forms is limited to the United States, its territories or possessions, and Puerto Rico; Canada is omitted. However, the forgery and alteration insuring agreement and the computer fraud insuring agreement in both the government crime forms and the commercial crime forms are subject to their own territory conditions, which provide worldwide coverage.

Who Needs Employee Theft Coverage?

Virtually all employers need employee theft (or employee dishonesty) coverage. Many organizations have experienced severe embezzlement losses committed by employees whom the organizations trusted so much that they did not see a need for employee theft insurance. Employee theft insurance is, in most cases, the most important crime coverage that an employer can buy.

Setting an appropriate limit for employee theft coverage can be difficult because embezzlement can occur undetected over many years, resulting in total losses that far exceed the amount that an employer would think was the maximum amount that could be taken by one employee. Consulting with the insured's financial officer and accountant might be a reasonable method for determining the appropriate amount of employee theft insurance for an account.

> **FOR FURTHER THOUGHT**
>
> **Underinsured Employee Theft Losses**
>
> The difficulty of determining an adequate amount of employee theft insurance can result in insureds being severely underinsured for that exposure. Many insureds have an "It can't happen to me" attitude about employee theft and fail to appreciate its catastrophic loss potential. Case histories that involve firms large and small, for-profit and not-for-profit, may focus attention on the problem and help insureds realize the need for stringent controls and high employee theft limits.
>
> In one four-month period, newspapers carried the following stories:
>
> - Just a week after a bookkeeper admitted stealing $150,000 from the Ohio Division of the American Cancer Society, the chief administrative officer was arrested and charged with fraud. He had wired $6.9 million from the Society's bank to his own account in Austria. (*The Columbus Dispatch*, June 9, 2000.)
>
> - A thirty-year employee of Harris Publishing Company was charged with stealing over $10 million by altering the payee on checks. She was a beloved figure in her hometown, known for her generosity to local charities. (*The New York Times*, August 5, 2000, p. B3.)
>
> - Starbucks lost $3.7 million to an employee who had worked for them for less than a year. She approved the payment of invoices from a fictitious consulting firm that she and her husband had created. (*The Wall Street Journal*, September 20, 2000, p. B2.)
>
> - A church in Forest Hills, N.Y., is trying to find out what its retired priest did with $2 million that he apparently took from the weekly collections. Auditors became suspicious when they noticed that ledger records of the total amount collected had been erased and rewritten. (*The New York Times*, October 6, 2000, p. B1.)
>
> These stories illustrate not that there was a sudden rash of embezzlements in this four-month period but that large thefts from lax organizations are frequent occurrences.

Forgery or Alteration

The forgery or alteration insuring agreement covers loss sustained by the insured because of:

> "forgery" or alteration of checks, drafts, promissory notes, or similar written promises, orders or directions to pay a sum certain in "money" that are
>
> (1) Made or drawn by or drawn upon you;
>
> (2) Made or drawn by one acting as your agent;
>
> or that are purported to have been so made or drawn.

In other words, the coverage responds to losses resulting from forgery or alteration of the *insured's* checks, drafts, etc., and not to losses resulting from the insured's acceptance of forged checks, etc., of *others*. Forgery or alteration coverage is summarized in Exhibit 1-3.

EXHIBIT 1-3

Summary of Forgery or Alteration Coverage

Causes of Loss	"Forgery" and alteration
Property Covered	Checks, drafts, promissory notes, or similar instruments made or drawn by the insured or the insured's agent
Where Coverage Applies	Worldwide

The form defines "forgery" as follows:

> "Forgery" means the signing of the name of another person or organization with intent to deceive; it does not mean a signature which consists in whole or in part of one's own name signed with or without authority, in any capacity, for any purpose.

The form does not define "alteration." As generally construed, alteration means something that has been done to an instrument that changes its meaning or terms without the consent of all parties to the instrument.[7] An example of alteration is changing the amount of a check from $100 to $2,100.

If the insured is sued for refusing to pay on any covered instrument because it may have been forged or altered, and if the insurer gives its written consent to the insured to defend against the suit, the insurer will pay the reasonable legal expenses that the insured incurs. Such expenses are payable in addition to the policy limit and are not subject to any deductible.

Forgery or alteration coverage does not apply to loss resulting from dishonest or criminal acts of employees, directors, and trustees. The employee theft insuring agreement will cover forgery or alteration committed against the insured by the insured's employees. (Some independently developed crime policies include forgery in the definition of employee theft.)

Endorsements are available for covering forgery or alteration of credit, debit, or charge cards; personal accounts of specified persons; and warehouse receipts and withdrawal orders.

Who Needs Forgery or Alteration Coverage?

Almost every organization is exposed to forgery or alteration losses, so the coverage is widely carried. Some firms do not purchase forgery and alteration coverage but instead rely on the general rule that the financial institution must bear the loss when it honors a forged or altered check. However, there are exceptions to this rule. Section 4-401 of the Uniform Commercial Code permits agreements that modify a bank's responsibility. Provisions to that effect are commonly included in the forms signed when a bank account is opened, but a bank cannot absolve itself of the duty to use ordinary care when honoring checks.

Selecting a limit of insurance is almost as difficult for forgery and alteration coverage as for employee theft. A common rule of thumb is to select the same dollar limit as that chosen for the employee theft. However, if the limit for employee theft has been carefully calculated, this method may overstate the amount of insurance needed for forgery and alteration: employees can steal other property in addition to funds.

The limit for forgery and alteration should probably equal the maximum amount that could be withdrawn from the firm's accounts in any ninety-day period. (Ninety days is used because monthly bank statements can be reconciled promptly upon receipt, and ninety days would provide adequate time to discover any forgeries or alterations.) The exposure should include not only funds on deposit but also amounts that might be paid using the automatic lines of credit that many firms establish with their banks. Because the premium for forgery and alteration is quite low, the insured's financial staff or accountants may not be willing to spend the time and effort to refine the limit.

Inside the Premises—Theft of Money and Securities

The insuring agreement titled **Inside the Premises—Theft of Money and Securities** covers money and securities inside the "premises" or a "banking premises" against an extremely broad scope of perils denoted by the words "theft, disappearance, and destruction." Inside the premises coverage for money and securities is summarized in Exhibit 1-4.

Recall that the policy definition of theft includes any type of "unlawful taking" of covered property "to the deprivation of the Insured." Hence, an insured loss (subject to exclusions) can be caused by burglary, robbery, unobserved theft, or any other unlawful taking of money or securities.

The form does not define "disappearance" or "destruction." The insured must prove that property has been destroyed if destruction is the cause of loss alleged in the claim. Disappearance is covered whether it is mysterious or not, and whether or not theft appears to be the cause of the disappearance. This broad scope of coverage is subject to several exclusions, to be described below.

EXHIBIT 1-4

Summary of Inside the Premises—Theft of Money and Securities Coverage

	Basic Coverage	Extension for Damage to Premises	Extension for Containers
Covered Causes of Loss	"Theft," disappearance, destruction	Actual or attempted "theft" of "money" or "securities"	Actual or attempted "theft" or unlawful entry
Covered Property	"Money," "securities"	The "premises" or their exterior	Locked safe, vault, cash register, cash box, or cash drawer
Where Coverage Applies	Inside the "premises" or "banking premises"	At the "premises"	Inside the "premises"

The insuring agreement covers loss of money and securities from within either the "premises" or "banking premises." "Premises" means the interior of that portion of any building the named insured occupies in conducting its business. "Banking premises" means the interior of that portion of any building occupied by a banking institution or similar safe depository.

The insuring agreement provides two extensions of the money and securities coverage, which apply to loss or damage to (1) the premises and (2) containers holding covered property. Neither of these extensions constitutes an additional amount of insurance. Any payment the insurer makes under these extensions is subject to the applicable limit of insurance.

Damage to Premises

The insurer agrees to pay for loss from damage to the "premises" or to their exterior that results from an actual or attempted theft of money or securities. The named insured must either own the premises or be liable for damage to them.

Loss of or Damage to Containers

The second extension deals with locked containers that hold money or securities. The insurer agrees to pay for the loss of or damage to a locked safe, vault, cash register, cash box, or cash drawer located inside the insured premises. Such loss or damage must result from actual or attempted theft of the container or from unlawful entry into the container. The extension will apply if, for example, burglars damage a safe by trying to break into it. Coverage will also apply if the burglars cart away the entire container in order to break into it somewhere else.

Who Needs Inside the Premises—Theft of Money and Securities Coverage?

Standard commercial property forms do not cover money and securities, so many businesses buy this crime coverage to insure money and securities on their premises. In some cases, businesses buy a less expensive form of money and securities coverage (endorsement CR 04 07) that covers money and securities inside the premises against the perils of robbery and safe burglary instead of the broader perils of theft, disappearance, or destruction. The alternative approach (which will be discussed in Chapter 2) might be preferred by a firm that keeps its money or securities in a safe or vault most of the time and is mainly concerned with safe burglary.

Many organizations use risk management techniques other than insurance—primarily retention, loss control, and avoidance—to treat this exposure. Most organizations keep only small amounts of cash on hand and have little exposure to securities loss. Many such organizations can retain any loss of money or securities. Loss control measures, such as silent alarms and frequent deposits, can reduce the exposure.

Inside the Premises—Robbery or Safe Burglary of Other Property

The insuring agreement titled **Inside the Premises—Robbery or Safe Burglary of Other Property** complements the inside the premises coverage discussed above. The insuring agreement discussed above covers *money and securities* inside the premises, and the insuring agreement discussed here covers *other property* inside the premises. Apart from the different types of property covered by each insuring agreement, the perils insured against by each insuring agreement are also different. The agreement previously discussed for money and securities insures against theft, disappearance, or destruction, whereas the agreement for other property insures against only robbery and safe burglary. Inside the Premises—Robbery or Safe Burglary of Other Property coverage is summarized in Exhibit 1-5 and described in more detail below.

Covered Causes of Loss

The covered causes of loss are (1) actual or attempted "robbery" of a "custodian" and (2) actual or attempted "safe burglary." These two perils are described in turn below.

"Robbery" of a "Custodian"

The policy definition of "robbery" is as follows:

> "Robbery" means the unlawful taking of property from the care and custody of a person by one who has:
>
> **a.** Caused or threatened to cause that person bodily harm; or
>
> **b.** Committed an obviously unlawful act witnessed by that person

EXHIBIT 1-5

Summary of Inside the Premises—Robbery or Safe Burglary of Other Property Coverage

	Basic Coverage	Extension for Damage to Premises	Extension for Containers
Covered Causes of Loss	Actual or attempted "robbery" of a "custodian" or "safe burglary"	Actual or attempted "robbery" or "safe burglary" of "other property"	Actual or attempted "robbery" or "safe burglary"
Covered Property	"Other property"	The "premises" or their exterior	Locked safe or vault
Where Coverage Applies	Inside the "premises"	At the "premises"	Inside the "premises"

The taking of property is considered robbery if the person taking the property has caused, or has only *threatened* to cause, bodily harm to the person having care or custody of the property. Bodily harm or a threat to cause harm is not required if the custodian witnesses an obviously unlawful act such as when someone runs out of the store with property that has not been paid for. However, the custodian must *witness* the unlawful act. If property is unlawfully taken without the custodian's observing the act, a "robbery" has not occurred.

To be covered, the property must also be taken from someone who meets the policy definition of "custodian," defined as follows:

> "Custodian" means you, or any of your partners or "members", or any "employee" while having care and custody of property inside the "premises", excluding any person while acting as a "watchperson" or janitor.

A common example of a custodian is a sales employee or cashier working inside the insured's store. The salesperson may either have been threatened by the thief or simply witnessed an "obviously unlawful act" such as a "smash and grab" theft from a display case or a show window.

It is important to remember that the definition of custodian excludes any person while acting as a "watchperson" or janitor. The policy definition of watchperson is "any person you retain specifically to have care and custody of property inside the 'premises' and has no other duties." The word "janitor" does not have a policy definition, so it takes its usual meaning. A typical dictionary definition of janitor includes either a doorkeeper or a person who cleans the premises, tends the heating system, and makes minor repairs.

Watchpersons are typically on the premises after regular business hours, and traditionally insurers have covered robbery of watchpersons under burglary forms (which essentially cover theft by breaking and entering a building).

Accordingly, robbery of a watchperson is covered under one of the optional crime insuring agreements (CR 04 06), which covers robbery of a watchperson as well as burglary.

Safe Burglary

The policy definition of "safe burglary," the other peril covered by the insuring agreement, is as follows:

> "Safe burglary" means the unlawful taking of:
>
> **a.** Property from within a locked safe or vault by a person unlawfully entering the safe or vault as evidenced by marks of forcible entry upon its exterior; or
>
> **b.** A safe or vault from inside the "premises".

Marks of forcible entry into the *premises* are not required. The burglar might have hidden within the premises or might have entered into the premises leaving no trace of force or violence—but that has no bearing on coverage as long as the burglar leaves marks of forcible entry *into the safe or vault*. However, the insurer can restrict coverage by endorsement (CR 35 10) to require forcible entry into the premises.

Coverage Extensions

The insuring agreement is subject to two coverage extensions. The first extension covers damage to the premises or their exterior resulting from actual or attempted robbery or safe burglary of "other property." The second extension covers loss of or damage to a locked safe or vault located inside the premises resulting from actual or attempted robbery or safe burglary.

Special Limit of Insurance

Inside the Premises—Robbery or Safe Burglary of Other Property is subject to a special limit of $5,000 per occurrence for the following types of property:

> (1) Precious metals, precious or semiprecious stones, pearls, furs, or completed or partially completed articles made of or containing such materials that constitute the principal value of such articles; or
>
> (2) Manuscripts, drawings, or records of any kind or the cost of reconstructing them or reproducing any information contained in them.

Who Needs Inside the Premises—Robbery or Safe Burglary of Other Property Coverage?

Many insureds do not buy this coverage because their contents are insured on a special-form basis that includes theft coverage (as under the Causes of Loss—Special Form). However, the coverage might be appropriate for an organization whose commercial property policy does not cover theft and whose principal crime loss exposures for "other property" inside the premises are robbery and safe burglary. Depending on its particular exposures, a business in this category might also want to buy optional burglary coverage (CR 04 06), which will be discussed in Chapter 2. Another alternative, which provides broader coverage than robbery and burglary coverage, is Inside the Premises—Theft of Other Property (CR 04 05), another one of the optional insuring agreements that will be discussed in Chapter 2.

Outside the Premises

The **outside the premises** insuring agreement covers money, securities, and other property while outside the premises and in the care and custody of either a "messenger" or an armored vehicle company. The policy definition of messenger is as follows:

> "Messenger" means you, or a relative of yours, or any of your partners or "members", or any "employee" while having care and custody of property outside the premises.

A messenger can be any of the same individuals who qualify as a custodian, as well as family members of the named insured. The principal difference between a custodian and a messenger is as follows:

- A custodian has care and custody of property *inside* the premises.
- A messenger has care and custody of property *outside* the premises.

An employee taking cash and checks to the bank for deposit in the insured's account is an example of a messenger.

The outside the premises insuring agreement does not cover all property against the same perils. Money and securities are covered against theft, disappearance, or destruction. Other property is covered against actual or attempted robbery. Outside the premises coverage is subject to the same $5,000 special limit of insurance that applies to Inside the Premises—Robbery or Safe Burglary of Other Property, as described above. Exhibit 1-6 summarizes outside the premises coverage.

EXHIBIT 1-6

Summary of Outside the Premises Coverage

	Coverage for "Money" and "Securities"	**Coverage for "Other Property"**
Covered Causes of Loss	"Theft," disappearance, destruction	Actual or attempted "robbery"
Where Coverage Applies	Outside the "premises" while in care or custody of a "messenger" or an armored car company and inside the U.S. (including its territories and possessions), Puerto Rico, and Canada	Outside the "premises" while in care or custody of a "messenger" or an armored car company and inside the U.S. (including its territories and possessions), Puerto Rico, and Canada

Who Needs Outside the Premises Coverage?

Standard commercial property coverage forms flatly exclude loss of money or securities. The only coverage that commercial property forms ordinarily provide for other types of property while away from the insured's premises comes by way of coverage extensions that are subject to low limits. Unless the insured has special-form coverage, theft is not a covered cause of loss for property on or off the premises. The Property in Transit extension of the Causes of Loss—Special Form covers theft of an entire package resulting from breaking into a locked vehicle, but that coverage is limited to $5,000 and does not cover robbery of a messenger. Thus, if an organization has significant off-premises messenger theft exposures for money, securities, or other property, outside the premises is an appropriate coverage. Examples of businesses that might buy outside the premises coverage are as follows:

- A retail store that does a large volume of cash transactions, whose managers make daily trips, by foot or motor vehicle, to the bank to deposit cash and checks. The loss exposure is robbery of money and securities from the messengers conveying the cash and checks to the bank.
- A bakery that uses its own vans and employee drivers to deliver its goods to grocery stores and coffee shops and is often paid in cash. The main loss exposure is robbery of money from the delivery van drivers, although "other property" in the form of baked goods could also be stolen.

Many organizations have annual transit insurance covering property shipped either on carriers' vehicles or on the insured's own vehicles. If an organization has a transit policy covering property shipped on its own vehicles, and if that policy includes theft as a covered peril, the organization may not need outside the premises coverage to insure "other property." However, if the organization has an off-premises exposure for money and securities in the custody of messengers, the organization will probably need outside the premises coverage because transit policies commonly exclude money and securities.

Computer Fraud

The almost universal use of computer systems among businesses has increased the opportunities for using computers to commit fraud and other criminal acts. The **computer fraud** insuring agreement provides a way for organizations to insure against loss of money, securities, and other property caused by:

> ... the use of any computer to fraudulently cause a transfer of that property from inside the "premises" or "banking premises":
>
> **a.** To a person (other than a "messenger") outside those "premises"; or
> **b.** To a place outside those "premises".

Computer fraud coverage is summarized in Exhibit 1-7.

The insuring agreement does not require that the computers used to commit the fraud be the property of the insured or even that they be located on the insured's premises. Coverage would apply if a nonemployee, using his or her own computer, gained access to the insured's computer system and directed shipments of property to unauthorized parties or made unauthorized transfers from the insured's bank accounts by gaining access to the bank's computer system.

EXHIBIT 1-7

Summary of Computer Fraud Coverage

Covered Cause of Loss	Use of a computer to fraudulently cause a transfer of covered property
Covered Property	"Money," "securities," and "other property"
Where Coverage Applies	The property must be transferred from inside the "premises" or a "banking premises" to a person or place anywhere else in the world

The various exclusions that apply to computer fraud coverage will be described later in this chapter. It is worth noting now, however, that the computer fraud insuring agreement does not cover loss caused by dishonest or criminal acts of employees, partners, members or managers of LLCs, directors, trustees, or representatives while acting alone or in collusion with other persons or while performing services for the named insured. Computer-related theft committed by the insured's own employees is insurable under the employee theft insuring agreement.

Apart from the limit of insurance shown in the policy declarations, computer fraud coverage is subject to a $5,000 per occurrence sublimit for loss of or damage to manuscripts, drawings, or records of any kind, including the cost of reconstructing them. The cost of reproducing data stored on computer media can be insured for higher limits under an electronic data processing (EDP) equipment policy.

Who Needs Computer Fraud Coverage?

Every organization should carefully analyze its potential for computer fraud losses, with input from its information systems department and financial officer. Some organizations may decide to treat the exposure exclusively with risk control measures, while other organizations may prefer to have insurance available if the risk control measures are not entirely successful. A factor to consider is that one breach in computer security could permit a fraudulent transfer of money, securities, or other property that amounted to a very severe loss.

Money Orders and Counterfeit Paper Currency

The **money orders and counterfeit paper currency** insuring agreement covers loss due to the insured's good-faith acceptance of the following:

    a. Money orders issued by any post office, express company or bank that are not paid upon presentation; or

    b. "Counterfeit" paper currency that is acquired during the regular course of business.

The insured must have accepted the money orders or counterfeit currency in exchange for merchandise, money, or services. Money orders and counterfeit paper currency coverage is summarized in Exhibit 1-8.

Who Needs Money Orders and Counterfeit Paper Currency Coverage?

The types of loss covered are seldom severe but can be frequent. Responding to the opinion of many insurers that insureds should control and retain these losses, ISO omitted money orders and counterfeit paper currency coverage from crime insurance forms when they were revised in 1985. A number of insurers soon offered the coverage on their own, and competitive pressures brought about its reintroduction in the 1995 ISO filing of crime form revisions. Still, many businesses choose not to insure this loss exposure. Training cashiers to detect counterfeit paper currency before accepting it or using devices that can detect counterfeit currency can help to prevent losses.

EXHIBIT 1-8

Summary of Money Orders and Counterfeit Paper Currency Coverage

Covered Cause of Loss	Good-faith acceptance of: (1) money orders that are not paid upon presentation or (2) "counterfeit" paper currency
Covered Property	Money orders issued by any post office, express company, or bank; and "counterfeit" paper currency acquired during the regular course of business
Where Coverage Applies	U.S. (including its territories and possessions), Puerto Rico, and Canada

EXCLUSIONS

The basic insuring agreements discussed above are subject to many exclusions contained in the ISO commercial and government crime forms. In these forms, the exclusions are divided into different groups depending on whether they apply to all insuring agreements or only to some insuring agreements. The exclusions are discussed below in the same groupings by which they are subdivided in the forms.

General Exclusions

The seven exclusions described below are applicable to any of the crime insuring agreements.

Acts Committed by You, Your Partners or Your Members

The exclusion eliminates coverage for loss resulting from theft or any other dishonest act committed by the named insured, the named insured's partners, or (if the named insured is a limited liability company) the named insured's members, whether acting alone or in collusion with other persons. The exclusion can present a major problem when providing employee theft coverage for large professional practices, such as those of accountants and attorneys, that have dozens or even hundreds of partners who in many ways resemble officers in other large organizations.

A partnership can cover theft committed by partners by purchasing endorsement CR 25 03, Include Partners as Employees, in connection with employee theft coverage. Similarly, a limited liability company can cover theft committed by its members by purchasing endorsement CR 25 04, Include Members of Limited Liability Company as Employees, in connection with employee theft coverage. Although both of these endorsements cover the additional exposure, each endorsement increases the policy deductible by an amount equal to the dishonest partner's or member's equity in the firm.

> **GOVERNMENT CRIME FORMS**
>
> ### Exclusions
>
> Because governmental entities do not have the same structure as business organizations, minor differences exist between some of the exclusions in the commercial crime forms and the corresponding exclusions in the government crime forms.
>
> The commercial form exclusion of "acts committed by you, your partners, or your members" is modified in the government forms to apply only to acts committed by you (the named insured). The reason for this modification is that governmental entities are not organized as partnerships or limited liability companies and therefore do not have partners or members.
>
> For similar reasons, the commercial form exclusion of "acts of employees, managers, directors, trustees, or representatives" is modified to apply to "acts of officials, employees, or representatives" in the government crime forms.

Acts of Employees, Managers, Directors, Trustees or Representatives

Apart from the employee theft insuring agreement, none of the crime insuring agreements are intended to cover theft or other dishonest acts committed by the named insured's employees, managers, directors, trustees, or authorized representatives. Consequently, the crime forms each contain an exclusion of such losses. The exclusion applies (1) whether such person was acting alone or in collusion with others and (2) while such person is performing services for the named insured or otherwise. This exclusion obviously does not apply to loss covered under the employee theft insuring agreement.

Governmental Action

Like virtually any policy covering property loss, the ISO crime forms exclude loss resulting from seizure or destruction of property by order of governmental authority.

Indirect Loss

The exclusion eliminates coverage for three types of loss other than physical loss of or damage to covered property: (1) business income losses; (2) payment of damages for which the insured is legally liable (other than compensatory damages arising directly from a loss covered by the policy); and (3) expenses incurred in establishing either the existence or the amount of loss under the policy.

Expenses that the insured incurs to establish the amount of loss can be covered by attaching endorsement CR 25 40 (Include Expenses Incurred To Establish the Amount of Loss). This endorsement provides coverage for reasonable costs paid to independent accounting, auditing, or other services used to determine the amount, but not the existence, of covered loss under employee theft, computer fraud, or both. Payment is limited to the lesser of a stated sublimit or a percentage of the covered expenses incurred.

Legal Expenses

The policy excludes expenses related to any legal action, except when covered under the forgery and alteration insuring agreement.

Nuclear

The exclusion eliminates coverage for loss resulting from nuclear reaction, nuclear radiation, or radioactive contamination.

War and Similar Actions

The policy excludes war in all its various forms, declared or not, including insurrection, rebellion, or revolution.

Exclusions Applicable Only to Employee Theft

The exclusions described below apply only to the employee theft insuring agreement.

Employee Canceled Under Prior Insurance

The insurer will not pay for loss caused by an employee who was canceled under any similar prior insurance and not reinstated since that last time of cancellation.

Inventory Shortages

The insurer will not pay for any loss that depends on inventory or profit-and-loss calculations to prove either the existence or the amount of the loss. This exclusion is commonly referred to as the **inventory shortages exclusion**. An inventory shortage is the difference between a physical inventory and the inventory shown in the insured's books and records.

Most businesses physically count and value their inventory only once a year. Between physical inventories, businesses estimate the value of goods on hand. To illustrate, assume that Smith Hardware Store took a physical inventory on

June 1, 2001, and that its goods have a markup on selling price of 33 1/3 percent (which means that one-third of the selling price is markup and two-thirds is cost). As of October 1, 2001, Smith might have estimated its inventory as shown in Exhibit 1-9.

EXHIBIT 1-9

Smith Hardware Inventory Calculation

6/1/2001 (at cost)		$100,000
Purchases since 6/1/2001 (at cost)		225,000
Total goods available for sale (at cost)		$325,000
Sales since 6/1/2001 (at selling price)	$300,000	
Less markup of 1/3	100,000	
Cost of goods sold after deducting markup		$200,000
Inventory on hand 10/1/2001 based on inventory calculation (at cost)		$125,000

If a physical inventory on October 1, 2001, showed only $75,000 in goods on hand, Smith might attribute the $50,000 shortage to employee theft, especially if an employee had been caught secretly selling some of the store's goods or if an employee had quit his job under suspicious circumstances. However, inventory shortages have many causes other than employee theft. Some of the causes include the following:

- Errors in count when receiving, shipping, or transferring material or when taking the physical inventory
- Failure to record material returned to vendors, shipped out for display, used as samples, or on consignment
- Failure to record material received, shipped, sold, or transferred to another location
- Shoplifting or theft by third parties, such as customers or employees of a guard service
- Damaged, spoiled, or destroyed material

Courts have upheld the intent that inventory or profit-and-loss computations are inadmissible as evidence in establishing that loss by employee dishonesty has occurred. However, some courts have permitted inventories or profit-and-loss computations to be used to establish the amount of the loss once employee dishonesty was established without relying on inventory computations.[8] The current ISO crime forms make the same distinction. The inventory shortages exclusion in those forms states that "where you establish wholly apart from such computations that you have sustained a loss, then you may offer your inventory records and actual physical count of inventory in support of the amount of loss claimed."

Trading

The policy definition of theft is potentially broad enough to include an employer's losses resulting from an employee's *unauthorized* trading in stocks, bonds, futures, commodities, or other similar items. However, because such losses can be catastrophic and because the rates for employee theft coverage do not contemplate them, the ISO crime forms exclude "loss resulting directly or indirectly from trading, whether in [the named insured's] name or in a genuine or fictitious account." Coverage for trading losses that meet the criteria for employee theft can be added by endorsement CR 25 16, Add Trading Coverage. The endorsement limits trading coverage to the amount of coverage shown in the endorsement and requires that the loss result directly from trading in a genuine account.

Warehouse Receipts

The warehouse receipts exclusion appears in the commercial crime forms only. It is omitted from the government crime forms. The exclusion eliminates coverage for "[l]oss resulting from fraudulent or dishonest signing, issuing, canceling or failing to cancel, a warehouse receipt or any papers connected with it." Such a loss might occur, for example, when an employee, in collusion with a customer, releases merchandise without canceling the receipt or issues a receipt without having received the merchandise. The customer could then make a claim for missing goods based on the fraudulent receipts. For coverage to apply, the employee's action must be fraudulent or dishonest—for example, accepting a bribe from the customer. A loss caused by an unintentional error would not be covered.

GOVERNMENT CRIME FORMS

Additional Exclusions

The government crime forms contain two additional exclusions that are not included in the commercial crime forms. These exclusions eliminate coverage for loss caused by (1) any employee required by law to be individually bonded or (2) any treasurer or tax collector. Some insurers will eliminate these exclusions by adding endorsement CR 25 12 (Include Treasurers or Tax Collectors as Employees). Coverage is also available under surety bonds designed specifically for public officials.

Occasionally a treasurer or tax collector is an independent contractor, not an employee. In that situation, merely removing the exclusion is not sufficient to afford coverage because independent contractors do not meet the policy definition of "employee." To cover employee theft committed by such agents, endorsement CR 25 02 (Include Designated Agents as Employees) or endorsement CR 25 41 (Include Designated Persons or Classes of Persons as Employees) can be added to the policy.

Exclusions Applicable to Inside the Premises and Outside the Premises

Eight exclusions apply specifically to the following insuring agreements, which will be referred to as insuring agreements 3, 4, and 5 in accordance with their numbering in the ISO commercial crime forms. (The same insuring agreements are numbered 4, 5, and 6 in the government versions of these forms.)

- Insuring agreement 3: Inside the Premises—Theft of Money and Securities
- Insuring agreement 4: Inside the Premises—Robbery or Safe Burglary of Other Property
- Insuring agreement 5: Outside the Premises

Accounting or Arithmetical Errors or Omissions

Insuring agreements 3, 4, and 5 do not cover losses resulting from accounting or arithmetical errors or omissions. Although many losses of this type are within the policy deductible, other losses could be sizable. The exposure falls within the general category of business risks that can be addressed by loss control measures, with any losses retained by the business.

Exchanges or Purchases

Insuring agreements 3, 4, and 5 exclude loss due to giving or surrendering property in an exchange or purchase. Thus, a fraudulent transaction or confidence scam that involves the loss of money, securities, or other property is not covered.

Fire

Insuring agreements 3, 4, and 5 do not cover loss resulting from fire, regardless of how the fire may be caused. However, the exclusion does not apply to fire loss or damage to safes or vaults or, under insuring agreement 3, to money and securities. (Loss of money or securities by fire is covered under the "destruction" peril in insuring agreement 3.)

Money Operated Devices

Insuring agreements 3, 4, and 5 do not cover loss of property from money operated devices (such as vending machines, amusement devices, or change machines) *unless* a continuous recording instrument inside the machine keeps track of the amount of money deposited. In the absence of a recording device, establishing the amount of the loss would be difficult or impossible.

Motor Vehicles or Equipment and Accessories

Insuring agreements 3, 4, and 5 do not cover loss of or damage to motor vehicles, trailers, or semi-trailers; or equipment and accessories attached to them. Theft of automobiles and related equipment can be insured under automobile physical damage coverage, and theft of mobile equipment can be insured under inland marine forms.

Transfer or Surrender of Property

This exclusion addresses two important exposures that may require special coverage. Both exposures involve transfer or surrender of property to someone outside the premises.

- The first exposure involves transfer or surrender of property to someone on the basis of unauthorized instructions.
- The second exposure involves surrendering property as the result of a threat to do bodily harm to a person or to damage or destroy property.

Many unauthorized instructions losses involve computer fraud, which can be insured under the computer fraud insuring agreement. Apart from computer fraud, it is possible to sustain a loss by voluntarily parting with property under the mistaken assumption that delivery was proper. If the unauthorized instructions were designed by an employee to defraud the employer, then the loss of property should be covered by employee theft insurance. Many unauthorized instructions losses can be prevented with the use of proper safeguards.

The exclusion of property surrendered as a result of a threat to harm a person or damage property contains an important exception. The exception states that the exclusion does not apply under the outside the premises insuring agreement if the insured (1) was unaware of any threat when the conveyance off premises began or (2) had knowledge of a threat when the conveyance began, but the loss was unrelated to the threat.

If, for example, a messenger conveying a bank deposit was robbed on the street at gunpoint, without any prior threat to the insured, insuring agreement 5 would cover the loss. In contrast, if the messenger conveyed money to an extortionist who had, before the conveyance began, kidnapped and threatened to kill the insured's family unless the money was given to him, insuring agreement 5 would not cover the loss. Some types of extortion losses can be covered under optional extortion endorsements that will be described in Chapter 2.

Vandalism

As noted earlier, insuring agreements 3 and 4 include coverage extensions for (1) damage to the premises and their exterior and (2) loss of or damage to various types of receptacles containing covered property, if directly caused by a covered peril. However, the vandalism exclusion eliminates coverage for damage to those types of property by vandalism or malicious mischief. Commercial property forms normally include coverage for damage to such property by vandalism or malicious mischief, including building damage caused by the breaking in or exiting of burglars.

Voluntary Parting With Title to or Possession of Property

The purpose of the voluntary parting exclusion is to eliminate coverage when the insured or an agent of the insured is tricked into *voluntarily* handing over property to a thief. For example, suppose a businessowner tells the firm's cashier that a bank messenger is to pick up money at a given time each day. If one day a wrongdoer impersonates the messenger and succeeds in getting the cashier to hand over the money *voluntarily*, the loss would not be covered by Inside the Premises—Theft of Money and Securities.

If the transfer of property is not completely *voluntary*—in other words, if the taking of property entails any violence or even a threat of violence by the taker—the exclusion does not apply. Similarly, if the property is taken without the involvement of the insured or the insured's agent (as in the case of a thief removing cash from a cash register without being observed), no voluntary transfer has occurred, and the exclusion is inapplicable.

Exclusion Applicable to Computer Fraud

In addition to the general exclusions discussed earlier, an inventory shortages exclusion also applies to the computer fraud insuring agreement. The exclusion is the same as the inventory shortages exclusion discussed earlier, except that it does not contain the exception that permits inventory records to be used in determining the *amount* of the loss claimed when the insured has already established, apart from such computations, that a covered loss has occurred.

SUMMARY

Because of the high frequency of crime losses, risk control techniques should be the first line of defense against such losses. For exposures that are beyond the organization's ability to control or retain, a wide variety of insurance coverages are available.

The ISO commercial crime program is available for insuring money, securities, and other property against a variety of perils, including (but not limited to) employee theft, forgery, alteration, theft, burglary, safe burglary, robbery, extortion, and computer fraud. The ISO commercial crime forms contain the seven insuring agreements listed below. Instead of summarizing these insuring agreements here, we suggest that you review the summary charts provided in the corresponding exhibits listed below:

Exhibit 1-2	Employee Theft
Exhibit 1-3	Forgery or Alteration
Exhibit 1-4	Inside the Premises—Theft of Money and Securities
Exhibit 1-5	Inside the Premises—Robbery or Safe Burglary of Other Property
Exhibit 1-6	Outside the Premises
Exhibit 1-7	Computer Fraud
Exhibit 1-8	Money Orders and Counterfeit Paper Currency

The ISO crime program also contains government crime forms that contain the same insuring agreements listed above, except that they have two alternative employee theft agreements, one applying the limit on a per loss basis and the other applying the limit on a per employee basis.

The commercial and government crime forms are subject to several general exclusions that apply to all insuring agreements as well as additional exclusions that apply to only one insuring agreement.

CHAPTER NOTES

1. "Preventing Crime on the Job," *Nation's Business*, July 1990, p. 36. The remainder of the over $50 billion in estimated crime loss would be other than employee theft/dishonesty crime losses. *The I.I.I. 1993 Fact Book* (New York: Insurance Information Institute, 1993), p. 94, reported $16 billion in crime losses based on FBI reports. FBI reports do not include embezzlement.
2. *Fact Book 2000* (New York: Insurance Information Institute, 1999), p. 3.10.
3. *Black's Law Dictionary*, 7th ed., under "unlawful act."
4. Employer's Administrative Services, Inc. v. Hartford Accident & Indemnity Co., 709 P2d (Ariz. Ct. App. 1985) cited in *Insurance Counsel Journal*, "Fidelity & Surety Law Survey," 1985, pp. 439–440. The court reached a similar decision in United States Fidelity & Guaranty Co. v. Three Garden Village Limited Partnership, 77 Md.App. 670,551 A2d 881 (1988) cited in *Insurance Counsel Journal*, "Fidelity & Surety Law Survey," 1989, p. 342.
5. Leedy Mortgage Co., 76 B.R. 440 (E.D. Pa. 1987), cited in *Insurance Counsel Journal*, "Fidelity & Surety Law Survey," 1988, p. 272.
6. American Commerce Insurance Brokers, Inc. v. Minnesota Mutual Fire and Casualty Co., Minn. Ct. App. NoC 9-94-499, 8/1/95. The court ruled that the claim should be treated as two series of acts, one being the theft of cash receipts and the other being the altering of the checks. The important point is that the agency had a $190,000 loss involving over 100 separate acts but collected only $20,000 because of the series-of-acts limitation.
7. *Black's Law Dictionary*, 7th ed., under "alteration."
8. For a discussion of court decisions on inventory shortages, see *FC&S Bulletins*, "Inventory Shortages Exclusion," Casualty & Surety Volume, Crime M.1-5 (May 1996).

Chapter 2

Commercial Crime Insurance, Part II

This chapter continues the survey of commercial crime insurance that began in Chapter 1. The main topics of this chapter are as follows:

- The optional crime insuring agreements for the ISO commercial crime forms, and how they supplement the basic insuring agreements discussed in Chapter 1.
- The conditions of the ISO commercial crime forms.
- Employee dishonesty insurance, and how it compares with employee theft insurance.

The appendix to this chapter lists and briefly describes several endorsements (in addition to the optional insuring agreements) that can be added to the ISO crime forms.

OPTIONAL CRIME INSURING AGREEMENTS

Any of twelve optional insuring agreements can be added by endorsement to the ISO crime coverage forms that were examined in Chapter 1. Exhibit 2-1 summarizes each of the optional insuring agreements, and the text provides additional discussion of each. In the interests of emphasizing the general purposes of the optional insuring agreements, the discussion omits some details of coverage. For complete coverage details, see the particular endorsements.

Clients' Property, CR 04 01

The property covered by the employee theft insuring agreement is limited to property (1) that the named insured owns or leases, (2) that the named insured holds for others, or (3) for which the named insured is legally liable, *except for property inside the premises of a client of the named insured.* The italicized words did not appear in the previous employee dishonesty forms. Under those forms, insurers frequently denied coverage for loss of clients' property on the grounds that the employee did not manifest intent to cause financial loss to the named insured.

For example, an employee of a cleaning service steals property belonging to customers whose offices the employee is cleaning. Unless the customer can hold the cleaning service legally liable for the theft, the cleaning service incurs no loss. The optional insuring agreement for clients' property provides a way to cover property inside a client's premises. The insurer agrees to pay claims only if they are presented to the insurer by the insured. The insurer is not obligated to pay claims submitted by the insured client.

EXHIBIT 2-1

Summaries of Optional Insuring Agreements

Optional Insuring Agreement	Covered Property	Covered Cause(s) of Loss
Clients' Property CR 04 01	"Money," "securities," or "other property": a. that the named insured's "client" owns or leases; b. that a "client" holds for others; or c. for which a "client" is legally liable; while the property is inside the "client's premises"	"Theft" committed by an identified "employee" ("Theft" means the unlawful taking of "money," "securities," or "other property" to the deprivation of the named insured's "client.")
Funds Transfer Fraud CR 04 02	"Funds," which the policy defines as "money" and "securities"	"Fraudulent instruction" directing a financial institution to transfer "funds" from the insured's "transfer account."
Extortion–Commercial Entities CR 04 03 **Extortion–Government Entities CR 04 04**	"Money," "securities," and "other property"	The surrender of covered property away from the "premises" because of a threat to do bodily harm to certain persons or to do damage to the "premises" or property inside the "premises"
Inside the Premises–Theft of Other Property CR 04 05	"Other property" inside the "premises"	"Theft" (including resulting damage to the "premises" or their exterior)
Inside the Premises–Robbery or Burglary of Other Property CR 04 06	"Other property" inside the "premises"	Actual or attempted "robbery" of a "watchperson" or "burglary"
Inside the Premises–Robbery or Safe Burglary of Money and Securities CR 04 07	"Money" and "securities" inside the "premises" "Money" and "securities" inside the "premises" or "banking premises" in a safe or vault	Actual or attempted "robbery" of a "custodian" Actual or attempted "safe burglary"

Optional Insuring Agreement	Covered Property	Covered Cause(s) of Loss
Employee Theft– Name or Position Schedule CR 04 08	"Money," "securities," and "other property"	"Theft" committed by an identified "employee"
	Policy definition of "employee" is changed to: (1) Any person named in the Schedule, if coverage applies on a Name Schedule basis; or (2) Any person engaged to perform the duties of a position shown in the Schedule, if coverage applies on a Position Schedule basis.	
Lessees of Safe Deposit Boxes CR 04 09	"Securities" in a safe deposit box in a vault inside the depository premises described in the policy; or temporarily elsewhere inside the same premises during the course of deposit or removal	"Theft," disappearance, or destruction
	"Other property" while in the same places where securities are covered, as above	"Burglary," "robbery," or vandalism
Securities Deposited With Others CR 04 10	"Securities" (a) while inside the premises of the "custodian" named in the policy, (b) while being conveyed by the "custodian" or an employee of the "custodian," and (c) while on deposit by the "custodian" for safekeeping in a depository	"Theft," disappearance, or destruction
Guests' Property CR 04 11	a. Guests' property in safe deposit boxes inside the premises b. Guests' property inside the premises or in the insured's possession	Any loss or damage for which the insured is legally liable, subject to exclusions
Safe Depository CR 04 12	Property of the insured depository's customers while inside the insured's premises. Two optional insuring agreements:	
	a. "Money," "securities," and "other property"	Any loss or damage for which the insured is legally liable, subject to exclusions
	b. "Securities" and "other property"	"Robbery," "burglary," destruction, or damage

Funds Transfer Fraud, CR 04 02

One of the major changes in the banking industry in recent years has been the rapid growth of electronic transfer of funds. Firms transfer millions of dollars from one account to another in single transactions, and the total volume is in the trillions of dollars a day.

The classic example of **funds transfer fraud** occurs when an interloper gains access to the transfer instruction and changes the account number so that the funds are transferred into the interloper's account. The use of computers to transmit these instructions has increased the potential for fraud. The question of whether a loss would fall on the bank or the firm requesting the transfer would depend on the particular facts and the law involved. The firm can cover its exposure to funds transfer fraud loss by endorsement to the ISO crime forms.

The Funds Transfer Fraud Endorsement provides coverage for loss of funds (defined as money and securities) resulting directly from a "fraudulent instruction" directing a financial institution to transfer funds from an insured's account. The endorsement defines "fraudulent instruction" to include electronic, telegraphic, cable, teletype, telefacsimile, or telephone instructions transmitted by someone other than the insured without the insured's knowledge or consent. "Fraudulent instruction" also includes forged written instructions, other than those described in the forgery insuring agreement. This coverage complements but does not replace forgery coverage. For complete protection, an insured needs both coverages.

Funds transfer fraud coverage also complements computer fraud coverage. To be covered under funds transfer fraud coverage, a loss does not have to involve a computer. The two coverages might overlap in some situations. For example, if a thief uses a computer to instruct the insured's bank to transfer funds to an account in another bank, both coverages might apply. In that event, the policy condition dealing with coverage under more than one insuring agreement would come into play. This condition limits recovery to the lesser of (1) the actual amount of the loss or (2) the sum of the limits of the applicable coverages.

Extortion, CR 04 03 and CR 04 04

Extortion is a crime in which the wrongdoer coerces another person to surrender money or property in order to obtain the release of a kidnapped person or to prevent the wrongdoer from carrying out a threat to damage or destroy property. Two optional crime coverage endorsements—one for commercial entities and one for governmental entities—are available for insuring loss due to extortion.

Both versions of the Extortion Endorsement cover the surrender of money, securities, or other property as a result of a threat communicated to the insured to do either of the following: (1) cause bodily harm to certain classes of persons who have been captured (or allegedly captured) or (2) cause damage to the "premises" or property inside the "premises." Under the endorsement for commercial entities, the person against whom harm is threatened must be captured or allegedly captured within the United States (including its territories or possessions), Puerto Rico, Canada, or any other location shown in the endorsement's schedule. The endorsement for government entities contains the same territory provision except that it omits Canada.

Under the endorsement for commercial entities, the capture (or alleged capture) of any of the following persons triggers coverage: a director, a trustee, a partner, a "member," a "manager," or an "employee" of the insured; a proprietor (if the insured is a sole proprietorship); and a relative or invitee of any of the foregoing persons. The comparable list of persons whose capture triggers coverage under the government version of the endorsement is limited to officials, employees, or representatives of the insured; and relatives or invitees of any of these persons.

In order to be covered, the first communication of the threat must occur during the policy period, and the surrender of the ransom must occur *away* from the insured premises. The endorsement requires the person receiving the threat to attempt to report the threat to an associate and to local law enforcement authorities before surrendering any money or other property.

> **FOR FURTHER THOUGHT**
>
> ### Kidnap and Ransom Insurance
>
> A number of specialty insurers, in both the U.S. and London markets, provide kidnap and ransom coverage that is broader in some respects than the ISO extortion endorsements. In addition to covering extortion losses resulting from threats to harm people or damage property, kidnap and ransom coverage can cover rewards paid to informants, loss of or damage to the property being transported in payment of an extortion demand, and additional expenses resulting from an extortion incident. Moreover, kidnap and ransom policies often apply on a worldwide basis, in contrast with the extortion endorsement's limitation to the United States and Canada unless additional locations are specified in the endorsement schedule or declarations.

Inside the Premises—Theft of Other Property, CR 04 05

This optional insuring agreement, summarized in Exhibit 2-1, provides a broader alternative to the basic insuring agreement titled Inside the Premises—Robbery or Safe Burglary of Other Property. The optional coverage, instead of being limited to robbery and safe burglary, covers theft, which the policy defines to include any unlawful taking of covered property to the deprivation of the insured. Thus, the definition of theft is broad enough to include the following perils:

- Burglary, robbery, and safe burglary
- Unobserved theft while the premises are open for business
- Theft by someone who enters the premises when they are closed without leaving the signs of forcible entry or exit required to establish a burglary

The Inside the Premises—Theft of Other Property Endorsement provides basically the same level of premises theft coverage as the Causes of Loss—Special Form. However, the special form has the following advantages for insureds:

1. The insurer cannot exclude coverage under the special form unless the insurer can prove that an exclusion applies.
2. The special form does not have any equivalent to the theft endorsement's exclusion of theft occurring during a fire inside the premises.
3. The limit of insurance for theft under the special form is the same as for all other perils covered by the policy; in contrast, separate crime coverages are frequently written for much lower limits of insurance than property coverages.
4. Loss of business income due to theft can be covered under a business income form attached to the special form. None of the crime coverage forms has any provision for insuring business income loss resulting from crime perils.

A disadvantage of the special form is that it applies a limit of $2,500 to theft of furs, jewelry, and similar valuables, and to patterns, dies, molds, and forms. The limit under the premises theft endorsement is $5,000, and it does not apply to patterns, dies, molds, and forms.

Inside the Premises—Robbery or Burglary of Other Property, CR 04 06

The Inside the Premises—Robbery or Burglary of Other Property Endorsement covers property other than money and securities inside the premises against two causes of loss: (1) actual or attempted burglary and (2) actual or attempted robbery of a watchperson.

It is important to remember that the only type of robbery covered by the endorsement is *robbery of a watchperson*. The policy definition of watchperson is "any person you retain specifically to have care and custody of property inside the 'premises' and who has no other duties." The endorsement does not cover robbery of a "custodian" (such as a store cashier) or any other person besides a "watchperson." If the insured wants both robbery (of a custodian) coverage and premises burglary coverage, the insured's crime policy must show limits for *both* of the following insuring agreements:

- Inside the Premises—Robbery or Safe Burglary of Other Property (Insuring Agreement 4 in the commercial crime forms)
- Inside the Premises—Robbery or Burglary of Other Property (endorsement CR 04 06)

Although coverage limited to burglary and watchperson robbery provides rather narrow crime protection, it may be suitable for businesses whose exposure to loss of "other property" is greatest when the premises are not open for business and when the property susceptible to loss is not enclosed in a safe or vault. It is also useful for firms for whom broader coverage is either unavailable or unaffordable.

Burglary

The endorsement defines **burglary** as follows:

> "Burglary" means the unlawful taking of property from inside the "premises" by a person unlawfully entering or leaving the "premises" as evidenced by marks of forcible entry or exit.

The references to "unlawfully leaving" and "forcible exit" make it clear that burglary includes a theft in which the thief legally enters the premises during regular working hours, conceals himself, and, after the building is locked for the night, unlawfully breaks out of the building to remove the stolen property.

The requirement that the break-in or break-out be evidenced by marks of forcible entry or exit—such as a broken window, a kicked-in door, or a damaged lock—is often crucial to determining whether coverage applies to a loss. If a door is inadvertently left unlocked, allowing a thief to enter and exit without leaving marks of forcible entry or exit, the loss will not be covered even if a theft has obviously occurred. This type of loss, as well as other non-burglary thefts, can be covered by endorsement CR 04 05, Inside the Premises—Theft of Other Property, or by the Causes of Loss—Special Form.

Robbery of a Watchperson

Inside the Premises—Robbery or Burglary of Other Property covers loss caused by robbery of a watchperson and can be broadened by endorsement (CR 35 02) to cover loss caused by robbery of a janitor. Recall that the basic insuring agreement titled Inside the Premises—Robbery or Safe Burglary of Other Property *excludes* robbery of a watchperson or a janitor even though it covers robbery of a "custodian."

Although it might at first glance seem illogical to divide the robbery exposure into separate insuring agreements, there are good reasons for doing so. First, robbery of a watchperson or janitor is closely related to burglary; a burglar who breaks into the premises might encounter a watchperson, changing what began as a burglary into a robbery.

Second, the separation offers insureds options to tailor coverage to their needs. For example, a merchant who places all of the firm's valuable property in a safe whenever the premises are closed might purchase Inside the Premises—Robbery and Safe Burglary of Other Property and retain the risk of loss caused by burglary or by robbery of a watchperson or janitor since there would be little of value exposed when those persons are on duty. In contrast, a firm whose stock in trade is bulky and of low unit value might want to retain the risk of robbery while open for business and want coverage only for burglary or for robbery of a watchperson while the premises are closed, when the thieves would have more time to steal the insured's property.

Inside the Premises—Robbery or Safe Burglary of Money and Securities, CR 04 07

The Inside the Premises—Robbery or Safe Burglary of Money and Securities Endorsement is a less expensive alternative to the basic crime insuring agreement titled Inside the Premises—Theft of Money and Securities. Instead of covering money and securities against loss caused by theft, disappearance, or destruction, endorsement CR 04 07 covers the same property against loss caused by robbery (of a custodian) or safe burglary. The main practical difference between the two levels of coverage is that the optional insuring agreement does not cover the following types of losses that are covered under the basic insuring agreement:

- Theft of covered property that is neither "robbery" of a custodian nor "safe burglary," such as ordinary burglary or unobserved theft
- Destruction or disappearance of covered property that is attributable to a peril other than robbery or safe burglary, such as destruction of money by a fire or hurricane

Despite these coverage differences, the optional insuring agreement provides a broad enough scope of coverage to satisfy the coverage needs of many insureds. In some cases, it may be the only coverage on money and securities that an underwriter is willing to provide.

Employee Theft—Name or Position Schedule, CR 04 08

The basic insuring agreement for employee theft, discussed in Chapter 1, applies on a *blanket* basis, covering employee theft committed by *any* employee (as defined) unless the policy specifically excludes the loss. In some cases, insureds prefer to obtain employee theft coverage on a *schedule* basis, which limits coverage to theft committed by an employee whose name (such as "William Stockdale") or position (such as "Bookkeeper") is listed in the policy. The Employee Theft—Name or Position Schedule Endorsement permits an insurer to substitute the schedule approach for the blanket employee theft insuring agreement. Schedule employee theft coverage is used primarily for small firms that have only one or two employees for whom coverage is desired.

The endorsement replaces the blanket definition of employee with the definition that follows:

> "Employee" means:
> (1) Any person named in the Schedule, if coverage applies on a Name Schedule basis; or
> (2) Any person you engage to perform the duties of a position shown in the Schedule, if coverage applies on a Position Schedule basis.

The substituted definition restricts coverage to theft committed by employees whose names or job titles are shown in the schedule contained in the endorsement. The schedule can be either of two types:

- **Name schedule**, which shows the names of covered employees, or
- **Position schedule**, which shows the titles of covered positions and indicates the number of persons who occupy each scheduled position.

In either case, the amount of coverage for each named person or each unnamed person in a scheduled position may vary depending on the employer's estimate of the amount that could be stolen by a person occupying that position. An example of an employee theft position schedule is shown in Exhibit 2-2.

EXHIBIT 2-2

Employee Theft Position Schedule

Titles of Covered Positions	Location of Covered Positions	Number of Employees in Each Position	Limit of Insurance on Each Employee	Deductible Amount on Each Employee
Bookkeeper	103 Main St.	1	$25,000	$500
Janitor	Blissville, IL	1	$10,000	$500

As compared with the name schedule, the position schedule has some advantages for the employer, because no reporting or policy changes are necessary when employees are replaced. The position schedule permits continuous coverage even though the individuals holding those positions may change. In contrast, the name schedule approach does not cover employees hired during the policy period until the insured notifies the insurer to add them to the schedule.

However, an employer with the position schedule can be penalized if, at the time of a loss, more employees occupy a given position than the number actually declared in the schedule. In those circumstances, the limit of insurance is reduced according to the following formula:

$$\frac{\text{Number of employees shown in the position}}{\text{Actual number of employees in the position}} \times \text{Limit} = \text{Reduced limit}$$

To illustrate, assume that a shipping clerk stole merchandise from her employer's warehouse. If the employer's position schedule showed only three shipping clerks when there were actually four in that position, and the limit shown for that position was $10,000, the most that the insurer would pay for the loss would be ³/₄ × $10,000, or $7,500.

Lessees of Safe Deposit Boxes, CR 04 09

Banks and other organizations maintain safe deposit boxes for the use of their customers. A bank customer can lease a safe deposit box and keep valuables locked in the box in order to prevent theft, damage, or destruction of the valuables. However, this risk control measure is not foolproof, and losses do occasionally occur. As a lessor, the bank or other depository is not an insurer of the property kept in the leased safe deposit box; it is liable only for losses resulting from its negligence.

The Lessees of Safe Deposit Boxes Endorsement enables a customer of a bank or depository to insure property that the customer keeps in a safe deposit box on the bank or depository premises. The endorsement provides two coverage options: (1) securities can be covered against theft, disappearance, or destruction; and (2) property other than money and securities can be insured against burglary, robbery, and vandalism.

The coverage enables the lessee (customer) to recover from its insurer for losses to covered property instead of having to prove that the lessor (bank or depository) was negligent and therefore legally liable to pay the loss.

The endorsement does not provide any benefit to the lessor. If the insurer pays a loss, it is subrogated to any recovery rights the depositor (lessee) may have against the lessor. Thus, the lessor still needs to have its own insurance on the property in its custody. Banks and other financial institutions can obtain this insurance under the Safe Depository Endorsement discussed later in this chapter. Depository companies that are ineligible for the financial institution policy can obtain similar coverage under the Safe Depository Endorsement discussed below.

Securities Deposited With Others, CR 04 10

In some cases, the owner of securities will place the securities in the temporary custody of another organization. For example, the custodian might be a creditor that is holding stock certificates as collateral or security for repayment of a loan by the owner of the stock. The Securities Deposited With Others Endorsement enables the owner of the securities to insure them while they are in the custodian's possession or on deposit by the custodian for safekeeping in a depository. The covered causes of loss under the endorsement are theft, disappearance, and destruction.

Guests' Property, CR 04 11

The Guests' Property Endorsement is designed for lodging facilities to protect themselves against liability because of property loss sustained by their guests. Although theft is a major source of loss, the endorsement provides broad coverage against non-crime losses as well. Traditionally, this type of coverage has been called *innkeepers liability insurance*. In the broad sense used here, "innkeeper" includes the owner or operator of any lodging facility—such as a hotel, a motel, a bed-and-breakfast, a resort, or even a dude ranch.

Under the common law, innkeepers are liable for all loss of a guest's property. This rule has been modified by statutes, which vary from state to state, to limit innkeeper liability for property of guests in some situations. One state, for example, limits liability for money, jewelry, negotiable instruments, and similar property to $1,500 if kept in a safe deposit box provided by the innkeeper. The innkeeper is not responsible for such types of property if the guest chooses not to keep it in a safe deposit box. The innkeeper's liability for other types of property not in a safe deposit box is limited to not more than $500. However, the innkeeper receives no limitation of liability for losses caused by the innkeeper's negligence.[1] Since the limitations of liability generally apply per guest, an innkeeper can incur a large liability loss if many guests' belongings are destroyed in one occurrence—even if the innkeeper was not negligent.

The Guests' Property Endorsement, summarized in Exhibit 2-1, covers loss to guests' property for which the insured is legally liable (subject to the applicable exclusions). If the insured is sued for refusing to pay for loss of guests' property and the insurer has given the insured its written consent to defend, the insurer will pay reasonable legal expenses incurred and paid by the insured. Covered legal expenses are payable in addition to the limit of insurance.

Safe Depository, CR 04 12

The Safe Depository Endorsement is designed to cover the liability of safe depository businesses for loss to their customers' property while inside the depository premises. This endorsement is rarely used because ISO rules limit eligibility to depositories other than financial institutions. Principally in large cities, some businesses exist whose sole service is providing safe deposit boxes, and they are eligible for the Safe Depository Endorsement.

CRIME POLICY CONDITIONS

The ISO crime forms each contain a long section titled Conditions. In the interests of (1) focusing attention on the conditions that are most important or unique to crime insurance and (2) avoiding repetition of routine conditions discussed in earlier chapters of this text, the following discussion omits some of the conditions. For complete details, see the actual forms. In the actual forms, the conditions are arranged in alphabetical order. They are discussed here in logical groupings.

Discovery Form Versus Loss Sustained Form

Each of the ISO crime coverage forms and policies comes in a discovery form and a loss sustained form, as shown in Exhibit 1-1 on page 1.3. The loss sustained approach has been the traditional approach for commercial crime insurance. A discovery form was not available under the ISO/SAA commercial crime program until 1997. The basic features of the discovery form and the loss sustained form can be summarized as follows:

- The **discovery form** covers losses that are first discovered during the policy period no matter when the loss occurred and regardless of whether the insured had previous coverage. Because underwriters may be unwilling to provide such expansive coverage for prior acts, an optional retroactive date endorsement is available to limit coverage for loss that was discovered during the policy period but that occurred before a specified retroactive date.

- The **loss sustained form** covers loss that occurs during the policy period and is discovered during the policy period or within one year after policy expiration. The loss sustained form also covers loss that occurs under a prior policy if insurance has been in effect continuously and the loss would have been covered under both the previous and the current insurance.

The discovery forms and the loss sustained forms differ from one another only in a few conditions, as summarized in Exhibit 2-3. These differences will be discussed in more detail below.

The choice between the loss sustained form and the discovery form has much more significance to employee theft insurance than to other crime coverages. Most crime losses other than employee theft are known when they happen (as in the case of a robbery) or are discovered shortly thereafter (as in a burglary discovered the next morning). Thus, for crime coverages other than employee theft, the policy in effect when the loss occurs will ordinarily be the one that applies to the loss, regardless of whether the applicable form is on a loss sustained or discovery basis. Employee theft losses, on the other hand, can go undetected for long periods, and thus the choice between the loss sustained form and the discovery form can have greater consequences for employee theft coverage. Accordingly, the discussion that follows mainly uses employee theft examples to illustrate the conditions applicable to the loss sustained form and the discovery form.

EXHIBIT 2-3

Conditions That Differ Between Loss Sustained Form and Discovery Form

Loss Sustained Form	Discovery Form
Loss Sustained condition expresses the coverage trigger.	*Discovery* condition expresses the coverage trigger.
Extended Period To Discover Loss condition provides a one-year period following policy expiration for discovering losses that occurred during the policy period.	Discovery form has same condition except that discovery period is one year for employee benefit plans only; sixty days for all other claims.
Loss Covered Under This Insurance and Prior Insurance Issued by Us or Any Affiliate condition.	Discovery form has no similar condition (other than the *Non-Cumulation* portion, below).
Loss Sustained During Prior Insurance condition.	Discovery form contains no similar condition.
Loss sustained form does not contain a *Non-Cumulation* condition, but the substance of that condition is contained in *Loss Covered Under This Insurance and Prior Insurance Issued by Us or Any Affiliate*.	*Non-Cumulation of Limit of Insurance* condition.

Loss Sustained Form

The Loss Sustained condition, contained only in the loss sustained form, states that the insurer will pay for loss that the named insured sustains through acts committed or events occurring during the policy period. Moreover, the insurer will pay a covered loss only if it is discovered by the insured during the policy period or within one year after the policy period ends, as set forth in the Extended Period To Discover Loss condition.

Extended Period To Discover Loss

To illustrate how the Extended Period To Discover Loss condition applies, assume that an employee theft loss occurred in the year 2000, during the term of an employee theft policy that ended on December 31, 2000, and was not replaced with another policy. If the loss is discovered anytime in 2001, it will be covered under the 2000 policy. If the loss is not discovered until sometime after 2001, it will not be covered under the 2000 policy, because the loss was discovered after the additional one-year discovery period.

In a slightly different situation, suppose that as soon as the 2000 policy expired, it was replaced with employee theft coverage (loss sustained basis) written by *another* insurance company. This replacement policy ran for calendar year 2001 and was then renewed on January 1, 2002. If a loss that occurred in 2000 was first discovered in 2002, the loss would not be covered under the 2000 policy, because the discovery period for that policy would have expired. In addition, one might conclude that the same loss would not be covered under the current (2002) policy, because the loss did not occur during the current policy period. However, the Loss Sustained During Prior Insurance condition of the loss sustained form remedies this problem, as discussed below.

Loss Sustained During Prior Insurance

This condition extends coverage in certain cases to apply to a loss *discovered* during the *current* policy's coverage period that *occurred* during the coverage period of any *prior* policy (issued by the present insurer or another insurer) and that would have been covered by the prior policy except that its discovery period had expired. Two additional conditions must be met:

1. The current insurance must have become effective at the same time the prior policy was canceled or terminated. Any gap in coverage between the past policy and the current policy eliminates coverage under this provision.

2. The loss must be one that would have been covered by the prior policy and by the *current* insurance had it been in effect at the time when the acts or events causing the loss during a prior policy period were committed.

If the above conditions are met, payment (by the current insurer) is limited to the *lesser* of (1) the amount recoverable under the current policy as of its *effective* date or (2) the amount that would have been payable under the prior insurance.

Without the Loss Sustained During Prior Insurance condition, an insurer would have difficulty selling employee theft coverage to any firm that already had the coverage with another insurer. If the insured switched insurance companies, the insured would (after the one-year reporting period of the prior policy ended) be without coverage for employee theft that occurred before the inception date of the new policy. The Loss Sustained During Prior Insurance condition, in effect, eliminates the "penalty" for changing insurance companies.

> **FOR FURTHER THOUGHT**
>
> **Superseded Suretyship**
>
> The condition that is now titled Loss Sustained During Prior Insurance was formerly titled Superseded Suretyship in fidelity bonds, the branch of suretyship from which employee theft insurance evolved. Some insurance practitioners still refer to this condition as the superseded suretyship provision instead of using the longer modern term.

Loss Covered Under This Insurance and Prior Insurance Issued by Us or Any Affiliate

In some cases, the same employee or employees may commit a series of related thefts over an extended period of time. In accordance with the policy definition of "occurrence," all of these thefts are considered to be a single occurrence. If the occurrence takes place over two policy periods, the loss may be covered under both policies, depending on when the loss is discovered. If the same insurer wrote both policies, the condition under discussion obligates the insurer only to pay the *higher* of the two applicable limits, not the sum of both limits. The final paragraph of this condition states that, regardless of the number of years that the policy remains in force or the number of premiums paid, the limit of insurance does not accumulate from year to year or period to period. (The discovery form expresses the same paragraph in its Non-Cumulation of Limit of Insurance condition.)

Discovery Form

The discovery form contains a Discovery clause, which states that losses are covered no matter when they occurred if they are first discovered during the policy period or during the additional period of time provided by the Extended Period To Discover Loss condition.

Discovery occurs when the insured first becomes aware of facts that would cause a reasonable person to assume that a loss covered by the policy has occurred. Mere suspicion is not sufficient to constitute discovery. The general rule followed by the courts of most states, first enunciated almost 100 years ago by the U.S. Supreme Court in a case involving a financial institution bond, holds that discovery has not occurred unless the insured has knowledge—not simply suspicion—of the existence of facts that would justify "a careful and prudent [person] in charging another with fraud or dishonesty."[2]

Extended Period To Discover Loss

The Extended Period To Discover Loss condition of the discovery form allows the insured only sixty days after termination or cancellation of the policy to discover loss that was sustained before policy termination or cancellation. However, a one-year discovery period applies with respect to employee benefit plans, and by using endorsement CR 20 04, the insurer can change the sixty-day discovery period to a shorter or longer period.

The extended period to discover loss terminates immediately upon the insured's obtaining other insurance replacing in whole or in part the insurance provided by the prior policy, whether or not the other insurance provides coverage for loss sustained before its effective date. If the new insurance is written on a discovery basis, it will provide coverage for newly discovered losses that occurred during prior policy periods. If the new insurance is written on a loss sustained basis, the Loss Sustained During Prior Insurance condition of the new policy will provide coverage for newly discovered losses that occurred during prior periods.

The Loss Sustained During Prior Insurance condition is omitted from the discovery form, because the discovery form covers any loss that is first discovered during its policy period no matter when the loss occurred—unless the policy has been limited by an optional retroactive date endorsement, as discussed below.

Retroactive Date Endorsement

Coverage for undiscovered losses no matter when they might have occurred can be a major advantage of the discovery form. An insured that has been in business for many years without employee theft insurance would be covered by a newly purchased policy for a loss that was discovered during the term of the new policy no matter when the loss originated.

This broad coverage can create an adverse selection problem as well as moral and morale hazards that an underwriter may not be willing to assume. To avoid this exposure, the underwriter can attach endorsement CR 20 05, Include Retroactive Date for Named Insured. Underwriters might also attach the endorsement if (1) they believe that the insured may have an unacceptable level of incurred but undiscovered prior losses or (2) an insured requests a large increase in the amount of coverage.

The endorsement provides that coverage is limited to losses the insured sustains through acts committed or events occurring after the retroactive date shown in the policy schedule and discovered during the policy period. If the retroactive date is set as the inception date of the policy, the policy will not cover any acts committed before the policy period.

Policy Bridge Endorsement

Commercial crime policies that have been written on a loss sustained basis may be renewed on a discovery basis. For insureds whose loss experience has been satisfactory, these renewal policies, in many cases, will not contain a retroactive date endorsement. Therefore, there will be overlapping coverage between the one-year discovery period in the expiring policy and the discovery basis coverage in the renewal policy. To smooth the transition, the endorsement titled Policy Bridge—Discovery Replacing Loss Sustained (CR 20 03) can be made a part of the renewal policy.

The **policy bridge endorsement** suspends the Other Insurance condition when the new policy replaces similar prior insurance that contained an extension of time to discover losses. The endorsement provides that losses discovered during the extended discovery period of the prior policy are not covered under the renewal policy unless the loss exceeds the limit of insurance in the prior policy. In that case, the renewal policy insurer will pay no more than the difference between the renewal policy limit and the expiring policy limit. Such a payment will not be subject to the new policy deductible.

No bridge endorsement is needed when a loss sustained form replaces a discovery form policy. The Loss Sustained During Prior Insurance provision in the loss sustained form will provide coverage for prior losses as previously discussed.

Interests Insured

Several conditions of the ISO crime forms are aimed at clarifying certain matters with respect to interests insured.

Ownership of Property; Interests Covered

The insurance applies only to property owned, leased, or held by the named insured or for which the named insured is legally liable. Moreover, the insurance is for the named insured's benefit only; it is not intended to provide rights or benefits to anyone else.

Joint Insured

The Joint Insured condition addresses situations in which more than one insured is named on a policy. This is common when two or more entities have the same ownership or control—for example, a parent corporation and its subsidiaries. In these cases, the first named insured acts not only for itself but also for all other insureds.

In addition, if any insured, partner, or officer of that insured knows any information relevant to the insurance, that knowledge is considered to be knowledge of every insured. For example, the Cancellation as to Any Employee condition (discussed earlier in connection with employee theft coverage) excludes coverage on an employee from the time that the insured learns that the employee has committed a theft or other dishonest act. Because of the Joint Insured condition, knowledge of a dishonest act by one insured would eliminate coverage with respect to that employee for all other insureds as well.

Another effect of this provision (when the policy includes joint insureds for employee theft coverage) is to provide employee theft coverage to *every* insured with respect to employees of *any other* insured.

Consolidation—Merger

If the covered organization consolidates or merges with another organization or purchases additional facilities, the policy automatically extends coverage to additional employees and premises for acts committed or events occurring within ninety days. The insurer must be notified within this ninety-day period of the consolidation or merger and pay the additional premium to extend coverage permanently. Because consolidations and mergers are much less common among government entities than among commercial enterprises, the government crime forms do not contain the Consolidation—Merger condition.

Claims Conditions

Several conditions describe the procedures and practices that will be used following a loss involving covered property.

Duties in the Event of Loss

The insured must perform the following duties after discovering a loss or situation that may be covered under the policy:

1. Notify the insurer as soon as possible.
2. Submit to an examination under oath at the insurer's request and give the insurer a signed statement of the insured's answers.
3. Give the insurer a detailed, sworn proof of loss within 120 days.
4. Cooperate with the insurer in the investigation and settlement of any claim.

For all of the crime insuring agreements except employee theft and forgery or alteration, the insured must also notify the police if the insured has any reason to believe that a covered loss involves a violation of the law.

Records

The Records condition requires the insured to keep records of all covered property so that the insurer can verify the amount of any loss. This clause emphasizes the obligation that an insured always has: to prove the amount of the loss. Failure to maintain adequate records can deprive an insured of coverage for a loss.

Valuation—Settlement

The Valuation—Settlement condition explains how money, securities, and other property will be valued for purposes of claim settlement. Subject to some exceptions and alternatives that will not be described here, losses are valued as follows:

- Covered loss of *money* is paid at the face value of the money.
- Covered loss of *securities* is paid at the market value of the securities at the close of business on the day the loss was discovered.
- Covered loss of or damage to *other property* (or to the "premises" or their exterior) is paid on a replacement cost basis without deduction for depreciation. However, the insurer will pay no more than the least of the following:
  1. The applicable limit of insurance
  2. The cost to replace the lost or damaged property with property of comparable material and quality
  3. The amount the insured actually spends that is necessary to repair or replace the lost or damaged property

Loss to property that is not actually repaired or replaced is paid on an actual cash value basis.

Deductible

The Deductible provision is contained in a separate section of the crime forms, not in the Conditions section. However, the deductible wording is of direct importance to claims settlement. No loss in any one occurrence is payable by the insurer unless the amount of loss exceeds the deductible amount. If the amount of loss exceeds the deductible amount, the insurer will pay the amount of the loss in excess of the deductible, up to the limit of insurance.

> **APPLICATIONS**
>
> Tri-State Supply Company has employee dishonesty coverage with a $50,000 limit and a $500 deductible. If one employee stole $4,000 of covered property, the insurer would pay the amount of loss in excess of the $500 deductible, or $3,500. If the amount of loss exceeded the limit of insurance, the insured would be able to recover the full amount of insurance. For example, on a loss of $50,500 or more, the insurer would pay the full $50,000 limit in excess of the $500 deductible. In other words, *the deductible is taken off the amount of the loss, not off the limit.*

Recoveries

After settlement for covered loss, the insurer may be able to recover property that has been stolen or otherwise lost. According to the Recoveries condition, if the insurer is successful in making any recoveries, the insurer is first allowed to recover its cost of obtaining the recovered property. Next the insured is reimbursed for any loss in excess of the limit of insurance and the deductible. Then the insurer is reimbursed up to the amount it made in settlement of the claim. Finally, in the unlikely event there is any remaining value to the recovered property, the insured is reimbursed for the deductible amount.

This procedure for sharing recoveries differs from the procedure in many other property insurance policies. In the ISO inland marine provisions, for example, it is usual for the net recovery to be applied first to what the insurer has paid in settlement of the loss. The balance, if any, goes to the insured.

> **APPLICATIONS**
>
> An employee of XYZ Company embezzled $500,000 and fled the country. XYZ's employee theft coverage had a limit of $200,000 and a $500 deductible. Accordingly, XYZ's insurer paid the full limit of $200,000. (Remember, the deductible is subtracted from the loss, not the limit.) The insurer hired a private detective, who recovered $400,000 of the money for a fee of $50,000 paid by the insurer. Out of the $400,000 recovered, the insurer would first recover the $50,000 it paid in recovery costs. Next, the insured would receive $299,500—the amount of its loss in excess of the limit of insurance and the deductible ($500,000 – $200,500). Finally, the insurer would receive the remaining $50,500 of the recovery proceeds, since at this stage the insurer is entitled to receive up to the full amount it paid in settlement. XYZ would not be able to recover the deductible amount.

Subrogation

The condition titled Transfer of Your Rights of Recovery Against Others to Us is more concisely known as a subrogation clause. Like most other insurance policies, a crime policy requires the insured to transfer its rights of recovery against others to the insurance company. Moreover, the insured must do nothing after loss to impair those rights.

Other Insurance

According to the Other Insurance condition, the insurance does not apply to loss recoverable under other insurance unless the other insurance is insufficient to cover the whole loss. In that case, the insurance will apply in excess of the other insurance, but only for an amount that, when added to the other insurance, does not exceed the limit of insurance.

GOVERNMENT CRIME FORMS

Indemnification and Faithful Performance

The government crime forms contain an indemnification condition not found in the commercial crime forms. The **indemnification condition** states that the insurer will indemnify any of the insured's officials who are required by law to provide faithful performance bonds against loss resulting from theft committed by employees who serve under these officials.

When such bonding requirements exist, the official may be held responsible to the insured public entity for loss resulting from theft committed by the official's subordinates. The indemnification condition confirms that the insurer will indemnify the official for such losses, enabling the official to indemnify the insured as required by law. This condition prevents the insured from having to proceed against its own officials to recover for employee theft committed by the officials' subordinates. The amount that the insurer will pay to indemnify an official of the insured is limited to the amount of insurance provided.

Faithful performance of duty coverage can be added to government crime policies by endorsement CR 25 19. The endorsement broadens employee theft coverage to include loss "resulting directly from the failure of any 'employee' to faithfully perform his or her duties as prescribed by law." This language provides coverage for various breaches of faithful performance that might not meet the criteria for employee theft.

If two crime policies containing this Other Insurance provision covered the same loss, each with sufficient limits, the insured could be put in the absurd position of having both insurers deny coverage altogether on the basis of this provision. If the insurers could not resolve the claim between themselves, a court would probably hold that the clauses are to be disregarded as "mutually repugnant." The loss would be apportioned between the two insurers as directed by the court, probably using proration by limits.

EMPLOYEE DISHONESTY COVERAGE

The crime insurance program jointly developed by ISO and the Surety Association of America (SAA), which was the predominant commercial crime program before ISO filed its current crime program, included employee *dishonesty* coverage forms instead of the current employee *theft* insuring agreements. The SAA Crime Protection Policy, which SAA introduced in 1999, uses the employee dishonesty approach, as do the Employee Dishonesty Coverage Form of the American Association of Insurance Services and some insurers' independently filed crime forms.

Thus, it is important for insurance professionals to understand the differences between employee theft coverage and employee dishonesty coverage. Even producers or insurance companies that have converted their entire books of business to the employee theft form will still want to know the terms and conditions of employee dishonesty coverage. One reason is to understand what their competitors are offering. Another is to have the understanding required to settle claims for acts that were committed while a prior employee dishonesty policy was in force.

The employee dishonesty insuring agreement from the SAA Crime Protection Policy is reproduced below.

> Employee Dishonesty
>
> We will pay for loss of, and loss from damage to, **money**, **securities** and **other property** resulting directly from dishonest acts committed by an **employee**, whether identified or not, acting alone or in collusion with other persons, with the manifest intent to:
>
> a. Cause you to sustain loss; and also
>
> b. Obtain financial benefit (other than employee benefits earned in the normal course of employment, including: salaries, commissions, fees, bonuses, promotions, awards, profit sharing or pensions) for:
>
>   (1) The **employee**; or
>
>   (2) Any person or organization intended by the **employee** to receive that benefit.
>
> © The Surety Association of America, used by permission.

Key components of employee dishonesty coverage that set it apart from employee theft coverage include the requirements for a "dishonest act," "manifest intent," and "financial benefit," as discussed below.

Dishonest Act

The policy provisions that define **employee dishonesty coverage** state that the employee's act must be dishonest, but the form does not define "dishonest." Therefore, "dishonest" takes its ordinary, reasonable meaning. Synonyms that dictionaries list for "dishonest" include "lying," "cheating," "deceiving," and "stealing." Thus, the phrase "dishonest act" denotes a broader range of offenses than "theft" as defined in the current ISO crime forms.

For example, an insured's purchasing manager might order office equipment from a supply house owned by his brother-in-law, knowing that the price charged by his relative was significantly higher than what other suppliers would have charged for the same equipment. The manager's behavior would not qualify as employee "theft" (as defined in the ISO crime forms), because the manager did not engage in "unlawful taking" of the employer's property. However, the manager's behavior would constitute a "dishonest act" that could (depending on additional criteria discussed below) be covered by employee dishonesty coverage.

Manifest Intent

Employee dishonesty forms also require that the employee must have acted with manifest intent to (1) cause a loss to the insured and (2) obtain financial benefit for the employee or for another person or entity that the employee wants to receive the benefit. This other person or entity might be a friend, a relative, or a favorite charity. Sometimes referred to as a "dual trigger," both elements of manifest intent must be present in order for coverage to apply. Thus, damage caused by a disgruntled employee who sets fire to his employer's property would not be covered. He undoubtedly intended to cause a loss to his employer, but he did not act with manifest intent to realize any financial benefit. In another case, a bank president failed to follow procedures when approving loans. The court found that he may have been dishonest in the broad sense of the term but held that the claim was not covered, because the bank president did not manifestly intend to cause a loss to the bank or to obtain personal profit for himself.[3]

Employee dishonesty forms usually do not define "manifest intent." However, *Webster's New World Collegiate Dictionary* (1997) defines "manifest" as "apparent to the senses . . . or to the mind" or "evident; obvious; clear; plain." Interpreting the words "manifest intent" has caused frequent coverage disputes. Some courts require specific proof that the employee intended to benefit from the dishonest act and to cause a loss to the employer.[4] Other courts have held that such specific proof of intent is not needed and have based coverage on a presumed intent to cause loss that is virtually certain to result from the dishonest act.[5] A claim by the employee that he or she did not intend to cause a loss to the employer is not conclusive. Such a claim would be evaluated in light of all the facts.[6]

In contrast with employee dishonesty forms, employee theft forms do not require manifest intent. The employee theft form does not require the insured to prove that the accused employee intended to cause a loss to the insured and obtain financial benefit for the employee or another person or entity. If, for example, an employee's only motive for stealing equipment from the employer was spite or revenge, and not financial benefit, employee theft insurance would still cover the loss.

Financial Benefit Other Than Employee Benefits

According to the language of the SAA employee dishonesty insuring agreement, the financial benefit that the dishonest employee seeks to obtain must be something "other than employee benefits earned in the normal course of employment, including: salaries, commissions, fees, bonuses, promotions, awards, profit sharing, or pensions."

For example, in the broadest sense of the term, it is dishonest for an employee to arrive late, leave early, and take three-hour lunches. The employer in such a case probably suffered a loss because it paid the employee a salary for work the employee did not perform. A claim for such loss would not be covered by employee dishonesty insurance because any salary earned in the normal course of employment does not satisfy the financial benefit other than employee benefits requirement.

More difficult cases arise when employees' dishonest acts increase the compensation they would otherwise have received. If a bookkeeper increases his salary from $400 to $600 per week without his employer's consent, can the employer submit a claim for the amount of the additional compensation received by the employee? Industry opinion is divided on this question. Some insurers hold that if the only financial benefit the employee received was salary, the claim does not meet the requirement of financial benefit other than salary. Others focus on the concept of *normal*. In their view, the extra $200 per week was not earned in the *normal* course of employment, and therefore employee dishonesty coverage applies.

Numerous court cases have dealt with claims for losses resulting from employees dishonestly inflating their earnings. These employees included salespersons who fraudulently misstated sales or leases, employees who manipulated timecards to receive payment for time they did not work, and employees who used other methods to inflate their compensation or bonuses.[7] However, almost all these cases involved older policy language, and many insurance practitioners would interpret the current employee dishonesty wording as allowing coverage for salaries inflated without the employer's authorization.[8] Some courts make a distinction where the insured does know about the payments. In a New York case, the insured's controller allegedly embezzled funds by paying himself unauthorized and excessive "salary, commission, and bonuses" from a payroll account over which he had exclusive control. The appellate division, reversing the lower court, held that if the insured's allegation that it did not knowingly make the payments to the controller was true, then the policy provision excluding coverage for benefits earned in the normal course of employment did not bar coverage.[9] The question, however, has not been settled. Some employee dishonesty insurers pay claims involving fraudulent salaries, while other insurers deny coverage.

Because employee *theft* coverage does not include a similar exclusion of employee benefits, it covers such claims as long as the employee's taking of additional salary or other employee benefits constitutes an unlawful act.

> **FOR FURTHER THOUGHT**
>
> ### SAA Crime Protection Policy
>
> Apart from the fact that the SAA Crime Protection Policy provides employee *dishonesty* coverage instead of employee *theft* coverage, this policy resembles the ISO commercial crime forms in many ways. The basic insuring agreements of the two forms are compared below.
>
> | ISO Commercial Crime Forms | SAA Crime Protection Policy |
> |---|---|
> | 1. Employee *Theft* | 1. Employee *Dishonesty* |
> | 2. Forgery or Alteration | 2. Forgery or Alteration |
> | 3. Inside the Premises—Theft of Money and Securities
4. Inside the Premises—Robbery or Safe Burglary of Other Property | 3. Inside the Premises
Includes the same coverages as ISO insuring agreements 3 and 4. |
> | 5. Outside the Premises | 4. Outside the Premises |
> | 6. Computer Fraud | 5. Computer Fraud |
> | 7. Money Orders and Counterfeit Paper Currency | 6. Money Orders and Counterfeit Paper Currency |
>
> A further difference between the ISO crime forms and the SAA Crime Protection Policy is that the ISO crime forms have both a loss sustained version and a discovery version, whereas the Crime Protection Policy is a discovery form only.

SUMMARY

Twelve optional insuring agreements are available by endorsement for adding additional or substitute coverages to the ISO commercial and government crime forms. Exhibit 2-1 summarizes the optional insuring agreements.

Each ISO crime form comes in either a discovery form or a loss sustained form. The discovery form covers losses that are first discovered during the policy period no matter when the loss occurred. The loss sustained form covers loss that occurs during the policy period and is discovered during the policy period or within one year after policy expiration. The loss sustained form also covers loss that occurs under a prior policy if insurance has been in effect continuously and the loss would have been covered under both the previous and the current insurance.

Because some crime policies provide employee *dishonesty* coverage instead of employee *theft* coverage, an insurance professional must understand the differences between these two similar coverages. In order for a dishonest act to be covered under employee dishonesty insurance, the employee who committed the act must have exhibited "manifest intent" to (1) cause a loss to the insured and (2) obtain financial benefit for the employee or for another person or entity. Moreover, the financial benefit must be something other than salary or other employee benefits earned in the normal course of employment. Employee theft insurance, which requires an "unlawful taking" of covered property to the deprivation of the insured, does not contain the above restrictions.

CHAPTER NOTES

1. General Business Law, *McKinney's Consolidated Laws of New York*, Book 19 (St. Paul, Minn.: West Publishing Co., 1988).
2. American Surety Co. of New York v. Pauley, 170 U.S. 133, as cited by Edward Etcheverry, "Discovery, Notice, Proof of Loss, and Suit Limitations," *Commercial Crime Policy* (Chicago: American Bar Association, 1997) p. 12–11.
3. Federal Deposit Insurance Corporation v. St. Paul Fire & Marine Ins. Co., 942 F. 2d 1032 (1991) cited in "Employee Dishonesty Insurance," *Malecki on Insurance*, July 1992, p. 2.
4. The various interpretations of "manifest intent" are discussed in more detail, with citations, by Andrew M. Reidy and Barbara M. Tapscott: "The Pitfalls of Fidelity Insurance," *The National Law Journal*, March 4, 1996; Michael Keeley, "Employee Dishonesty Claims: Discerning the Employee's Manifest Intent," 30 *Tort and Insurance Law Journal* 915 (1995); and Michael Keeley and Harvey Koch, "Employee Dishonesty: The Essential Elements of Coverage Under Insuring Agreement A," in Duncan Clore, ed., *Financial Institution Bonds*, 2d ed. (American Bar Association, 1998).
5. Liberty National Bank v. Aetna Life & Casualty, 568 F. Supp 860, 868 (D.N.J. 1983).
6. Federal Deposit Insurance Corp. v. United Pacific Insurance Co., 20 F.3d 1070, 1078 (10th Cir. 1994).
7. James B. Lansing Sound, Inc. v. National Union Fire Ins. Co., 801 F.2d at 1567, and Efrain Dickson v. State Farm Lloyds, 944 S.W. 2d 666.
8. See, for example, Bruce Hillman, "Insurers Should Do the Right Thing in Judging Claims," *National Underwriter* (P&C edition), May 13, 1996, p. 13.
9. Klyn v. Travelers Indem. Co., 709 N.Y.S. 2d 780 (App. Div. 4th Dep't. 2000). The decision quoted Federal Deposit Ins. Corp. v. St. Paul Fire & Marine Ins. Co., 738 F Supp 1146, 1160 (*mod on other grounds* 942 F.2d 1032); "Where the employer does not knowingly pay funds to its employee under the belief that the funds have been honestly earned, but is instead unaware of the employee's receipt of the funds or pays the lost funds for some purpose other than the employee's compensation, the employee has committed pure embezzlement which is recoverable under the [policy]."

Appendix: Summary of Selected ISO Crime Endorsements

This appendix is not a complete listing of ISO crime endorsements but is included to give examples of how the ISO crime forms can be modified by endorsement to meet special needs. For a complete listing of endorsements, refer to the appropriate ISO reference materials.

Form No.	Form Name	Description
CR 20 02	Policy Change (Loss Sustained Form)	Shows the name of the insured, effective date of the change, and kind of change made to amend the policy.
CR 20 03	Policy Bridge—Discovery Replacing Loss Sustained	Provides excess coverage for loss that occurred during prior insurance. (Suspends the other insurance condition when a discovery policy replaces a loss sustained policy that included an extension of time to discover losses.)
CR 20 05	Include Retroactive Date for Named Insured	Limits coverage to losses the insured sustains through acts committed or events occurring after the retroactive date shown in the policy schedule and discovered during the policy period. (Used with discovery form only.)
CR 20 08	Convert to an Aggregate Limit of Insurance	Limits the total recoveries under the policy to a predetermined amount regardless of the number of occurrences during the policy period.
CR 20 09	Annual Territorial Limits	Amends Territory condition by adding or deleting territories as shown in the schedule.
CR 20 16	Provide Notice of Cancellation to Another Entity	Requires the insurer to notify listed entity that coverage is canceled.
CR 20 19	Obligee	Allows a higher body of government to be named as the insurance beneficiary.
CR 25 01	Exclude Designated Persons or Classes of Persons as Employees	Excludes employee theft coverage for specific persons, classes of persons (e.g., controlling stockholders), or employees.
CR 25 02	Include Designated Agents as Employees	Extends the definition of "employee" to include the insured's designated agents (e.g., independent contractors) listed in a schedule on the endorsement.

Form No.	Form Name	Description
CR 25 03 honest	Include Partners as Employees	Provides employee theft protection to the partners in an enterprise who have sustained loss because of the acts of a dishonest partner.
CR 25 04	Include Members of a Limited Liability Company as Employees	Amends definition of "employee" to include members of an insured limited liability company.
CR 25 05	Include Leased Workers as Employees	Provides employee theft coverage for leased employees.
CR 25 07	Include Specified Directors or Trustees on Committees as Employees	Extends definition of "employee" for not-for-profit insureds.
CR 25 08	Include Specified Non-Compensated Officers as Employees	Provides coverage for the officers not compensated as employees by the insured.
CR 25 09	Include Volunteer Workers as Employees	Extends definition of "employee" to include volunteers.
CR 25 16	Add Trading Coverage	Provides limited coverage for trading losses.
CR 25 17	Add Warehouse Receipts Coverage	Schedules a limit for loss from the fraudulent or dishonest signing, issuing, canceling, or failing to cancel a warehouse receipt.
CR 25 18	Add Faithful Performance of Duty Coverage	Provides coverage to a fraternal order or similar organization for failure of an "employee" to faithfully perform duties prescribed by its constitution and by-laws.
CR 25 19	Add Faithful Performance of Duty Coverage for Government Employees	Provides coverage to a governmental entity for failure of an "employee" to faithfully perform duties prescribed by law.
CR 25 20	Add Credit, Debit or Charge Card Forgery	Provides coverage for loss if a "written instrument" (i.e., credit, debit, or charge card) is involved. (Used by corporations that provide credit cards for business purposes to employees.)
CR 25 21	Add Warehouse Receipts Forgery	Provides coverage for loss from forged warehouse receipts or withdrawal orders.
CR 25 22	Include Personal Accounts of Specified Persons	Provides coverage for personal accounts of specified persons (e.g., loss from the unauthorized use of a credit card).
CR 25 34	Add Schedule Excess Limit of Insurance for Specified Employees or Positions	Provides an excess limit of insurance on specified employees above the limit provided by blanket employee theft coverage.

Form No.	Form Name	Description
CR 25 37	Change Schedule (Loss Sustained Form)	Changes the names of covered employees or covered positions when employee theft coverage is written on a schedule basis.
CR 35 01	Exclude Specified Property	Reduces coverage by excluding loss of scheduled property.
CR 35 04	Increased Limit for Specified Property Subject to Special Limit of Insurance	Increases the $5,000 sublimit for specified property.
CR 35 06	Limit Coverage to Office Equipment	Limits covered property to office equipment for purposes of Inside the Premises coverage.
CR 35 08	Limit Coverage to Specified Portion of Premises	Limits Inside the Premises coverage to loss occurring in a specified part of the premises.
CR 35 09	Add Protective Devices or Services	Requires the insured to maintain protective devices or services described in the endorsement.
CR 35 14	Reduce Limit of Insurance for Designated Premises	Reduces limit of insurance for listed premises.
CR 35 15	Decrease Limit of Insurance While Premises Not Open for Business	Lowers the limit of insurance while the premises are not open for business and a custodian is not on duty.
CR 35 19	Limit Coverage to Fixtures, Fittings or Appliances, or Property in Public Entrances, Hallways or Storerooms	Limits coverage to fixtures, fittings or appliances, or property in public entrances, hallways, or storerooms.
CR 35 20	Add Property of Others	Provides coverage for the property of others in addition to the basic coverage for the property of the insured.
CR 35 21	Include Theft of Outdoor Signs	Provides coverage for outdoor signs.
CR 35 22	Require Record of Checks	Requires the insured to make either a photograph or a descriptive record of checks the insured accepts.
CR 35 23	Extend Definition of Premises to Include Portion of Grounds Enclosed by Fence or Wall	Expands premises to include the enclosed grounds.
CR 35 24	Increase Limit of Insurance for Specified Periods	Provides a temporary increase for the limit of insurance during known periods of high activity. (Also known as the peak-season endorsement.)

Form No.	Form Name	Description
CR 35 25	Include Selling Price or Processing Charge	Changes the Valuation—Settlement condition to value finished goods at selling price and to include processing charges in the value of raw material or goods in process.
CR 35 26	Extend Premises to Entire Plot of Ground Under Your Control	Expands the definition of premises to include the entire plot of ground under the insured's control at the address shown in the schedule.
CR 35 27	Include Covered Property in Custody of Designated Agents	Provides coverage for the insured's property on the premises of an agent listed.

Chapter 3

Financial Institution Bonds

Few industries have crime loss exposures equal to those faced by financial institutions, such as banks, savings and loan associations, and securities dealers. The SAA maintains several different forms, called **financial institution bonds**, to cover these exposures. The names of the SAA bond forms, as well as two additional policies developed by SAA for financial institutions, are listed in Exhibit 3-1.

Forms differing from the SAA bonds are available from both domestic and London insurers. A significant number of financial institutions, particularly the larger ones, have at least part of their insurance placed in London. In addition, some insurers market independently developed package policies that include financial institution bond coverages, as well as other property and casualty coverages.

The SAA financial institution bonds are similar in many ways to the commercial crime forms already discussed. The differences are in large part accounted for by the nature of the loss exposures faced by financial institutions and the state and federal regulations requiring that financial institutions be protected by insurance against crime losses. Furthermore, financial industry trade groups, such as the American Bankers Association, have been influential in shaping the SAA financial institution bonds to provide greater protection for their members.

There is only historical significance to the fact that these insurance contracts are called "bonds." At one time, a condition of being employed by a bank or other financial institution was that employees give their bonds as to their honesty. Employees would pay a surety company to "guarantee" their honesty, and the surety company would bond the employee. After the simplification of insurance forms in the 1980s, employee dishonesty insurance continued to be called a "fidelity bond." Because employee dishonesty is a major concern in underwriting financial institution coverage, these forms were traditionally handled by an insurance company's bond department.

Form 24 is the only financial institution bond discussed in any detail here. The other bonds follow similar formats with clauses added or deleted to reflect

> **EXHIBIT 3-1**
>
> **SAA Financial Institution Forms**
>
> | Name of Form | Used To Insure |
> |---|---|
> | Form No. 14 | Stockbrokers and investment bankers |
> | Form No. 15 | Mortgage bankers and finance companies |
> | Form No. 23 | Credit unions |
> | Form No. 24 | Commercial banks, savings banks, and savings and loan associations |
> | Form No. 25 | Insurance companies |
> | Excess Bank Employee Dishonesty Bond, Form No. 28 | Commercial banks |
> | Combination Safe Depository Policy | All of the above |
> | Computer Crime Policy | All of the above |

the differing nature of the exposures they are designed to cover. This chapter concludes with brief descriptions of the other SAA forms designed for financial institutions. The appendix to this chapter lists and briefly describes the various riders (endorsements) that can be added to financial institution bonds.

FORM 24 FOR BANKS AND SAVINGS INSTITUTIONS

Standard Form No. 24, used to insure commercial banks and savings and loan associations, is one of the most widely used of the SAA financial institution forms.

For many years, this form was called the **Bankers Blanket Bond**, and that term is still often used as a generic description of this type of insurance.

Insuring Agreements

Form 24 contains the six insuring agreements listed below. Agreements A, B, C, and F are required components of the policy. Agreements D and E, though printed in the form, are optional. Also optional is a computer systems rider.

A. Fidelity
B. On Premises
C. In Transit
D. Forgery or Alteration
E. Securities
F. Counterfeit Currency

Each insuring agreement is summarized below, with emphasis on the differences between the financial institution bond coverage and the commercial crime coverage forms described earlier.

Fidelity

The agreement titled "Fidelity" (the historical name for employee dishonesty coverage) is the most important element of the bond; employee dishonesty accounts for the vast majority of losses, as well as the most severe losses. The fidelity agreement covers loss caused by dishonest or fraudulent acts committed by "employees." The definition of "employee" in the financial institution bond is broader than that in the Employee Dishonesty Coverage Form because it includes (1) attorneys and their employees retained by the insured while performing legal services for the insured and (2) corporations or partnerships and their employees performing data processing of checks or other records for the insured.

Fidelity coverage in the financial institution bond forms requires that the employee's acts be committed with the manifest intent to (1) cause the insured to sustain loss and (2) obtain financial benefit for the employee or another person or entity. The manifest intent requirements were discussed in Chapter 2 in connection with employee dishonesty insurance.

On Premises

The on-premises agreement provides coverage that is broader than that of any of the other crime forms discussed so far. It covers almost any kind of personal property (including money and securities) located at any office or premises anywhere in the world against an extremely broad range of perils.

The definition of covered "property" in the policy is extremely broad, encompassing money, securities, and personal property other than securities:

> Property means Money, Certificated Securities, Uncertificated Securities of any Federal Reserve Bank of the United States, Negotiable Instruments, Certificates of Deposit, Documents of Title, Acceptances, Evidences of Debt, Security Agreements, Withdrawal Orders, Certificates of Origin or Title, Letters of Credit, insurance policies, abstracts of title, deeds and mortgages on real estate, revenue and other stamps, tokens, unsold state lottery tickets, books of account and other records, whether recorded in writing or electronically, gems, jewelry, precious metals in bars or ingots, and tangible items of personal property which are not hereinbefore enumerated.

The Uniform Commercial Code is often used as a reference for defining specific terms within this definition of covered "property." The on-premises coverage insures such "property" against loss by robbery, burglary, misplacement, and mysterious unexplained disappearance, as well as damage to or destruction of the property, while the property is "lodged or deposited within offices or premises located anywhere." To be covered against the perils listed above, the property need not be at premises of the insured. The property could be at another banking premises in a foreign country, for example, and still be covered. Loss caused by riot or civil commotion outside the United States and Canada is excluded, however.

Additional covered perils, if committed by a person present at the *insured's* premises, are theft, false pretense, and common-law or statutory larceny.

However, the on-premises coverage excludes employee dishonesty losses covered by the fidelity insuring agreement of the bond.

On-premises coverage also applies to loss of or damage to furnishings, fixtures, supplies, or equipment within a covered office of the insured if caused by actual or attempted larceny, theft, burglary, or robbery, or by vandalism or malicious mischief. Damage to the office building itself by actual or attempted larceny, theft, burglary, or robbery is also covered. Damage to the *interior* of the office building by vandalism or malicious mischief is covered as well. However, to be covered for the losses described in this paragraph, the insured must either own or be legally liable for the furnishings, fixtures, supplies, equipment, or office.

Form 24 excludes fire loss to real property, furniture, fixtures, and other similar items. If, for example, burglars set the office on fire, loss by fire to money (or any other "property" as defined) would be covered, but fire damage to furnishings, fixtures, and the building would not be covered. However, the insured's commercial property insurance will generally cover fire loss caused by criminals, as well as damage to furnishings, fixtures, supplies, and equipment within the insured's offices resulting from larceny, burglary, robbery, or vandalism.

This overlap between the financial institution bond and the commercial property policy does not generally create a problem because the deductibles on financial institution bonds are usually much higher than those on commercial property policies. When the loss exceeds both deductibles or the deductibles are the same, a dispute can arise between the two insurers because the Other Insurance provision in each policy typically states that each policy is excess over any other insurance. Using the same insurer for both the financial institution bond and for the commercial property insurance, when that option is possible, can avoid such problems. Several insurers have developed package policies for financial institutions that combine bond coverages and commercial property and liability forms in one policy.

In Transit

The in-transit coverage agreement insures "property" (as defined above) while in transit anywhere in the custody of certain types of individuals or organizations as described below. The covered perils are "robbery, common-law or statutory larceny, theft, misplacement, mysterious unexplainable disappearance, being lost or made away with, and damage thereto or destruction thereof."

The property in transit must either be (1) in the custody of a natural person acting as messenger or (2) in the custody of a transportation company and being transported in an armored vehicle. However, certain types of lower-risk property specified in the bond are also covered while in the custody of a transportation company and being transported in a conveyance *other than* an armored motor vehicle. These types of property include (1) records, (2) certificated securities issued in registered form and not endorsed, and (3) negotiable instruments not payable to bearer or not endorsed. The insurance provided by this insuring agreement is excess over any valid and collectible insurance of the transportation company.

Forgery or Alteration

Although the forgery or alteration insuring agreement appears in the standard bond form, it is an optional coverage. Appropriate entries on the declarations page indicate whether it has been purchased. The insuring agreement covers loss resulting from forgery of a signature or alteration involving most types of negotiable instruments and certain other listed instruments. Losses resulting from written instructions directed toward the insured that have been altered or bear a forged signature are also covered.

The term **forgery** is defined to mean only the signing of the name of another with the intent to deceive. It does not include the genuine but unauthorized signature of the signer. A genuine but unauthorized signature could be, for example, a corporate officer's signature on a check that exceeds the officer's authority. Although this may be a dishonest act covered by Agreement A—Fidelity, it would not constitute forgery or alteration. Machine-produced signatures are treated the same as handwritten signatures under the forgery or alteration insuring agreement.

> **FOR FURTHER THOUGHT**
>
> **Unauthorized Signature Not a Forgery**
>
> John Doe, an insurance agent, issues bogus policies to customers. He collects checks from his customers drawn to the order of XYZ Insurance Company. Doe deposits those checks into account #1234, which he controls at his bank. He endorses the checks as follows:
>
> > John Doe, agent for XYZ Insurance Company
> > For deposit to account #1234
>
> Although this is an unauthorized signature, the signature is not a forgery as defined in the bond because it consists in part of a genuine signature.

Securities

The insuring agreement for securities, also optional, covers loss sustained by the insured because of its reliance on certain listed instruments that bear a forged signature, that are altered, or that are counterfeit or stolen. Often, these are instruments that the bank holds as collateral for a loan. The bank may sustain a loss when it attempts to sell the securities after default on the loan and then discovers that the instruments are counterfeit. The securities insuring agreement would cover such a loss. Another possible loss situation involves the forged signature of a spouse on a second mortgage on a home, which may invalidate the mortgage.

Counterfeit Currency

The counterfeit currency insuring agreement covers loss when the bank, acting in good faith, receives any counterfeited money of the United States, Canada, or another country in which the insured maintains a branch office.

Computer Systems

An optional computer systems rider (endorsement) can be added to the bond to cover loss resulting from the introduction of false data or programs into a computer system used by the bank. Because the fidelity insuring agreement covers such acts committed by employees, the computer systems rider applies to acts of nonemployees who gain access to the system. This coverage can be modified to fit specific exposures.

Exclusions

The financial institution bond contains several exclusions. Some of the more significant ones are as follows:

- Loan Exclusion
- Exclusion of Property Contained in Customers' Safe Deposit Boxes
- Trading Exclusion
- Uncollected Funds Exclusion
- Extortion Exclusion

Loan Exclusion

If the insured advances funds to a borrower with the expectation of repayment in the normal course of business, but such repayment is not made, the bond excludes coverage for the resulting loss. The intent of the policy is to provide coverage for dishonest acts, not unfortunate decisions regarding granting credit. Thus, as with many of the exclusions in the bond, an exception to the loan exclusion provides coverage if employee dishonesty is involved. In the fidelity insuring agreement, loss arising through loan activity is covered only if the employee acts in collusion with other parties to the loan transaction and receives a financial benefit of at least $2,500.

Exclusion of Property Contained in Customers' Safe Deposit Boxes

The bond does not cover loss resulting from the burglary or robbery of customers' property from safe deposit boxes unless the loss is caused by dishonesty on the part of a bank employee. The separate Combination Safe Depository Policy for financial institutions covers this exposure.

Trading Exclusion

Loss caused through *trading activity* in stocks, bonds, futures, commodities, or other similar items is not covered under the fidelity insuring agreement, even if employee dishonesty is involved. Trading coverage, however, can be purchased for an additional premium. The coverage for trading activities would still be subject to the manifest intent requirement of the fidelity insuring agreement. See the following discussion of "rogue trading."

> ### FOR FURTHER THOUGHT
>
> **Rogue Trading**
>
> In 1996, one of London's oldest and most respected banking firms, the Banngs Investment Group, discovered that one of its traders had run up $1.2 billion in losses in unauthorized trades in stock index futures. Later that year, Daiwa Bank in New York discovered that unauthorized securities trading by a single broker cost it $1.1 billion.
>
> The trading exclusion in SAA financial institution bonds excludes losses of this type, often referred to as "rogue trading." Even if the policy is extended to cover trading losses, losses of this type will probably not be covered because of the "manifest intent" requirement. In many of these cases, the huge losses arise from the employee's unauthorized efforts to make profits for the firm. These actions may be unwise and dishonest, but the employee usually does not manifest an intent to cause the employer to sustain a loss. On the contrary, rogue traders usually expect to reap huge profits for their firms.
>
> To close this coverage gap, underwriting syndicates at Lloyd's and other entities developed a policy that covers loss resulting from unauthorized trading. This policy will cover such loss even if the insured cannot show that the employee had personal gain as one of his or her motives.
>
> To be eligible for coverage, financial institutions must show that they have internal controls in place, such as written trading policies and independent oversight of trading activities. Initial interest in the coverage came from the largest national and global institutions that face huge exposures (trade press reports discuss limits as high as $400 million), but coverage could be just as important for smaller firms.
>
> Based on articles by Stephanie D. Esters, "Lloyd's Introduces Rogue Trading Policy," *National Underwriter,* Property & Casualty ed., October 20, 1997, p. 9; and Rodd Zolkos, "Policies Covering `Rogue Trading' Timely in Finance," *Business Insurance,* February 23, 1998, pp. 3 and 14.

Uncollected Funds Exclusion

The uncollected funds exclusion eliminates coverage for loss involving items of deposit that "are not finally paid for any reason." For example, the bond does not cover losses sustained because the bank honored a bad check or another item of deposit. The simplest way of managing this exposure is not to pay the item until it is collected through the clearing process.

Extortion Exclusion

Although the financial institution bond excludes loss by extortion, SAA riders can be added to the bond to cover, for an additional premium, threats against persons or property.

Coverage Trigger and Bond Term

Financial institution bonds apply on a discovery basis, covering loss sustained by the insured at any time but discovered during the bond period. If the bond is replaced by another "discovery basis" bond, the new bond will cover all losses discovered during the new bond period, regardless of when they occurred. Under normal circumstances, no need exists for a discovery period under the old policy or for a superseded suretyship provision under the new policy. If the bond is canceled, regulators require that the insured must replace it immediately. The replacement bond would cover any claim discovered after its inception until it expires, no matter when the loss occurred.

The term of a financial institution bond can be either continuous or for a fixed period, usually one year.

- If continuous, the term starts with the date shown in the declarations and runs continuously until canceled.
- If for a specified term, the bond period ends on the termination date shown in the declarations or in an endorsement.

The Loss Sustained Rider can be added to change the bond to respond to a covered loss that is both sustained by the insured and discovered during the bond period. A discovery period and superseded suretyship provision generally apply to the loss sustained form.

Limits of Liability

An aggregate limit of liability applies to the entire bond. In addition, a single-loss limit applies to each of the basic insuring agreements (insuring agreements A, B, C, and F). Optional insuring agreements (insuring agreements D and E) may have a single-loss limit in an amount less than that of the basic insuring agreements.

Deductibles

The SAA manual requires a minimum $1,000 deductible. There is no maximum deductible. In practice, most bonds are issued with deductibles much larger than $1,000. Deductibles for the largest financial institutions can run into the millions of dollars and are coordinated with sophisticated loss funding plans.

Notice of Loss

Like most other insurance policies, financial institution bonds require that the insured give prompt notice of loss to the insurer. Unlike most other policies, the financial institution bond adds the requirement that the report be made within thirty days of the discovery of loss. This requirement can create problems for insureds. Insureds are often reluctant to report dishonesty losses, perhaps because they believe that such losses reflect on the firm's management supervision. In one case, a bank officer supposedly disappeared with $5 million and a company car. The bank immediately reported the theft of the car but delayed for months before reporting the embezzlement.[1] Failure to promptly report a discovered loss can jeopardize coverage.

The requirement for prompt reporting has led to frequent litigation. In some jurisdictions, the insurer must show that it has been prejudiced by the insured's delay in giving notice. In others, the notice provision is considered a condition precedent, and failure to give timely notice defeats the insured's claim.[2]

Unlike many commercial policies, financial institution bonds do not require that police be notified if a law may have been broken.

BONDS FOR OTHER FINANCIAL INSTITUTIONS

Standard Form No. 24 is designed to meet the insurance needs of commercial banks, savings banks, and savings and loan associations. Other types of financial institutions have different exposures to loss, and four other financial institution bond forms are available to match their requirements:

1. Standard Form No. 14, for broker/dealers
2. Standard Form No. 15, for mortgage bankers and finance companies
3. Standard Form No. 23, for credit unions
4. Standard Form No. 25, for insurance companies

The details of coverage vary by form, depending on the exposures and needs of the particular type of financial institution for which each bond form is intended. For example, Forms 14 and 15 contain the same six insuring agreements that appear in Form 24 because the exposures are similar. Form 23 contains fidelity, on-premises, and in-transit insuring agreements because those are the most likely exposures for credit unions. Form 25 contains all but the counterfeit currency insuring agreement.

Because of changes in the financial services industry, the operations of different types of institutions are starting to overlap. For that reason, the bonds for these institutions are becoming increasingly similar. However, there are still differences between the forms. This text will contrast Forms 14 and 25 with Form 24, concluding with a brief description of Forms 15 and 23.

Form 14 for Broker/Dealers

Form 14 is designed to cover securities brokers and dealers. The volume of business handled by these firms is staggering, amounting to many billions of dollars a day worldwide. Form 14 is very similar to Form 24 for banks, but noteworthy differences exist in three areas: (1) coverage for partners, (2) insuring agreements, and (3) other provisions.

Coverage for Partners

Embezzlement or other dishonest acts committed by partners would not be covered under the wording used in Form 24 because partners would not meet the definition of employee. Although the omission of coverage for dishonest acts of partners does not create any problem for banks, it would for broker/dealers, which are often organized as partnerships. These partnerships may have dozens or even hundreds of partners. To meet this need for coverage, Form 14 includes partners in the definition of employee. If the insured or the underwriter desires, coverage for partners can be eliminated by an entry on the declarations page.

Coverage available for loss caused directly or indirectly by partners is excess over the partner's financial interest in the insured partnership and, of course, the policy deductible. For example, if a partner had a financial interest in the insured partnership equal to $500,000 and caused a loss to the firm of $1,250,000, the coverage would be limited to $750,000, less the deductible.

Insuring Agreements

The insuring agreements in Forms 14 and 24 are similar. The most important difference concerns trading losses. The trading exclusion in Form 24 (for banks) eliminates coverage for all losses resulting directly or indirectly from trading. (Coverage is available by rider.) In Form 14 (for broker/dealers), the exclusion applies only to customers' accounts. It does not apply to trading losses in the firm's account.

Furthermore, the exclusion pertaining to transactions in a customer's account does not apply to the unlawful withdrawal and conversion of money, securities, or precious metals directly from a customer's account by an employee of the insured—provided such unlawful withdrawal and conversion are covered under the fidelity insuring agreement.

Thus, for example, Form 14 provides coverage when an employee transfers money from a customer's account to his or her own account. It does not apply to a loss sustained by a customer because the value of a security declines, nor does it apply to losses resulting from "churning." Churning refers to sales activity initiated or encouraged by the salesperson solely to generate commissions.

The requirement of manifest intent discussed in connection with Form 24 applies to Form 14 as well. The rogue trading coverage discussed earlier would therefore be appropriate for broker/dealers.

The major differences between the insuring agreements for banks and those for broker/dealers are summarized in Exhibit 3-2.

Other Provisions

The exclusions in Form 14 are identical in almost all respects to those found in Form 24 with only a few minor differences. Some exclusions, such as the exclusion of loss of property in customer safe deposit boxes, are omitted in Form 14 because they do not pertain to the operations of broker/dealers. A few others are added or changed to reflect the different exposures of the two classes. Two have already been mentioned: (1) the exclusion of loss caused by a partner to the extent of the partner's financial interest in the firm and (2) the amendment of the trading loss exclusion to apply only to trading in customers' accounts. Some of the other exclusions added to Form 14 are as follows:

EXHIBIT 3-2

Major Differences Between Insuring Agreements in Form 14 for Broker/Dealers and Form 24 for Banks

Insuring Agreement	Differences from Form 24
Fidelity	Form 14 does not have a limitation on losses resulting from loans because loans are not part of their business.
	Form 14 limits coverage for transactions in a customer's account to the unlawful withdrawal and conversion of money, securities, or precious metals directly from a customer's account.
	Form 14 has no exclusion of trading in the firm's account.
	Form 24 excludes coverage for all trading loss, although some trading coverage can be added by endorsement, which would cover both customer and house accounts.
On Premises	No difference in coverage.
In Transit	No difference in coverage.
Forgery or Alteration	Unlike Form 24, Form 14 does not provide that telegraphic, cable, or teletype instructions sent by an impostor shall be deemed to be a forgery. Underwriters regard forgery or alteration of these types of instructions as an unacceptably increased risk for stockbrokers compared to other financial institutions.
Securities	Form 14 provides coverage for fewer types of securities than Form 24 does. For example, Form 24 includes documents of title in the list of securities, whereas Form 14 does not.
Counterfeit Currency	No difference in coverage.

- Dishonest acts of a nonemployee who is a securities, commodities, money, mortgage, real estate, loan, insurance, property management, or investment banking broker, agent, or representative
- Loss from investment advice or guarantees
- Loss due to liability for unlawfully disclosing or acting on nonpublic information

Form 25 for Insurance Companies

Most of the roughly 8,000 property, casualty, life, and health insurance companies operating in the United States are insured using **Financial Institution Bond Form No. 25.** Form 25 is very similar to Form 14 and Form 24. A few differences tailor the coverage specifically to the needs of insurance companies. Important differences are summarized below.

Limitation on Coverage for Loan Losses

Form 25 does not include the limitation found in Form 24 that fidelity losses due to loans are not covered unless the employee received a financial benefit of at least $2,500. Such loans are generally not a part of insurance company operations, so no limitation is required.

Theft and False Pretense Coverage

Theft and false pretenses are not named as covered perils in the On Premises insuring agreement of Form 25; they are specifically included in both Form 14 and Form 24. Although Form 25, like Form 14 and Form 24, includes coverage for common-law and statutory larceny, some states hold that false pretense losses are not included within the definition of larceny.

Office Locations Covered

Form 25 covers only the insured's offices located in the United States and Canada unless other offices are listed in the declarations. Form 14 and Form 24 cover loss of property within any office or premises, wherever located.

Property on Deposit

Unlike Form 14 and Form 24, Form 25 specifically includes property deposited with any political subdivision of the United States or Canada. (Insurance companies are frequently required to deposit securities with states or provinces to do business in the jurisdiction.)

Exclusions

Form 25 excludes loss resulting from contractual or extra-contractual liability, such as bad-faith claim handling. Because banks and stockbrokers do not face this exposure, Forms 14 and 24 do not include this exclusion.

Forgery Coverage

Forgery coverage in Form 25 includes forgery of policy loan documents and policy assignment forms. Forgery of negotiable instruments is only for those made or drawn by or drawn upon the insured. It does not include coverage for forged fund transfer instructions. As previously noted, Form 14 does not cover forgery or alteration of telegraphic, cable, or teletype instructions. Form 24 covers forgery or alteration of many types of documents that a bank would usually receive.

Form 15 for Mortgage Bankers and Finance Companies

Form 15 for mortgage bankers and finance companies is also very similar to Form 24. The few differences between Form 15 and Form 24 relate to the differences between the loss exposures of mortgage bankers and the loss exposures of commercial banks. For example, Form 15 does not cover forgery of registered or bearer obligations because mortgage bankers and finance companies do not face this exposure. They do not open bank accounts for their clients, and they do not issue registered checks.

Form 23 for Credit Unions

Form 23 is seldom used. Most credit unions are insured by an independently developed policy issued by an insurance company that specializes in credit unions.

OTHER FINANCIAL INSTITUTION BONDS AND POLICIES

The following three forms complete the SAA portfolio of coverages for financial institutions:

- Excess Bank Employee Dishonesty Bond, Form 28
- Computer Crime Policy for Financial Institutions
- Combination Safe Depository Policy for Financial Institutions

Form 28 is available only to banks. The computer crime form can be written for any organization eligible for any financial institution form. The combination safe depository policy can be written for any financial institution that provides safe deposit facilities.

Excess Bank Employee Dishonesty Bond

One of the most important questions facing the officers of a bank is how much coverage to buy; the possibility of a catastrophic loss is real. Fidelity losses to banks have been known to exceed $50 million caused by a single employee.

One method of covering large loss exposures is by means of the **Excess Bank Employee Dishonesty Bond, Form 28**. This bond is usually written for amounts of $1 million or more and covers as excess over other applicable bonds and insurance. It is an acceptable method of covering large losses caused by employee dishonesty, the peril most likely to cause extremely large losses. Lesser amounts are subject to loss from burglary and robbery, for example, so that the limits in a financial institution bond may be sufficient for those exposures.

This form is only available to banks. Other financial institutions desiring higher fidelity limits can increase the limit in their financial institution bond or purchase a nonstandard excess fidelity bond.

Computer Crime Policy

Advances in data processing have transformed the operations of financial institutions. They are now almost totally dependent on computers and computer data. Damage to computer systems and data can cause enormous loss to a financial institution. Although the computer systems of financial institutions generally have high levels of security, no system can be completely invulnerable to the acts of a knowledgeable criminal or a determined hacker.

To insure losses from criminal activity involving computers, the SAA developed its **Computer Crime Policy for Financial Institutions.** The policy, which is a companion to financial institution bonds, contains seven insuring agreements:

1. Computer systems fraud
2. Data processing service operations
3. Voice-initiated transfer fraud
4. Telefacsimile transfer fraud
5. Destruction of data or programs by hacker
6. Destruction of data or programs by virus
7. Voice computer system fraud

(Agreements 1, 3, and 4 above are also available as riders for Form 24.)

The core of the policy is the computer systems fraud agreement; all the other insuring agreements are optional. The computer systems fraud coverage insures loss caused by someone who has entered or changed electronic data or computer programs in the insured's computer system. However, this insuring agreement does not cover loss caused by employee dishonesty, which the financial institution bond covers.

The data processing service operations insuring agreement is designed for insureds that perform data processing services for others under contract. It covers loss sustained by the insured's clients caused by fraudulent entries or changes in the insured's computer system if the insured is legally liable to its client.

Insuring agreements 3 and 4 cover the fraudulent transfer of funds based on telephone or fax instructions given by someone pretending to be either a customer or an employee in another office. Security measures are required, and, when the transfer exceeds the amount specified in the policy, the transaction must be confirmed by a call-back to verify the instructions.

Insuring agreements 5 and 6 cover the cost required to restore data or programs damaged by a computer hacker or a computer virus. Repairing the damage may involve simple duplication of data from backup copies or complex restoration requiring skilled programmers and consultants. Both electronic data and computer programs are covered if they can be repaired by duplication; however, only computer programs are covered if they must be restored.

The hacker insuring agreement covers "malicious destruction of, or damage to, electronic data or computer programs." The virus insuring agreement covers the insured's computer system "if damage or destruction was caused by a computer program which was written or altered to incorporate a hidden instruction designed to destroy or damage electronic data or computer programs."

Insuring agreement 7 covers loss resulting from unauthorized voice telephone call charges. The charges can result from fraudulent use of codes or passwords to access the insured's voice communications network.

Like financial institution bonds, the computer crime policy provides coverage on a discovery basis. The policy in effect when the loss is discovered provides coverage; it does not matter when the loss occurred or whether the insured had insurance at that time.

In addition to financial institutions, many other types of organizations are susceptible to some or all of the perils described above. The computer fraud insuring agreement discussed in Chapter 1 and the funds transfer fraud insuring agreement discussed in Chapter 2 can be used to cover many of these perils. In addition, nonstandard forms used by some insurers can provide other computer crime coverages for organizations that are not eligible for financial institution bonds.

Combination Safe Depository Policy

Many financial institutions provide safe depository facilities for their customers and are thus exposed to legal liability for the loss of their customers' property. In addition, the institutions may want to cover customers' property, even when they are not legally liable for its loss to maintain customer goodwill. The **Combination Safe Depository Policy for Financial Institutions** can be used to provide coverage for these exposures.

The policy has two coverage options:

- Liability of the Depository
- Loss of Customers' Property; Premises Damage

The Liability of the Depository agreement covers almost all causes of loss to the extent of the financial institution's legal liability. The Loss of Customers' Property agreement includes coverage for damage to the insured's premises resulting from actual or attempted burglary or robbery or destruction of customers' property. Coverage for customers' property can either include or exclude money. Each coverage is subject to its own limit of insurance.

The combination safe depository policy can be written for organizations not eligible for financial institution bonds.

SUMMARY

Financial institutions obtain crime insurance under specialized forms called financial institution bonds. Financial Institution Bond Form No. 24, used to insure commercial banks and savings and loan associations, includes insuring agreements for fidelity (employee dishonesty), on premises, in transit, forgery or alteration, securities, and counterfeit currency. Other crime-related coverages can be added by rider (endorsement). The Excess Bank Employee Dishonesty Bond, Form 28, can be used to provide an additional layer of employee dishonesty coverage above the fidelity limit provided by Form 24.

Financial institution bonds similar to Form 24 are available for insuring securities brokers and dealers (Form 14), finance companies (Form 15), credit unions (Form 23), and insurance companies (Form 25). Separate policies for insuring computer crime and safe depository loss exposures of financial institutions are also available.

CHAPTER NOTES

1. R. Mark Keenan and Pablo Quinones, "Unraveling the Mystery of Insurance Coverage for Criminal Losses—It's No Shame to Claim," *Insurance Advocate*, May 16, 1998, p. 18.
2. Andrew M. Reidy and Barbara M. Tapscott, "The Pitfalls of Fidelity Insurance," *The National Law Journal*, March 4, 1996.

Appendix: Summary of Riders for SAA Financial Institution Bonds and Policies

Form #	Form Name	Form or Policy	Type of Organization	Description
SR 6185	Agents Fidelity Insuring Agreement	25	Insurance companies	Covers specifically named or described agents for life insurance companies. Schedules a separate single loss limit of liability for each agent.
SR 5376a	Exclusion of Industrial Agents Rider	25	Insurance companies	Excludes industrial agents, as employees, for life insurance companies.
SR 5976c	Agents Rider	24	Commercial banks, savings banks, and savings and loan associations	Includes, as employees, scheduled agents elected or appointed by the insured to perform duties that are ordinary in the course of the insured's business.
SR 6182a	Aggregate Limit— Reinstate or Increase	14, 15, 24, 25, 28, CCP	Financial institutions (other than credit unions)	Reinstates or increases aggregate limit mid-term.
SR 6035b	Amendatory Rider for Credit Union Blanket Bond	23	Credit unions	Revises Insuring Clause (a) by adding exclusions and provides definition for forgery.
SR 6183	Definition of Employee— Attorneys	25	Insurance companies	Includes, as employees, attorneys.
SR 5922b	Exclude Closing Attorneys	24	Commercial banks, savings banks, and savings and loan associations	Excludes closing attorneys.

Form #	Form Name	Form or Policy	Type of Organization	Description
SR 5347b	Closing Attorneys Rider—Title Insurance Companies	15	Mortgage bankers and finance companies	Covers attorneys retained to assist in real property closings or in making mortgage loans; also covers their employees.
SR 5886g	Automated Teller Machine Exclusion: Blanket "On Premises" Coverage: Schedule of Excluded Locations of Unattended Devices	24	Commercial banks, savings banks, and savings and loan associations	Provides limited "on premises" coverage. Covers ATMs against burglary and other perils within an office of the insured or other locations not excluded.
SR 6026a	Automated Teller Machine Exclusion: Blanket "On Premises" Coverage: Schedule of Excluded Locations of Unattended Devices	23	Credit unions	Provides limited "on premises" coverage. Covers ATMs against burglary and other perils within an office of the insured or other locations not excluded.
SR 5149b	Add a Branch Rider	23	Credit unions	Covers a branch office.
SR 5035c	Eliminate Branch Offices	14, 15, 23, 24, 25	Financial institutions	Excludes branch offices.
SR 5531	Rider Canceling an Existing Rider—Discovery Form	14, 15, 24, 25, 28	Financial institutions (other than credit unions)	Cancels or terminates an existing rider on a discovery form.
SR 5150b	Rider Canceling an Existing	14, 15, 23, 24, 25, 28	Financial institutions	Cancels or terminates an existing rider on a loss sustained form.

Continued on next page.

Form #	Form Name	Form or Policy	Type of Organization	Description
SR 5150b continued	Rider—Loss Sustained Form			
SR 5083c	General Cancellation Clause Rider	14, 15, 23, 24, 25, 28	Financial institutions	Provides a general notice of cancellation.
SR 5969a	Cancellation Rider [National Association of Securities Dealers]	14	Stockbrokers and dealers	Provides a notice of cancellation to the National Association of Securities Dealers. Used to comply with statutory or departmental authorities.
SR 5769c	Cancellation Rider [New York Stock Exchange]	14	Stockbrokers and dealers	Provides a notice of cancellation to the New York Stock Exchange. Used to comply with statutory or departmental authorities.
SR 5777b	Cancellation Rider [any recognized stock exchange, other than the New York Stock Exchange]	14	Stockbrokers and dealers	Provides a notice of cancellation to any recognized stock exchange, other than the New York Stock Exchange. Used to comply with statutory or departmental authorities.
SR 5834c	S.E.C.—Sole Insured Cancellation Clause Rider	14	Stockbrokers and dealers	Provides a notice of cancellation to the Securities and Exchange Commission for a Registered Management Investment Company covered as the sole insured. Used to comply with statutory or departmental authorities.
SR 5971a	S.E.C.—Joint Insured Cancellation Clause Rider	14	Stockbrokers and dealers	Provides a notice of cancellation to the Securities and Exchange Commission for Registered Management Investment Companies covered as joint insureds. Used to comply with statutory or departmental authorities.

Form #	Form Name	Form or Policy	Type of Organization	Description
SR 6004a	Cancellation Rider [Securities Investor Protection Corp.]	14	Stockbrokers and dealers	Provides a notice of cancellation to the Securities Investor Protection Corporation for the insured registered with the commission but not a member of a national securities association. Used to comply with statutory or departmental authorities.
SR 5923c	Cancellation Rider [National Credit Union Admn.]	23	Credit unions	Provides a 60-day notice of cancellation by the underwriter and provides, when appropriate, a notice of cancellation to the National Credit Union Administration. Used to comply with statutory or departmental authorities.
SR 5795d	SBA Cancellation Rider	15, 24	Mortgage bankers and finance companies; commercial banks, savings banks, and savings and loan associations	Provides a notice of cancellation to the Small Business Administration. Used to comply with statutory or departmental authorities.
SR 5967e	Central Handling of Securities	14, 24, 25	Stockbrokers and dealers; commercial banks, savings banks, savings and loan associations; insurance companies	Covers certificated securities while they are at a depository in a scheduled location. Covers the insured's interest in property recorded on the depository books.
SR 5151a	Change of Name or Address Rider	14, 15, 23, 24, 25, 28	Financial institutions	Provides the insured's change of name or address.

Form #	Form Name	Form or Policy	Type of Organization	Description
SR 6151a	Coinsurance Rider	14, 15, 24, 25, 28	Financial institutions	Provides a coinsurance provision for bonds with a single limit of liability on the declarations page.
SR 6149c	Computer Systems Fraud Insuring Agreement	24	Commercial banks, savings banks, and savings and loan associations	Covers the insured's proprietary system or one listed on the form for loss from the fraudulent entry of data or an unauthorized change or program. Loss includes property transferred, paid, or delivered from a covered computer system.
SR 6196	Computer Systems Fraud Insuring Agreement	14, 15, 25	Stockbrokers and dealers; mortgage bankers and finance companies; insurance companies	Covers the insured's proprietary system or one listed on the form for loss from fraudulent entry of data or an unauthorized change or program. Loss includes property transferred, paid, or delivered from a covered computer system.
SR 6133b	Computer Systems Fraud Insuring Clause	23	Credit unions	Covers the insured's proprietary system or one listed on the form for loss from fraudulent entry of data or an unauthorized change or program. Loss includes property transferred, paid, or delivered from a covered computer system.
SR 5262a	Concurrent Insurance Rider	14, 15, 23, 24, 25, 28	Financial institutions	Adds the additional insurance requirement. Used when a bond is issued concurrently with another bond.
SR 5261b	Cosurety Rider	14, 15, 24, 25, 28	Financial institutions (other than credit unions)	Adds the cosurety provision for loss participation. Used when two or more underwriters intend to share in the same layer of bond coverage or limit of liability.

Form #	Form Name	Form or Policy	Type of Organization	Description
SR 5887d	Credit, Debit, Charge, Access, Convenience, Identification or Other Card Exclusion	23	Credit unions	Excludes loss from credit, debit, or charge cards that obtain credit from, or gain access to, automated or electronic funds transfer systems.
SR 5851b	Data Processing Rider	23	Credit unions	Adds, as employees, data processing insureds and their partners, officers, employees.
SR 6100e	Delete Data Processing Coverage	14, 15, 24, 25	Financial institutions (other than credit unions)	Deletes coverage for data processing losses.
SR 6150c	Amend Declarations Page—Discovery Form	14, 15, 24, 25	Financial institutions (other than credit unions)	Adds a nonmidterm change to the declaration page for the discovery form.
SR 6172b	Amend Declarations Page—Loss Sustained Form	28	Commercial banks	Adds a nonmidterm change to the declaration page for the loss sustained form.
SR 6158	Amend Declarations Page—Standard Form No. 18	28	Commercial banks	Renews or extends the bond period or reinstates or increases the aggregate limit.
SR 6198	Amend Declarations Page	CCP	Financial institutions	Adds a change to declaration page.
SR 6170	Amend Declarations Page	CSD Policy	Financial institutions	Adds a nonmidterm change to the declaration page.
SR 5861b	Deductible Rider—Form No. 23	23	Credit unions	Provides a deductible amount for all insuring clauses.

Form #	Form Name	Form or Policy	Type of Organization	Description
SR 5711c	Clause (D) Aggregate Deductible Rider	23	Credit unions	Provides an aggregate deductible for Insuring Clause (D) for credit union blanket bond.
SR 6137b	joint Insured Varying Single Loss Deductible Rider	14, 15, 24, 25, 28	Financial institutions (other than credit unions)	Provides different deductible amounts for different joint insureds.
SR 5797b	Rider [Real Estate Investment Trusts (REIT)]	15	Mortgage bankers and finance companies	Covers directors or trustees of the insured. Used for Real Estate Investment Trusts.
SR 5673a	Draft-Signers Rider	25	Insurance companies	Includes, as employees, persons authorized to sign drafts on behalf of the insured who are empowered contractually to settle the insured's claims.
SR 5784b	Rider [Reduced Premium]	14	Stockbrokers and dealers	Provides a reduced premium for the insured with no employees.
SR 6059a	Effective Time Rider	23	Credit unions	Changes the time of inception or termination from noon to 12:01 A.M.
SR 6163	Exclusion (f) Rider	CSD Policy	Financial institutions	Replaces exclusion (f) with loss due to any fraudulent, dishonest, or criminal act by an officer or employee acting alone or in collusion.
SR 5935i	Extortion—Threats to Persons Rider	14, 15, 24, 25	Financial institutions (other than credit unions)	Adds loss of property surrendered from the insured's office as a result of threat to do bodily harm to any person. Extends coverage to a relative or invitee of specific insureds. Provides an optional coinsurance agreement.

Form #	Form Name	Form or Policy	Type of Organization	Description
SR 5943e	Extortion—Threats to Persons Rider	23	Credit unions	Adds loss of property surrendered from the insured's office as a result of threat to do bodily harm to any person. Extends coverage to relative or invitee of specific insureds. Provides an optional coinsurance agreement.
SR 6003e	Extortion—Threats to Property Rider	14, 15, 24, 25	Financial institutions (other than credit unions)	Adds loss of property surrendered from the insured's office as a result of threat to property. Provides a mandatory coinsurance agreement.
SR 6000e	Extortion—Threats to Property Rider	23	Credit unions	Adds loss of property surrendered from the insured's office as a result of threat to property. Provides a mandatory coinsurance agreement.
SR 5936e	Extortion Exclusion Rider	23	Credit unions	Excludes loss from surrender of property away from the insured's office.
SR 5956b	Extortion—Threats to Persons Rider—Branch Office Exclusion	14, 15, 23, 24, 25	Financial institutions	Excludes named locations.
SR 5991a	Extortion—Threats to Property Rider—Branch Office Exclusion	14, 15, 23, 24, 25	Financial institutions	Excludes named locations.
SR 5380b	Faithful Performance Rider	23	Credit unions	Adds dishonest or fraudulent acts with manifest intent of the employee, adds exclusions, and provides the definition of forgery.

Form #	Form Name	Form or Policy	Type of Organization	Description
SR 5697a	Foreign Employees Rider	28	Commercial banks	Covers employees in scheduled foreign branch offices.
SR 5609g	Fraudulent Mortgages Insuring Agreement	24	Commercial banks, savings banks, and savings and loan associations	Covers loss resulting from the insured having a defective security instrument because the signature was obtained by trick, artifice, fraud, or false pretense.
SR 6186	Freddie Mac, Fannie Mae or Ginnie Mae	14, 15, 23	Stockbrokers and dealers; mortgage bankers and finance companies; credit unions	Provides the loss-payee and notification agreement that suggests the underwriter make a good faith effort to give a thirty-day cancellation notice. Used to comply with the rules and regulations of secondary mortgage markets.
SR 5955c	Holding Company—As joint Insured	14, 15, 23, 24, 25, 28	Financial institutions	Adds the holding company as joint insured.
SR 5907a	Insuring Agreement (G) Rider	14	Stockbrokers and dealers	Covers facsimile signatures for an assignment or substitution.
SR 5379	Insuring Clause (D) Rider	23	Credit unions	Covers forgery or alteration.
SR 5297c	Increase-Decrease Rider	23	Credit unions	Increases or decreases coverage for forgery, alteration, or misplacement.
SR 5109a	Adding or Deducting Insureds Rider	14, 15, 23, 24, 25, 28	Financial institutions	Adds or subtracts joint insureds.
SR 5398a	joint Insured Rider—Loss Sustained Form	23	Credit unions	Covers joint insureds.
SR 5046d	Increase-Decrease Rider	23	Credit unions	Increases or decreases the amount of the bond.

Form #	Form Name	Form or Policy	Type of Organization	Description
SR 6111c	Delete Loan Participation Coverage	24	Commercial banks, savings banks, and savings and loan associations	Deletes coverage for underlying securities used as collateral for participation on a loan.
SR 6110e	Loss Sustained Rider	14, 15, 24, 25, 28	Financial institutions (other than credit unions)	Converts the discovery bond form to the loss sustained form.
SR 5077d	Maintenance Employees Rider	24	Commercial banks, savings banks, and savings and loan associations	Excludes building and maintenance employees in listed positions.
SR 5377	Misplacement Rider	23	Credit unions	Covers misplacement and mysterious unexplainable disappearance.
SR 5804e	Bank Money Order Issuer Rider	24	Commercial banks, savings banks, and savings and loan associations	Covers commercial bank money order issuers and their partners, officers, and employees.
SR 6168	Partnership Coverage	14	Stockbrokers and dealers	Covers a partner's dishonest and fraudulent acts.
SR 6145b	ERISA Rider	14, 15, 23, 24, 25, 28	Financial institutions	Limits employees to directors, trustees, or others handling funds or other property of a plan that the insured owns, operates, or controls.
SR 5558	Premises Rider	23	Credit unions	Covers property in Alaska, Hawaii, Puerto Rico, or Virgin Islands.
SR 5604a	Property Rider	25	Insurance companies	Covers property lodged or deposited with the government of a country other than the U.S. and Canada.

Form #	Form Name	Form or Policy	Type of Organization	Description
SR 6139a	National Association of Securities Dealers Rider	14	Stockbrokers and dealers	Covers a registered representative or registered principal associated with the insured who is not a sole proprietor, sole stockholder, director, or trustee of the insured.
SR 6191	Delete Restoration Coverage for Computer Programs	CCP	Financial institutions	Deletes restoration coverage for computer programs.
SR 6188	Retroactive Date Rider/Endorsement	14, 15, 24, 25, 28, CCP	Financial institutions	Adds a retroactive date for all insureds.
SR 6193	Retroactive Date Rider/Endorsement—Joint Insured	14, 15, 24, 25, 28, CCP	Financial institutions	Adds a retroactive date for specified joint insureds.
SR 6199	Retroactive Date Rider/Endorsement—Merger, Consolidation or Purchase of Assets	14, 15, 24, 25, 28, CCP	Financial institutions	Adds a retroactive date for merger, consolidation, or purchase of assets.
SR 5885	Safe Deposit Box Exclusion Rider	23	Credit unions	Excludes loss for property in a safe deposit box.
SR 6157b	Savings and Loan Association Rider	24	Commercial banks, savings banks, and savings and loan associations	Covers expenses for audits or examinations required by state or federal authorities resulting from a loss caused by the dishonest or fraudulent acts of employees.

Form #	Form Name	Form or Policy	Type of Organization	Description
SR 6171a	Savings Bank	24	Commercial banks, savings banks, and savings and loan associations	Covers a director or trustee employed as a salaried, pensioned, or elected official while acting as a member of a committee elected or appointed by the insured's board of directors or trustees.
SR 5869g	Servicing Contractors Insuring Agreement—Discovery Form	24	Commercial banks, savings banks, and savings and loan associations	Covers fraudulent or dishonest acts committed with manifest intent by a servicing contractor. Covers the loss of money that the servicing contractor fails to pay to the insured or fails to disburse to the insured according to the insured's instructions.
SR 5583d	Excludes Servicing Contractors	24	Commercial banks, savings banks, and savings and loan associations	Excludes coverage for specified banks, savings and loan associations, and banking institutions acting as servicing contractors.
SR 6152	Single Limit	CSD Policy	Financial institutions	Adds a single total limit for Insuring Agreements A and B.
SR 5089b	Statutory Coverage Rider	24	Commercial banks, savings banks, and savings and loan associations	Covers loss to savings and loan associations other than loss caused by described fraudulent or dishonest acts. Used to comply with statutes.
SR 6195	Telefacsimile Transfer Fraud Insuring Agreement	24	Commercial banks, savings banks, and savings and loan associations	Covers loss from fax transfer fraud.
SR 7000	Telefacsimile Transfer Fraud Insuring Clause	23	Credit unions	Covers loss from fax transfer fraud

Form #	Form Name	Form or Policy	Type of Organization	Description
SR 5965	Termination Section Amendatory Rider	23	Credit unions	Deletes the termination conditions and limitations. Used to comply with federal regulation.
SR 6027f	Trading Loss Rider	15, 24, 25	Mortgage bankers and finance companies; commercial banks, savings banks, and savings and loan associations; insurance companies	Covers loss from trading. Includes a Single Loss Limit of Liability.
SR 6095b	Trading Loss Rider	23	Credit unions	Covers loss from trading. Specifies an amount for the trading loss as part of, and not in addition to, the Limit of Liability.
SR 6220	Transit Cash Letter Insuring Agreement	24	Commercial banks, savings banks, and savings and loan associations	Covers loss from a transit cash letter.
SR 6064b	Uncollected Funds Exclusion	23	Credit unions	Excludes loss from the payout or withdrawal of uncollected funds for deposit.
SR 5856c	U.S. Savings Notes Rider	23	Credit unions	Includes U.S. savings notes under the Redemption of U.S. Savings Bonds provision.
SR 5307b	Valuation Clause Rider	14	Stockbrokers and dealers	Provides an alternative method for evaluating securities at the time of loss.
SR 5155b	Verification Certificate	14, 15, 23, 24, 25, 28	Financial institutions	Certifies bond ownership.
SR 6184a	Voice Initiated Transfer Fraud Insuring Agreement	24	Commercial banks, savings banks, and savings and loan associations	Covers loss from voice-initiated transfer fraud.

Form #	Form Name	Form or Policy	Type of Organization	Description
SR 6187b	Voice Initiated Transfer Fraud Insuring Clause	23	Credit unions	Covers financial institutions that rely on telephone instructions for authorization to transfer funds through a scheduled computer system. Requires a dollar amount for transfers above which telephone instructions are recorded electronically.

Note: The letter at the end of the form number changes each time the rider is amended. For example, the letter "c" means that the rider has been revised three times.

Chapter 4

Underwriting and Loss Control, Part I

Underwriters determine what risks the insurer will assume and avoid, the premium to be charged for the risks assumed, and the policy terms and conditions under which those risks will be assumed. Loss control attempts to prevent losses from occurring or to minimize the size of losses that do occur. Loss control personnel assist the underwriter by providing reliable information about the risk for the underwriting process. In addition, loss control might make some risks acceptable to the insurer that would not be acceptable in the absence of loss control.

Effective underwriting of commercial crime insurance and financial institution bonds comes principally from knowing how applicants manage their operations. Applicants that have effective loss control programs are usually good prospects for crime insurance. However, rate increases are unlikely to compensate for an insured's lax security or sloppy management.

The underwriting considerations for commercial crime coverages and those for financial institution bonds are the same in most respects. Chapters 4 and 5 discuss these common underwriting considerations as well as some additional underwriting considerations that are unique to commercial crime coverages or financial institution bonds.

This chapter describes sources of underwriting information, how underwriters evaluate applicants, and what controls underwriters recommend. Chapter 5 examines additional underwriting information and loss control measures and the factors underwriters consider when they calculate final premiums.

SOURCES OF UNDERWRITING INFORMATION

The application is the underwriter's primary tool for evaluating crime and financial institution risks. For certain classes of business, insurers create supplemental questionnaires. Answers to supplemental questionnaires fill information gaps and help underwriters decide whether an applicant meets the underwriting guidelines. Depending on the applicant's line of business, underwriters use financial reports, information from agents and brokers, and other documents to better understand the risk.

Application

Several sections in the crime applications for commercial businesses and financial institutions are similar, though they might not appear in the same sequence. Exhibits 4-1 and 4-2 are the ACORD Commercial Insurance Application and the ACORD Crime Section.[1] The Surety Association of America's Financial Institution Bond applications vary by type of bond and have slight variations by state to satisfy state laws. For example, some states require fraud warning statements in the application.

Named Insured and Location

The named insured should be properly listed on the application because the named insured has certain rights and responsibilities under the insurance contract. For example, the insurer mails notice of cancellation to the named insured. As mentioned in previous chapters, policy definitions often refer to the named insured. In addition, the first named insured has specific responsibilities to act for itself and on behalf of every other insured. Thus, the named insured should be properly identified to ensure that coverage is in order. Producers can help applicants complete this section accurately. An accurate description of the named insured also influences eligibility for coverage. For example, credit unions or financial institutions are not eligible insureds in a crime insurance policy. In addition, named insureds can create new exposures and affect how exclusions and conditions apply. For example, in some crime forms the named insured must notify police if there is any reason to believe the loss involved a violation of law.

Properly listing all the locations the applicant wants to insure is also important. The application asks for the mailing address and the location of all other existing locations the applicant wants to insure. This information affects rates and where the insurer mails cancellation notices. In addition, if a loss occurs at an unlisted location, coverage might not apply.

Coverages, Endorsements, Limits of Liability, and Deductibles

Most applications have a section listing the available coverages. In Exhibit 4-2 the application lists ISO commercial crime coverages and includes columns for specifying the liability limits and deductibles. The application also provides space to list other coverages or endorsements. Underwriters pay close attention to requested endorsements. When a requested endorsement, such as the Include Volunteer Workers as Employees endorsement, extends the definition of "employee," the underwriter might need additional information about the exposures and controls the applicant is using.

Underwriters evaluate whether the limits are adequate considering loss trends and the applicant's needs. For example, employee theft or dishonesty losses are sometimes not discovered immediately. The policy limit is all that is available for losses regardless of when they are discovered. Thus, policy limits should be adequate to cover losses whenever they are discovered.

EXHIBIT 4-1

ACORD Commercial Insurance Application

[ACORD Commercial Insurance Application form, Applicant Information Section (ACORD 125, 2000/08). The form includes the following sections and fields:]

Header fields: Producer, Phone (A/C, No, Ext), Fax (A/C, No.), Code, Sub Code, Agency Customer ID, Carrier, NAIC Code, Underwriter, Underwriter Off., Date, Policies or Program Requested, Policy Number.

Indicate Sections Attached: Property; Glass and Sign; Accounts Receivable/Valuable Papers; Crime/Miscellaneous Crime; Transportation/Motor Truck Cargo; Equipment Floater; Installation/Builders Risk; Electronic Data Proc; Commercial General Liability; Business Auto; Truckers/Motor Carrier; Garage and Dealers; Vehicle Schedule; Boiler & Machinery; Workers Compensation; Umbrella.

Status of Transaction: Quote; Issue Policy; Renew; Bound (Give Date and/or Attach Copy) — Date, Time, AM/PM; Change; Cancel.

Package Policy Information: Enter this information when common dates and terms apply to several lines, or for monoline policies. Proposed Eff Date, Proposed Exp Date, Billing Plan (Direct Bill / Agency Bill), Payment Plan, Audit.

Applicant Information: Name (First Named Insured & Other Named Insureds); FEIN or Soc Sec # (of First Named Insured); Phone (A/C, No, Ext); Internet Address; Mailing Address Incl ZIP+4 (of First Named Insured); Individual; Corporation; Subchapter "S" Corporation; Not For Profit Org; CR Bureau Name; ID Number; Year Bus Started; Partnership; Joint Venture; Limited Corporation; Inspection Contact; Phone (A/C, No, Ext); Accounting Records Contact; Phone (A/C, No, Ext).

Premises Information: Loc #; Bld #; Street, City, County, State, ZIP+4; City Limits (Inside/Outside); Interest (Owner/Tenant); Yr Built; Part Occupied. [Three rows provided.]

Nature of Business/Description of Operations by Premise(s)

General Information — Explain all "Yes" responses:

1. Is the applicant a subsidiary of another entity or does the applicant have any subsidiaries?
2. Is a formal safety program in operation?
3. Any exposure to flammables, explosives, chemicals?
4. Any catastrophe exposure?
5. Any other insurance with this company or being submitted?
6. Any policy or coverage declined, cancelled or non-renewed during the prior 3 years? Not applicable in MO.
7. Any past losses or claims relating to sexual abuse or molestation allegations, discrimination or negligent hiring?
8. During the last five years (ten in RI), has any applicant been convicted of any degree of the crime of arson? In RI, this question must be answered by any applicant for property insurance. Failure to disclose the existence of an arson conviction is a misdemeanor punishable by a sentence of up to one year of imprisonment.
9. Any uncorrected fire code violations?
10. Any bankruptcies, tax or credit liens against the applicant in the past 5 years?

Remarks/Processing Instructions

ANY PERSON WHO KNOWINGLY AND WITH INTENT TO DEFRAUD ANY INSURANCE COMPANY OR ANOTHER PERSON FILES AN APPLICATION FOR INSURANCE OR STATEMENT OF CLAIM CONTAINING ANY MATERIALLY FALSE INFORMATION, OR CONCEALS FOR THE PURPOSE OF MISLEADING, INFORMATION CONCERNING ANY FACT MATERIAL THERETO, COMMITS A FRAUDULENT INSURANCE ACT, WHICH IS A CRIME AND SUBJECTS THE PERSON TO CRIMINAL AND [NY: SUBSTANTIAL] CIVIL PENALTIES. (NOT APPLICABLE IN CO, HI, NE, OH, OK, OR, VT; IN DC, LA, ME AND VA, INSURANCE BENEFITS MAY ALSO BE DENIED)

Applicant's Signature   Producer's Signature

ACORD 125 (2000/08)   PLEASE COMPLETE REVERSE SIDE   © ACORD CORPORATION 1993

4.4 Commercial Crime Insurance and Financial Institution Bonds

PRIOR CARRIER INFORMATION

LINE	CATEGORY						
COMMERCIAL GENERAL LIABILITY	CARRIER						
	POLICY NUMBER						
	POLICY TYPE	CLAIMS MADE / OCCURRENCE	CLAIMS MADE / OCCURRENCE	CLAIMS MADE / OCCURRENCE	CLAIMS MADE / OCCURRENCE	CLAIMS MADE / OCCURRENCE	
	RETRO DATE						
	EFF-EXP DATE						
	GENERAL AGGREGATE (LIMITS)						
	PRODUCTS COMP OP AGGREGATE						
	PERSONAL & ADV INJ						
	EACH OCCURRENCE						
	FIRE DAMAGE						
	MEDICAL EXPENSE						
	BODILY INJURY — OCCURRENCE / AGGREGATE						
	PROPERTY DAMAGE — OCCURRENCE / AGGREGATE						
	COMBINED SINGLE LIMIT						
	MODIFICATION FACTOR						
	TOTAL PREMIUM						
AUTOMOBILE LIABILITY	CARRIER						
	POLICY NUMBER						
	POLICY TYPE						
	EFF-EXP DATE						
	COMBINED SINGLE LIMIT						
	BODILY INJURY — EA PERSON / EA ACCIDENT						
	PROPERTY DAMAGE						
	MODIFICATION FACTOR						
	TOTAL PREMIUM						
PROPERTY	CARRIER						
	POLICY NUMBER						
	POLICY TYPE						
	EFF-EXP DATE						
	BUILDING AMT						
	PERS PROP AMT						
	MODIFICATION FACTOR						
	TOTAL PREMIUM						
	CARRIER						
	POLICY NUMBER						
	POLICY TYPE						
	EFF-EXP DATE						
	LIMIT						
	MODIFICATION FACTOR						
	TOTAL PREMIUM						

LOSS HISTORY

ENTER ALL CLAIMS OR LOSSES (REGARDLESS OF FAULT AND WHETHER OR NOT INSURED) OR OCCURRENCES THAT MAY GIVE RISE TO CLAIMS FOR THE PRIOR 5 YEARS (3 YEARS IN KS & NY)   CHK HERE IF NONE   SEE ATTACHED LOSS SUMMARY

DATE OF OCCURRENCE	LINE	TYPE/DESCRIPTION OF OCCURRENCE OR CLAIM	DATE OF CLAIM	AMOUNT PAID	AMOUNT RESERVED	CLAIM STATUS
						OPEN
						CLOSED
						OPEN
						CLOSED

REMARKS   NOTE: FIDELITY REQUIRES A FIVE YEAR LOSS HISTORY

NOTICE OF INSURANCE INFORMATION PRACTICES
PERSONAL INFORMATION ABOUT YOU, INCLUDING INFORMATION FROM A CREDIT REPORT, MAY BE COLLECTED FROM PERSONS OTHER THAN YOU IN CONNECTION WITH THIS APPLICATION FOR INSURANCE AND SUBSEQUENT POLICY RENEWALS. SUCH INFORMATION AS WELL AS OTHER PERSONAL AND PRIVILEGED INFORMATION COLLECTED BY US OR OUR AGENTS MAY IN CERTAIN CIRCUMSTANCES BE DISCLOSED TO THIRD PARTIES. YOU HAVE THE RIGHT TO REVIEW YOUR PERSONAL INFORMATION IN OUR FILES AND CAN REQUEST CORRECTION OF ANY INACCURACIES. A MORE DETAILED DESCRIPTION OF YOUR RIGHTS AND OUR PRACTICES REGARDING SUCH INFORMATION IS AVAILABLE UPON REQUEST. CONTACT YOUR AGENT OR BROKER FOR INSTRUCTION ON HOW TO SUBMIT A REQUEST TO US.

ACORD 125 (2000/08)

EXHIBIT 4-2

ACORD Crime Section

ACORD™ CRIME SECTION 2000

PRODUCER	PHONE (A/C, No, Ext):	APPLICANT (First Named Insured)				DATE
	FAX (A/C, No):					
		EFFECTIVE DATE	EXPIRATION DATE	DIRECT BILL	PAYMENT PLAN	AUDIT
				AGENCY BILL		
CODE: SUB CODE:		FOR COMPANY USE ONLY			BASIS FOR COVERAGE	
AGENCY CUSTOMER ID:					DISCOVERY	
					LOSS SUSTAINED	

COVERAGE FORM	LIMIT	DEDUCTIBLE	COVERAGE FORM	LIMIT	DEDUCTIBLE
EMPLOYEE THEFT ☐ BLANKET ☐ SCHEDULE ☐ ERISA	$		INSIDE THE PREMISES ROBBERY OR BURGLARY OF OTHER PROPERTY ☐ BLANKET ☐ SCHEDULE	$	
TOTAL ASSET VALUE $	$		OUTSIDE THE PREMISES MONEY AND SECURITIES	$	
EMPLOYEE THEFT GOVERNMENTAL CRIME ☐ BLANKET ☐ SCHEDULE	$		OTHER PROPERTY ☐ BLANKET ☐ SCHEDULE	$	
FORGERY OR ALTERATION	$		COMPUTER FRAUD	$	
INSIDE THE PREMISES THEFT OF MONEY AND SECURITIES ☐ BLANKET ☐ SCHEDULE	$		MONEY ORDERS AND COUNTERFEIT PAPER CURRENCY	$	

COVERAGE ENDORSEMENTS

ERISA EMPLOYEE THEFT - ADDITIONAL INFORMATION

NAME OF PLAN	PRINCIPAL ADDRESS	NUMBER OF TRUSTEES, EMPLOYEES, ETC HANDLING PLAN ASSETS	NUMBER OF PLAN PARTICIPANTS

IS THERE A LICENSED SECURITIES FIRM RESPONSIBLE FOR INVESTING OF FUNDS UNDER PLAN(S)? ☐ YES ☐ NO

CLASSIFICATION OF EMPLOYEES/LOCATIONS

LIST ALL OFFICERS AND EMPLOYEES (Including those construed to be employees by endorsement), OTHER THAN AGENTS AND PARTNERS, WHO HANDLE OR HAVE CUSTODY OF MONEY, SECURITIES OR OTHER PROPERTY, INCLUDING, IN ANY EVENT, THE POSITIONS LISTED BELOW:

NUMBER OF:	NUMBER OF:	NUMBER OF:	NUMBER OF:
ACCOUNTANTS AND ASSTS	COLLECTORS	LOCKER ROOM ATTENDANTS	STOCK CLERKS
ADJUSTERS	COMPUTER PROGRAMMERS	MAITRE D'S AND ASSTS	STOREKEEPERS
ADMINISTRATORS AND ASSTS	COMPTROLLERS AND ASSTS	MANAGERS AND ASSTS	STOREROOM PERSONNEL
APPRAISERS AND CLERKS ACTING AS APPRAISERS	CREDIT CLERKS AND MANAGERS	MEDICAL DIRECTORS	SUPERINTENDENTS AND ASSTS
ATTORNEYS	CUSTODIANS	MESSENGERS, OUTSIDE	SUPERVISORS AND ASSTS
AUDITORS AND ASSTS	DELIVERY PERSONS	PAYROLL DISTRIBUTORS	TAXI DRIVERS
BOOKKEEPERS	DEMONSTRATORS	PURCHASING AGENTS AND ASSTS	TEACHERS HAVING CUSTODY OF MONEY OR SECURITIES
BUS DRIVERS	DIETITIANS WHO ORDER FOOD	RECEIVING CLERKS	TIMEKEEPERS AND ASSTS
BUYERS AND ASSTS	DRIVERS AND DRIVERS' HELPERS	REFINERY GAUGERS OF OIL COMPANIES HANDLING REFINED GASOLINE AND OILS	TRUCK DRIVERS
CANVASSERS (Door-to-door salespeople)	FOOD INSPECTORS	SALESPEOPLE	WAREHOUSE PERSONNEL
CASHIERS AND ASSTS	HEAD PHARMACISTS	SECURITY PERSONNEL	WINE CELLAR PERSONNEL
CHAIRPERSONS	INSTRUCTORS HAVING CUSTODY OF MONEY OR SECURITIES	SERVICE STATION ATTENDANTS	WINE STEWARDS/ESSES
CHEFS WHO ORDER FOOD	JANITORS	SHIPPING CLERKS	ALL OTHER OFFICERS AND EMPLOYEES NOT LISTED ABOVE
NUMBER OF OFFICERS:	TOTAL NUMBER OF OTHER EMPLOYEES:	MANUFACTURERS, PROCESSORS, WHOLESALERS OR DISTRIBUTORS; NUMBER OF RETAIL LOCATIONS:	ALL OTHER CLASSES; NUMBER OF LOCATIONS OTHER THAN HOME OR HEAD OFFICES:

REMARKS

ACORD 141C (2000/08) ATTACH TO APPLICANT INFORMATION SECTION © ACORD CORPORATION 1980

4.6 Commercial Crime Insurance and Financial Institution Bonds

CONTROLS AND AUDIT PROCEDURES

AUDITS

1. IS THERE AN AUDIT BY? ☐ CPA ☐ PUBLIC ACCOUNTANT ☐ STAFF ☐ OTHER: _____

5. DATE OF COMPLETION OF LAST AUDIT OF: CASH & ACCOUNTS _____ INVENTORY _____

2. NAME AND ADDRESS OF PERSON OR FIRM PERFORMING AUDIT

6. WERE ANY DISCREPANCIES OR LOOSE PRACTICES COMMENTED UPON IN THIS AUDIT? IF "YES", SUBMIT A COPY OF THE AUDIT AND AUDITOR'S COMMENTS. ☐ YES ☐ NO

7. AUDIT FREQUENCY? ☐ ANNUAL ☐ SEMI-ANNUAL ☐ QUARTERLY ☐ OTHER: _____

3. ALL LOCATIONS AUDITED? ☐ YES ☐ NO

8. DOES AUDIT INCLUDE INVENTORY? ☐ YES ☐ NO

4. IS AUDIT MADE IN ACCORDANCE WITH GENERALLY ACCEPTED AUDITING STANDARDS AND SO CERTIFIED? IF NO, EXPLAIN SCOPE OF AUDIT. ☐ YES ☐ NO

9. AUDIT REPORT IS RENDERED TO: ☐ OWNER ☐ PARTNERS ☐ BOARD OF DIRECTORS ☐ OTHER: _____

BANKING/OTHER

1. ARE BANK ACCOUNTS RECONCILED BY SOMEONE NOT AUTHORIZED TO DEPOSIT OR WITHDRAW? ☐ YES ☐ NO

3. WILL SECURITIES BE SUBJECT TO JOINT CONTROL OF TWO OR MORE RESPONSIBLE EMPLOYEES? ☐ YES ☐ NO

2. IS COUNTERSIGNATURE OF CHECKS REQUIRED? IF NOT, WHO SIGNS CONTROLS? ☐ YES ☐ NO

4. ARE ALL OFFICERS AND EMPLOYEES REQUIRED TO TAKE ANNUAL VACATIONS OF AT LEAST FIVE CONSECUTIVE BUSINESS DAYS? ☐ YES ☐ NO

MONEY - SECURITIES

ENTER THE EXPOSURES FOR EACH CATEGORY. AMOUNTS ENTERED SHOULD BE MAXIMUM EXPOSURE.

TYPE	MONEY	CHECKS FOR DEPOSIT	CHECKS FOR ACCOUNTS PAYABLE	PAYROLL CHECKS	MONEY OVERNIGHT	SECURITIES (IN BANK/SAFE DEPOSIT)
INSIDE	$	$	$	$	$	$
MESSENGER #1	$	$	$	$	$	
MESSENGER #2	$	$	$	$	$	

PROPERTY

DESCRIPTION OF PROPERTY, MERCHANDISE, STOCK, ETC	MAXIMUM VALUE

GENERAL INFORMATION

BUSINESS HOURS	AVG # EMPLOYEES ON DUTY	CHECKS STAMPED FOR DEPOSIT ONLY	FREQUENCY OF DEPOSITS	NIGHT DEPOSITORY USED	ANNUAL GROSS SALES OR RECEIPTS FOR LAST FISCAL YEAR	DOES PREMISES HAVE DOUBLE CYLINDER DOOR LOCKS? YES NO	OTHER INFORMATION

SAFE/VAULT

MANUFACTURER	LABEL	CLASS	DOOR TYPE ROUND	DOOR TYPE SQUARE	COMBINATION LOCKS OUTER	INNER	CHEST	THICKNESS DOOR (EXCL BOLTWORK)	WALL
	UL								
	SMNA								
	UL								
	SMNA								

MESSENGER PROTECTION

MESS'GR #	# OF GUARDS PER MESSENGER	PRIVATE CONVEYANCE USED?	SAFETY SATCHEL USED?	MESS'GR #	# OF GUARDS PER MESSENGER	PRIVATE CONVEYANCE USED?	SAFETY SATCHEL USED?
		☐ YES ☐ NO	☐ YES ☐ NO			☐ YES ☐ NO	☐ YES ☐ NO

PREMISES/SAFE PROTECTION

ALARM TYPE: ☐ HOLD-UP ☐ PREMISES ☐ SAFE

ALARM DESCRIPTION: ☐ LOCAL GONG ☐ CENTRAL STATION ☐ POLICE CONNECT ☐ WITH KEYS

GRADE: ___

EXTENT OF PROTECTION — SAFE/VAULT ___ PREMISES ___ PARTIAL 1 2 3 COMPLETE

ALARM INSTALLED AND SERVICED BY: _____

 # GUARDS ___ **# WATCH PERSONS** ___

WATCHPERSONS: ☐ RPT/CENT ST ☐ CLOCK HRLY ☐ DON'T SIGNAL

ACCESSIBLE OPENINGS & PROTECTION: _____

OTHER PROTECTION (Fences, Floodlights, etc): _____

CERTIFICATE NUMBER: _____

EXPIRATION DATE: _____

REMARKS

ANY PERSON WHO KNOWINGLY AND WITH INTENT TO DEFRAUD ANY INSURANCE COMPANY OR ANOTHER PERSON FILES AN APPLICATION FOR INSURANCE OR STATEMENT OF CLAIM CONTAINING ANY MATERIALLY FALSE INFORMATION, OR CONCEALS FOR THE PURPOSE OF MISLEADING INFORMATION CONCERNING ANY FACT MATERIAL THERETO, COMMITS A FRAUDULENT INSURANCE ACT, WHICH IS A CRIME AND SUBJECTS THE PERSON TO CRIMINAL AND [NY:SUBSTANTIAL] CIVIL PENALTIES. (NOT APPLICABLE IN CO, HI, NE, OH, OK, OR, VT; IN DC, LA, ME AND VA, INSURANCE BENEFITS MAY ALSO BE DENIED)

ACORD 141C (2000/08)   USE ADDITIONAL FORMS IF MORE THAN ONE LOCATION

FOR FURTHER THOUGHT

Underinsured Crime Losses

The absence of any coinsurance provision in crime policies and the difficulty of determining an adequate amount of crime insurance can result in insureds' being severely underinsured for crime losses, particularly employee theft or dishonesty losses. Insureds often have an "It can't happen to me" attitude about crime and fail to appreciate the catastrophic potential of some of these exposures. Case histories that involve both large and small firms may focus attention on the problem and help insureds realize the need for stringent controls and high employee dishonesty limits.

The Clock Collector

An executive stole $12.5 million from a specialty-chemical manufacturer over nine years and used the money to purchase antique clocks. As vice president in charge of strategic development, he had sole authority to approve international marketing expenses, and he changed more than 150 invoices for his clock purchases into bills payable by his employer. He earned a six-figure salary, was a member of the management committee, and was extremely well respected by his co-workers until a routine audit disclosed his dishonesty.

Club Cha-Cha

The chief financial officer of a meat exporter stole $95 million from his employer. He issued checks to himself for seven years and covered the shortage by securing loans for his employer from various banks with whom the firm did business. He had sole control over finances, enabling him to pay off earlier loans by arranging even more loans. Prosecutors charged that the officer had used the money to buy beachfront condominiums, citrus ranches, and even a nightclub named Club Cha-Cha.

The Shoemaker's Children

Like the proverbial shoemaker's children without shoes, insurance agents often have little or no employee dishonesty coverage. The bookkeeper of one small insurance broker embezzled $190,000 by pocketing cash payments, inserting her own name as payee on customers' checks and issuing unauthorized payroll and petty cash checks to herself. The agency had employee dishonesty coverage with a limit of only $10,000.

The Clock Collector and Club Cha-Cha cases were reported by Gary Strauss, "Embezzlement Growth Is `Dramatic,'" *USA Today*, January, 13, 1998, p. 2A. The Shoemaker's Children case is derived from the court decision of American Commerce Insurance Brokers, Inc. v. Minnesota Mutual Fire and Casualty Co., Minn. Ct. App. NoC9-94-499, 8/1/95.

Rating Factors

Rating information found on the application includes the following:

- Number of employees
- Classification of employees
- Number of locations
- Optional coverages and endorsements

The number and classification of the employees to be insured are important rating factors in both commercial crime and financial institution bond forms. Proper listing of the employees and their classifications produces a more accurate premium and alerts underwriters to exposures they might otherwise overlook. The crime application classifies employees by type of employment. Each position listed in the classification section is a ratable employee for premium purposes. The premium includes separate charges for all corporate officers, except owner-officers who are excluded from coverage, so the total number of officers should be listed. For blanket employee theft or dishonesty coverage, the total number of other employees is important. The premium reflects charges for those employees in addition to the charges for officers and listed employees. For financial institution bonds, the application should specify the number of salaried officers, employees, retained attorneys, and persons employed through employment contractors.

Underwriters evaluate the application's list of employees to verify that the list corresponds with the class of business. For example, if a manufacturer is applying for blanket employee theft coverage, the application might list only warehouse personnel as employees. Additional questions should come to the underwriter's mind because the applicant could also have shipping and delivery exposures that involve shipping, stock, and receiving clerks.

The number of locations the applicant wants to insure is another necessary rating factor. Underwriters of financial institutions want to know whether each location is a full-service, limited-use, or specific-use location.

Optional coverages also affect rating because they change the policy coverage. Applications often ask specific questions relating to optional coverages. Underwriters might follow up with even more questions. Applications might include requests for extortion coverage, unattended automated teller machines (ATMs) coverage, servicing contractor's coverage, or loan participation coverage. For extortion coverage, underwriters evaluate how the applicant's security procedures affect the extortion risk. Underwriters might ask the following questions:

- To what foreign countries do covered employees travel?
- How frequently do covered employees travel abroad?
- What are their travel schedules?
- Does the applicant want to exclude any foreign locations?

For unattended ATMs, the application specifies the amount of coverage the applicant wants, the size of the deductible, and which locations the applicant wants to include or exclude. For servicing contractors coverage, the application lists the name and location of the mortgage servicer, and the underwriter might want to know the amount that will be serviced. The underwriter might also ask for copies of the servicing contracts. Finally, for loan participation coverage, the underwriter might ask what the loan-to-deposit ratio is or request balance sheet information as supporting documentation.

Audit Procedures and Controls

Commercial crime and financial institution bond applications ask about the applicant's audit procedures and money handling controls. The ACORD crime application labels the section "Controls"; most financial institution bond applications label it "Audit Procedures." These sections provide underwriters with basic information about the applicant's internal and external controls. Underwriters might ask applicants to submit additional information.

Producers can help applicants understand what an audit is when they complete this section. Many applicants believe that because they engaged a CPA's services, they have had an audit. This is not necessarily true. CPA services vary. For example, an applicant might hire a CPA to do its taxes but not to do an independent audit of financial statements. Another applicant might engage a CPA to review only the accounts and records before the applicant submits them to the board of directors. An **audit** is a formal examination of accounts to verify their correctness. The key word is "verify." If the accountant's report uses the word "compile" or "review," the accountant did not actually audit the books and records or verify the authenticity of the figures. A **compilation report** is an unaudited statement based on management-provided information or statements. That information has not been audited or reviewed and the accountant expresses no opinion or assurance about that information. A **review** consists of inquiries concerning the applicant's accounting practices and procedures for recording, classifying, and summarizing accounting transactions, and analytical procedures to compare previous statements and expected results. All information included in the statements is a representation of management. The review states that no material changes are required for the financial statements to conform to generally accepted accounting practices. A compilation or review does not assess the integrity of the applicant's internal controls to ensure that the numbers the applicant presented to the CPA are accurate.

Questions about controls go beyond whether a CPA has conducted an audit. Underwriters might ask the following questions:

- How often does the applicant have external and internal audits performed?
- Who conducts the audits?
- How often does the applicant submit the reports to the board of directors?
- Who reconciles bank accounts?
- Does the applicant require countersignatures on checks?
- How does the applicant handle securities?

Depending on the type of coverage requested, applicants might provide detailed information about the safes and vaults on their premises and any protection devices, such as alarms, inside and around the premises.

Loss History

The application's loss history section is important because loss experience can be used to predict future losses, although risk factors can change over time. Full disclosure of loss information to the underwriter is mandatory. Applicants can explain in the comments section what corrective measures they have taken. Underwriters usually want at least three years' history. In some cases underwriters ask only for a history of losses that the new policy would cover and losses that exceed the requested deductible. Loss history also influences the final premium.

Supplemental Information

The basic application is not always enough. For example, many commercial crime insurers have created supplemental questionnaires for auto dealers and title companies because their operations are unique. For financial institution bonds, the underwriting process is more involved. Besides requiring financial reports, which will be discussed later, underwriters ask applicants to complete additional questionnaires. The questionnaires ask applicants to describe their internal controls, computer systems controls, policies and procedures for wire transfers, and the equipment that protects money, securities, and the safe deposit facility.

When applicants request optional coverage or endorsements, insurers might ask them to respond to detailed supplemental questionnaires. Underwriters ask financial institutions seeking computer systems coverage to schedule the systems they want covered, describe them, and provide operating details. In particular, underwriters want information about security, the volume of money processed, the nature of the money transactions, and the use of outside contractors and service bureaus.

In addition to supplemental questionnaires, underwriters might ask for:

- A brief description of what each of the operating subsidiaries does. Underwriters might ask applicants to describe the volume and mix of business, specify the percentage of ownership by the parent or holding company, and provide a separate schedule of such items as employees and locations.
- The background and history of the organization, such as the date the business was established; the dates of recent mergers or acquisitions; the type of organization (proprietorship, partnership, or corporation); the turnover rate of employees and their dates of hire; management changes; and the nature of the ownership, including major shareholders, organizations, or entities that own, control, and operate the business.
- Detailed information on the applicant's internal controls.

Financial Reports

At a minimum, underwriters examine the applicant's most recent annual report, CPA audit, management letter, and response. Financial institution bond underwriters might ask for information from two to three prior years. Because applicants prepare their own annual reports, which will naturally present the most positive picture possible, underwriters also review the CPA audit, management letter, and response. As mentioned earlier, the CPA audit must verify the accuracy of the accounts. Many audit firms have their own name for the audit report to management, but auditors and insurance underwriters use the generic term **management letter.** Auditors who detect weaknesses in the internal controls system will state their recommendations, also called reportable conditions, in the management letter. CPAs are not required to report these but are encouraged to do so by their governing principles. Underwriters should see the complete management letter and the applicant management's comments, or response, to the recommendations. Underwriters seek to confirm that management has taken corrective measures or implemented suitable alternatives.

Agents and Brokers

Agents and brokers serve as the local underwriters. Particularly in small towns, the applicant is located "just down the street" from the agent. These agents or brokers usually know everyone in town and can vouch for the applicant. Understandably, agents and brokers will present their clients in the best possible light. However, they are obligated to disclose to insurer underwriters any relevant information and to provide information to assist in making a decision. Insurer underwriters should cultivate good relations with reputable agents and brokers who will deal in good faith and present accurate underwriting information.

Other Documents

In many cases crime underwriting does not require more information than that which can be obtained from the sources discussed above. However, underwriting of financial institutions might require additional in-depth investigation. Exhibit 4-3 lists other documents underwriters might review for financial institution bonds. Some of these documents are considered confidential. Underwriters should take great care to keep them secure. Financial institutions might be prohibited from releasing some information by federal regulation.

EXHIBIT 4-3

Sources of Financial Institution Bond Underwriting Information

- Internal financial statements
- Brochures and advertising information
- Bylaws and articles of incorporation
- Regulatory reports
- Prospectuses or proxy statements
- Resumes of key personnel and board members

Continued on next page.

- Standard operating procedure documents
- Indemnity agreements
- Leases
- Contracts with vendors
- General standard operating procedures for high-exposure operating divisions or subsidiaries (for example, a bank's loan policy)
- Administrative documents for welfare, pension, and benefits plans, or the annual report of employee benefit plans
- Organizational charts
- Monthly board reports
- Litigation reports
- Short-term and long-term business plans or strategic plans
- Internal audit reports for particular departments or responsibility centers

Sometimes underwriters visit the applicant's facility to review documents or observe how the applicant carries out procedures. If applicants consider their documents sensitive or confidential, underwriters review the material on the applicant's premises under controlled conditions without obtaining any copies. If an underwriter suspects the applicant is not implementing good security procedures, he or she might ask to do a walk-through of the applicant's operations to review the physical and operational security procedures.

UNDERWRITING CONSIDERATIONS

Underwriting commercial crime coverages or financial institution bonds entails looking at many aspects of the applicant's organization. How far they look depends on the complexity of the risk and the coverages the applicant requests. Most commercial crime underwriters are satisfied after they examine the applicant's ownership and organizational structure. Financial institution bond underwriters usually investigate further, looking at historical growth, future plans, economic environment, business plans, management, boards of directors, and financial stability.

Ownership

Four common categories of business ownership are: sole proprietorship, partnership, corporation, and joint venture.[2] Each has different implications for how the business should be underwritten. Ownership also affects the applicant's operating philosophy, which in turn affects loss control.

Sole Proprietorships and Partnerships

A **sole proprietorship** is the simplest form of business in which one person owns all the business's assets. A **partnership** is a joint undertaking based on an express or implied agreement between two or more persons to operate a business for profit. Whether an applicant is a sole proprietorship or a partnership influences employee dishonesty underwriting because employee dishonesty coverage applies only to the insured's employees. If John Jones, the sole proprietor of Jones Grocery Store, steals from his store, the loss he causes to his business is not covered. If an employee steals from the store, the loss to the grocery store is covered. The same principle applies to partnerships. A partner might be a victim of a crime, but employee dishonesty coverage will not apply if the partner is the culprit. As mentioned in Chapter 2, an endorsement is available to cover dishonest acts of partners.

In sole proprietorships and partnerships, underwriters want the sole proprietor or partners to be involved with the internal controls of the operation. For example, if the proprietor or partner signs all checks or reconciles the monthly bank statement, the underwriter is more comfortable providing employee dishonesty coverage because the proprietor or partner is more likely to notice irregularities that might indicate employee dishonesty.

Corporations

A **corporation** is a form of business created by statute and is owned by shareholders and managed by a board of directors. Corporations might be close or professional corporations. Close corporations, also known as closely held, family, or privately held corporations, are owned by members of a family or by only a few individuals. They present two underwriting considerations. First, if a family member, as owner-officer, performs all the record keeping for money and securities or controls day-today operations, the underwriter should attach an endorsement excluding the owner-officer from employee dishonesty coverage. Then, if the owner-officer steals from the business, the loss would not be covered. The endorsement saves the insured money because there is no premium charge for the owner-officers. The second consideration concerns noncompensated owner-officers. An example is the principal owner's spouse who reconciles the monthly bank accounts. If the applicant asks to include the spouse in coverage, with the noncompensated officers endorsement, the underwriter should request further underwriting information to ensure that appropriate controls are in place to manage the exposure.

Professional corporations are formed by professionals such as physicians, lawyers, dentists, or accountants. These corporations might be identified by the letters P.C. (professional corporation), S.C. (service corporation), or P.A. (professional association). Forming a professional corporation rather than a partnership negates the partner exclusion. Thus, underwriters should pay special attention to the internal controls for professional corporations. For example, an employee who does not have check-signing authority should reconcile the bank statement at least monthly to maintain controls.

Absentee ownership is an underwriting concern because absentee owners often abdicate their management duties to the institution's operating management. Absentee owners who fail to monitor and oversee the activities of their management are more likely to experience losses. Large financial institutions, with ownership spread over many shareholders, are less likely to have problems with an absentee owner ignoring or misdirecting the entity's operations.

Large corporations might have multiple locations and engage in a variety of operations. Underwriters of large corporations generally ask for more information than what the basic application provides. They ask the applicant to complete supplemental questionnaires, or they insist that the applicant's CPA evaluate the applicant's internal controls as part of a set of agreed-upon procedures in nonaudit situations. The ownership of large corporations can influence the applicant's operating philosophy. Significant shareholders, those with 10 percent or more of the outstanding voting shares, have a sizable influence on the organization. Underwriters should carefully scrutinize operating managers with major ownership interests because people with executive management responsibility also have the greatest opportunity to steal.

Financial institution underwriters are watchful for owners who take control of an institution and use its assets for the benefit of their other businesses. For example, in the 1980s developers took control of savings and loans and other thrift institutions through stock ownership and then diverted the assets to investments in highly speculative real estate transactions. This abuse caused severe losses for financial institutions.

Joint Ventures

A **joint venture** resembles a partnership. Two or more persons combine their efforts or property for a single or related transactions or projects. The joint venture ends when the transactions or projects are completed. For example, several contractors might jointly build and sell houses in a single development. When the development is completed, the joint venture ends.

Joint ventures can be insured two ways. If one party to the joint venture is clearly the managing entity, the joint venturers might be named as joint insureds on the managing entity's commercial crime policy or financial institution bond. If all entities equally manage the joint venture, a policy or bond could name the venture as the named insured, consisting of the related parties. For example, the policy might state "XYZ Development Project, a joint venture of X Corporation and Z Corporation." Most crime underwriters insist that each entity carry its own crime insurance policy in addition to coverage for the joint venture. This is especially true for employee dishonesty insurance. This precaution protects the insurer from claims for activities outside the scope of the joint venture.

Other

Other organizational forms include syndicates, joint stock companies, business trusts, cooperatives, and limited liability companies. Statutes often govern how and when these organizations can be formed. The underwriter should request a full description of the organization or might obtain that information from the Internet. A copy of the entity's state license to do business would provide the information but might be impractical to obtain. From this information the underwriter can determine what coverage is appropriate and how best to control losses.

Organizational Structure

Underwriters examine their applicants' organizational structure and analyze how well management oversees it. An applicant's organizational structure varies by its managerial skills and style, its scope of activity, and its geographic and marketing territory. Large companies might have many specialized departments and managers whose roles and decision-making responsibilities are very specific. Small companies might have a few people assuming multiple management and decision-making roles.

Underwriters can evaluate each department for safeguards and internal controls. For example, an underwriter might find that an understaffed department with few management, supervisory, or audit personnel had a breakdown of its internal controls. If the breakdown is serious, the underwriter will decide if the entire risk is unacceptable.

Each organizational structure presents its own risk management needs. For example, a large manufacturing company might have compartmental functions and management so that no one employee can cause a single large loss. A small business might have one trusted employee to oversee bookkeeping and inventory, thus exposing itself to a large loss.

Basic functions of any business include:

- Hiring employees
- Managing cash through accounts payable, accounts receivable, and investments
- Submitting documents to regulators or governmental authorities, including taxes, public disclosure documents, and licenses
- Managing the day-to-day operations of the company, including planning, marketing, auditing, and operating management information systems

Beyond these core functions, however, businesses distinguish themselves by the products and services they offer. Successful underwriters understand how services and products present loss exposures. After the underwriter learns what functions are operating within the business and how, the next step is to assess what exposures they represent. Just one function of the many within a business can represent a significant exposure. For example, an insurer's claim department presents many employee dishonesty exposures. A claim representative could embezzle funds by creating false claim files, forging checks, or accepting kickbacks from repair facilities. Inefficient claim-reporting and record-keeping systems increase the opportunity for an employee to steal without timely detection. Just one function of the many within a business can represent significant exposure potential.

ADDITIONAL UNDERWRITING CONSIDERATIONS FOR FINANCIAL INSTITUTIONS

Commercial crime underwriters often obtain enough information about a business from the sources discussed above. Financial institution underwriters generally look further by examining the institution's historical growth and future plans, economic environment, business plan, management, board of directors, and financial strength.

Historical Growth

An applicant's historical growth in assets, number of employees, number of locations, and territory covered, as well as the speed of that growth, are all risk factors. Underwriters assess how management maintained managerial and internal control over the operations during growth. For instance, territorial expansion tests how well management adapts to new locations. It tests management's ability to attract qualified personnel, adapt to the new legal environments in their new territories, and focus on the products and services they are experienced in supporting. Underwriters are more confident about writing coverage on financial institutions that have successfully managed past growth than they are about ones that have not handled growth well.

An applicant's mergers and acquisitions history reveals a great deal about how it handles growth. With each merger or acquisition, management must integrate new people, products, and approaches into the existing operations. Underwriters look for changes in the corporate culture and products and identify new risks associated with such changes. Especially for discovery form coverage, underwriters analyze acquisitions to be sure they are acceptable risks before extending coverage.

Economic Environment

Underwriters study the general makeup of the local and regional economies because economic changes can affect a financial institution's success. For example, products and services should be compatible with consumers' needs. Potential economic opportunities affect the timing for introducing certain products that could strengthen or weaken the institution's portfolio. Underwriters must be sensitive to economic changes that might create difficulties for an applicant and adjust pricing accordingly.

Business Plan

A financial institution's short-term business plan and long-term strategic plan reveal the institution's expectations of current management, its financial projections, and its plans for current or new products and services. Underwriters look at plans for expansion. In particular, they pay attention to the opening and closing of locations, the special treatment of specific operations, significant drops in revenue, and changes in the mix of products and services. As underwriters examine business plans, they evaluate market changes or shifts by performing a peer analysis. **Peer analysis** compares the applicant's approach to business with the competition's approach to business. Peer analysis, whether conducted by the underwriter or by an independent consultant, is an important tool for underwriters to use when comparing financial statements, management styles, and internal control procedures.

This analysis gives an underwriter a relative view of the risk potential of the applicant compared to competitors.

Because underwriters prefer long-term relationships with financial institutions, they need to know whether management plans to be acquired by, or to acquire, another business. The underwriter learns from the financial institution's management what criteria would cause management to change its current position or philosophy about a merger or acquisition.

Management

Underwriters study a financial institution's corporate culture and management philosophy when they evaluate it. They also review key managers' experience in their areas of responsibility, knowledge about the territory, their reputation within the community, and their reputation among their peers. Key managers' general education and managerial philosophies also help underwriters characterize a financial institution's management style.

Management changes at the board or executive level could mean a new direction for the institution's goals, objectives, products, and services. Underwriters evaluate the new management's quality and depth and the plans for an orderly transfer of responsibilities in important operating areas. Management sets the ethical and performance standards for the institution. In addition to changes within the management team, underwriters evaluate management's ability to support other organizational structure changes and potential new exposures.

Board of Directors

The board of directors is ultimately responsible for the success of a business. Underwriters distinguish between inside and outside directors, because outside directors' viewpoints are generally more independent than those of inside directors. Underwriters note the directors' backgrounds and might request information about each director's expertise, knowledge, experience in the community, and participation in overseeing the institution.

Besides analyzing individual board members' qualifications, underwriters note the number of board meetings held each year and which board members attend. They check how often the board conducts special meetings or appoints special committees. They review who serves on the committees governing important activities, such as the asset-liability, audit, executive, loan, compliance, investment, and compensation committees. Underwriters examine the relationship between management and the board to ensure that the board is sufficiently involved to meet its responsibilities.

In addition to examining the general reports to board members, underwriters are interested in informal discussions between management and the board. Informal discussions reveal how well management communicates with the board about new products or services, mergers and acquisitions, major offerings, and potential risks relating to the institution's financial statements, capital structure, and profitability.

Financial Strength

Underwriters examine a financial institution's financial strength based on financial reports. Financial reports came to underwriters' attention in the late 1970s when they discovered the correlation between poor financial performance and underwriting losses by fraud. Underwriters apply a **CAMELS** analysis. CAMELS stands for:

- Capital
- Asset quality
- Management
- Earnings
- Liquidity
- Sensitivity to market risk

CAMELS refers to the Uniform Financial Institution's Rating System (UFIRS). Each financial institution is assigned a composite rating based on an evaluation of the factors listed. The composite rating is a number from 1 to 5, with 1 indicating the highest rating and 5 the lowest.

Analysis of an institution's capital structure shows whether it complies with all regulatory guidelines and meets peer averages. A review of assets reveals whether the institution has adequately diversified its investments and whether the investments are performing at necessary levels. In addition, the volume of past due accounts affects asset quality. As discussed earlier, underwriters look for a solid, stable management team with a good track record and years of experience. In an earnings analysis, the underwriter wants to see a consistently profitable operation that derives its income from its main operation, not from nonrecurring events. Underwriters do liquidity analyses to determine whether the institution can meet short-term obligations without relying on risky investments. Finally, underwriters evaluate a financial institution's vulnerability to market risk. For financial institutions with no active foreign exchange or trading operations, market risk primarily reflects exposure to changes in interest rates.

A common way to measure financial institution performance is through ratio analysis, complemented by trend analysis. The usual sources of financial information are the applicant's audit reports and call reports. **Call reports** are one kind of regulatory report that financial institutions submit to the Federal Financial Institution Examination Council or to the Federal Deposit Insurance Corporation. Call reports are consolidated reports of condition and income for banks. Different forms are used for banks with domestic and foreign offices and for banks with total assets of different sizes.[3]

Other regulatory reports sometimes available to underwriters include FOCUS reports, annual statements, and other special supporting reports financial institutions must submit to the Securities and Exchange Commission (SEC) and other governmental bodies, including such reports as 10Ks, 8Qs, and prospectuses. **FOCUS** is an acronym for the Financial and Operational Combined Uniform Single report. Broker-dealers are required to file this report monthly and quarterly with self-regulatory organizations (SROs) such as the National Association of Securities Dealers. SROs include exchanges, securities associations, and clearing organizations registered with the Securities and Exchange Commission and required by federal securities laws to be self-policing. The FOCUS report contains figures on capital, earnings, trade flow, and other required details. FOCUS reports are nonpublic.[4]

Besides regulatory reports, underwriters can consult financial reporting services, such as Sheshunoff, Moody's, Standard and Poor's, Best's, and Value Line. Less frequently, underwriters review information from the *Wall Street Journal* and investment banker and broker-dealer reports. Many of these sources, including call reports, are available on the Internet. Exhibit 4-4 lists other information that underwriters study when they conduct a financial analysis.

EXHIBIT 4-4

Information for Analysis of Financial Strength

- Debt structure
- Sources of capital
- Debt history
- Types of investments
- Interest rate management
- Tax effects on transactions
- Leveraged transactions
- Margins
- Profit and loss
- Litigation
- Uninsured losses
- Fixed costs
- Break-even analyses

These issues and many more influence the financial well-being of an institution. Managers' financial strategies and the predictability of their results are short-term. Most institutions' financial models are not highly successful at projecting profitability beyond twelve to eighteen months. Even those predictions are suspect under certain economic conditions. Underwriters compare management's predictions to historical trends, the institution's current financial condition, and management's commitment to its stated strategic plan.

Capital Ratio

In accounting, a business's capital represents its net worth. Generally, a financial institution with a high capital ratio can absorb losses better than one with a low capital ratio. Underwriters often use two capital ratios: the equity capital ratio and the primary capital ratio.

Equity Capital Ratio

The equity capital ratio is:

$$\frac{\text{Equity capital}}{\text{Average total assets}} = \text{Equity capital ratio}$$

Equity capital is the total value of the institution's preferred stock, surplus, common stock, undivided profits and capital reserves, and net unrealized holding gains (or losses) on available-for-sale securities. Average total assets are used to lessen the effect of periodic changes in total assets. However, ratios might use ending assets rather than average total assets. Exhibit 4-5 shows a balance sheet from Metro Bank's call report.

Following the assets and liabilities section is the equity capital section. The total equity capital for Metro Bank is $18,677,000. When that total is divided by total assets of $165,012,000, the resulting ratio is 11.3 percent. This ratio looks strong compared to the range of 7 to 8 percent that underwriters prefer for community banks.

Primary Capital Ratio

The second of the two capital ratios commonly used by financial institution bond underwriters is the primary capital ratio, expressed as follows:

$$\frac{\text{Primary capital}}{\text{Average total assets}} = \text{Primary capital ratio}$$

Primary capital is equity capital plus loan loss reserves. Loan loss reserves are monies that financial institutions set aside in anticipation of expected loan write-offs. The amount of loan loss reserves depends on the quality of the loan portfolio. Average total assets are used to lessen the effect of periodic changes in total assets. However, the ratio might use ending assets rather than average total assets. Metro Bank's loan loss reserves appear in Exhibit 4-5 in the assets section under item 4.c. as "Less: Allowance for loan and lease losses." The underwriter calculates the primary capital ratio as follows:

Equity capital	$18,677,000
Loan loss reserves	+955,000
Primary capital	$19,632,000

$19,632,000 / $165,012,000 = 11.9%

Underwriters prefer applicants with stronger percentages for the equity capital ratio than for the primary capital ratio. Capital ratios that are materially lower than peer or expected averages might indicate poor management of the institution's loan portfolio and investment strategies. Underwriters look for trends to be sure an institution is stable. They also confirm that the ratios meet regulatory standards, though in some states the department of financial institutions might have lower standards than what the underwriter prefers.

Institutions that exercise poor judgment, such as underwriting risky commercial loans or investing in junk (poor investment grade) bonds, put themselves at a much greater risk of failure than those that operate more conservatively. Financial institution underwriters need to examine the lending or investing philosophies of the institutions they are reviewing.

Asset Quality Ratios

Asset quality ratios evaluate the quality of the financial institution's loan portfolios. Two ratios underwriters apply are:

EXHIBIT 4-5

Balance Sheet

Legal Title of Bank

City

State Zip Code

FDIC Certificate Number

FFIEC 041
Page RC-1

10

Consolidated Report of Condition for Insured Commercial and State-Chartered Savings Banks for June 30, 2001

All schedules are to be reported in thousands of dollars. Unless otherwise indicated, report the amount outstanding as of the last business day of the quarter.

Schedule RC—Balance Sheet

Dollar Amounts in Thousands

		RCON	Bil	Mil	Thou	
ASSETS						
1. Cash and balances due from depository institutions (from Schedule RC-A):						
a. Noninterest-bearing balances and currency and coin[1]		0081		8	672	1.a.
b. Interest-bearing balances[2]		0071			43	1.b.
2. Securities:						
a. Held-to-maturity securities (from Schedule RC-B, column A)		1754			0	2.a.
b. Available-for-sale securities (from Schedule RC-B, column D)		1773		78	435	2.b.
3. Federal funds sold and securities purchased under agreements to resell		1350		3	600	3.
4. Loans and lease financing receivables (from Schedule RC-C):						
a. **Loans and leases held for sale**		5369				4.a.
b. **Loans and leases, net of unearned income**	B528 / 70 487					4.b.
c. LESS: Allowance for loan and lease losses	3123 / 955					4.c.
d. **Loans and leases, net of unearned income and allowance** (item 4.b minus 4.c)		B529		69	532	4.d.
5. Trading assets (from Schedule RC-D)		3545			0	5.
6. Premises and fixed assets (including capitalized leases)		2145		1	782	6.
7. Other real estate owned (from Schedule RC-M)		2150			0	7.
8. Investments in unconsolidated subsidiaries and associated companies (from Schedule RC-M)		2130			0	8.
9. Customers' liability to this bank on acceptances outstanding		2155			0	9.
10. Intangible assets:						
a. **Goodwill**		3163			0	10.a.
b. **Other intangible assets** (from Schedule RC-M)		0426			0	10.b.
11. Other assets (from Schedule RC-F)		2160		2	948	11.
12. **Total assets** (sum of items 1 through 11)		2170		165	012	12.

[1] Includes cash items in process of collection and unposted debits.
[2] Includes time certificates of deposit not held for trading.

Continued on next page.

FFIEC 041
Page RC-2

Schedule RC—Continued

	Dollar Amounts in Thousands	RCON	Bil	Mil	Thou	
LIABILITIES						
13. Deposits:						
a. In domestic offices (sum of totals of columns A and C from Schedule RC-E)		2200		145	191	13.a.
(1) Noninterest-bearing[1]	6631			29	060	13.a.(1)
(2) Interest-bearing	6636			116	131	13.a.(2)
b. Not applicable						
14. Federal funds purchased and securities sold under agreements to repurchase		2800			0	14.
15. Trading liabilities (from Schedule RC-D)		3548			0	15.
16. **Other borrowed money** (includes mortgage indebtedness and obligations under capitalized leases) (from Schedule RC-M)		3190			165	16.
17. Not applicable						
18. Bank's liability on acceptances executed and outstanding		2920			0	18.
19. Subordinated notes and debentures[2]		3200			0	19.
20. Other liabilities (from Schedule RC-G)		2930			979	20.
21. Total liabilities (sum of items 13 through 20)		2948		146	335	21.
22. **Minority interest in consolidated subsidiaries**		3000			0	22.
EQUITY CAPITAL						
23. Perpetual preferred stock and related surplus		3838			0	23.
24. Common stock		3230			900	24.
25. Surplus (exclude all surplus related to preferred stock)		3839		1	340	25.
26. a. Retained earnings		3632		15	458	26.a.
b. **Accumulated other comprehensive income**[3]		B530			979	26.b.
27. **Other equity capital components**[4]		A130			0	27.
28. Total equity capital (sum of items 23 through 27)		3210		18	677	28.
29. Total liabilities, minority interest, and equity capital (sum of items 21, 22, and 28)		3300		165	012	29.

Memorandum
To be reported with the March Report of Condition.

1. Indicate in the box at the right the number of the statement below that best describes the most comprehensive level of auditing work performed for the bank by independent external auditors as of any date during 2000

	RCON	Number	
	6724	N/A	M.1.

1 = Independent audit of the bank conducted in accordance with generally accepted auditing standards by a certified public accounting firm which submits a report on the bank

2 = Independent audit of the bank's parent holding company conducted in accordance with generally accepted auditing standards by a certified public accounting firm which submits a report on the consolidated holding company (but not on the bank separately)

3 = **Attestation on bank management's assertion on the effectiveness of the bank's internal control over financial reporting by a certified public accounting firm**

4 = Directors' examination of the bank conducted in accordance with generally accepted auditing standards by a certified public accounting firm (may be required by state chartering authority)

5 = Directors' examination of the bank performed by other external auditors (may be required by state chartering authority)

6 = Review of the bank's financial statements by external auditors

7 = Compilation of the bank's financial statements by external auditors

8 = Other audit procedures (excluding tax preparation work)

9 = No external audit work

---

[1] Includes total demand deposits and noninterest-bearing time and savings deposits.
[2] Includes limited-life preferred stock and related surplus.
[3] Includes net unrealized holding gains (losses) on available-for-sale securities, accumulated net gains (losses) on cash flow hedges, and minimum pension liability adjustments.
[4] Includes treasury stock and unearned Employee Stock Ownership Plan shares.

$$\frac{\text{Nonperforming assets}}{\text{Total assets}}$$

and

$$\frac{\text{Loan loss reserves}}{\text{Nonperforming assets}}$$

Nonperforming assets are foreclosed real estate or delinquent loans (loans the borrower is not repaying according to the terms of the contract). Nonperforming assets are not a specific line on the balance sheet. Underwriters derive this figure from parts of the call report and from audit reports. An underwriter prefers a **nonperforming-assets-to-total-assets ratio** below 2 percent. If Metro Bank's nonperforming assets are $3,330,000, the nonperforming-assets-to-total-assets ratio comes close to meeting the criterion:

$$\$3,330,000 / \$165,012,000 = 2.02\%$$

The **loan-loss-reserve-to-nonperforming-assets ratio reflects** how much cushion the institution has against future write-offs or its ability to adjust profits to cover the write-offs. Institutions that make risky loans should have a higher ratio than institutions making low-risk loans. A ratio of 70 to 80 percent is not uncommon for institutions with risky loans. Metro Bank's loan-loss-reserves-to-nonperforming-assets ratio is:

$$\$955,000 / \$3,330,000 = 28.7\%$$

Because Metro Bank is making low-risk loans, this is a favorable ratio.

The ratio changes quarterly for most institutions, based on changes in the loan loss reserves. Significant swings in loan loss reserves directly affect profitability and capital. Financial institutions should show a history of maintaining sufficient quarterly or annual profits to cover reserve adjustments.

The loan mix for a lending operation is important to underwriters because it influences trends on nonperforming assets. Well-collateralized loans, such as single-family dwellings, make up a conservative portfolio. However, if the institution engages in highly leveraged transactions, such as loans to unstable, third-world businesses, speculative commercial real estate developers, or developers in an already overbuilt community, an underwriter should be more cautious. Other risky lending strategies include loans to leveraged-buyout participants, loans to venture capitalists or recapitalization companies, and stock loans on poorly performing organizations or weakened financial institutions.

Equity Ratios

Equity measures the institution's ability to sustain losses in earnings. The stronger the institution is, the more easily it can attract additional funds for growth. **Equity ratios** show how well a financial institution can attract additional capital for growth. Underwriters commonly use the return-on-equity (ROE) ratio:

$$\frac{\text{Net income}}{\text{Equity capital}} = \text{Return on equity (ROE)}$$

For large financial institutions, this ratio is generally 6 to 7 percent although stockholders might prefer a higher percentage to compete favorably with investment alternatives. Underwriters prefer that small, localized institutions have a higher ratio. The net income figure comes from the financial institution's income statement. If Metro Bank's net income is $3,500,000, the ROE would be:

$$\$3,500,000 / \$18,677,000 = 18.7\%$$

Metro Bank's ratio is well within the acceptable range.

Liquidity Ratios

Liquidity ratios generally measure the degree to which assets are funded by stable rather than unstable liabilities. Underwriters consider different information for financial institutions, insurance companies, and securities firms.

Financial Institution Liquidity Ratios

Underwriters use three ratios to measure liquidity:

- Loans-to-deposits ratio
- Securities-to-assets ratio
- Large-deposits-and-borrowings-to-deposits ratio

The loans-to-deposits ratio is the simplest to calculate. The loans-to-deposits ratio, particularly for banks, should not be too high and might typically be 65 to 70 percent. An acceptable loans-to-deposits ratio differs based on where the institution is located and whether it is a savings and loan association or a commercial bank. Metro Bank's reported total loans on line 4.b. in Exhibit 4-5 and its reported total deposits on line 13.a. give it a loans-to-deposits ratio as follows:

$$\$70,487,000 / \$145,191,000 = 48.5\%$$

This is a conservative ratio that underwriters would view favorably if other ratios are favorable. By comparing different ratios, underwriters can assure that an institution is not sacrificing earnings to maintain liquidity.

Institutions can usually liquidate securities more easily and at less cost than they can liquidate loans. Thus, the securities-to-assets ratio complements the loans-to-deposits ratio by providing another indicator of liquidity. A high ratio is desirable for liquidity. Large deposits and borrowings are generally less stable and more expensive sources of funding than core deposits. A low ratio is desirable.

Insurance Company Liquidity Ratios

When underwriting insurance companies, underwriters study the Annual Statement. The Annual Statement contains information on the following:

- Total investments, real estate investment, type and quality of securities, tax effects, and trading positions.

- Securities not required to be marked to market (not required to be posted at the sale value of the security at the time of reporting).
- Reserving practices. (Understated reserves lead to overstated profits. Statutory reserves might not be sufficient.)
- Reinsurance and the reinsurer's ability to respond to claims.
- Litigation, errors or omissions, large claims that are unreserved, and claims that are in suit.
- The ratio of premiums written to stockholders' equity.

Securities Firm Liquidity Ratios

Tools for analyzing a securities firm are the monthly FOCUS reports, current prospectuses, annual reports, and 10Ks. Securities brokers and dealers must comply with net capital requirements, which evolve from SEC Rule 15c3-1 requiring that brokers and dealers maintain a minimum amount of net capital. Basic net capital is total ownership equity, including allowable subordinated liabilities, minus nonallowable assets, and certain securities positions on contractual securities commitments, subordinated securities borrowings, and various trading and investment positions.

There are two methods of computing net capital requirements. One requires an amount equal to the greater of $100,000 or 2 percent of the aggregate debt items rising from customer transactions as defined. The other method multiplies $6\,^2/_3$ percent times the total aggregate indebtedness. The monthly FOCUS report provides the data for this calculation.

One unusual element in the computation is the allowance of subordinated debt to support the net capital requirements. If subordinated debt represents a significant portion of net capital, the firm might be subject to long-term financial dependence or to the whims of those holding the debt.

Other considerations are the size and nature of the organization's in-house trading account and the economic value of the account; litigation arising from customers; breaches of rules and regulations causing costly fines and penalties; and the nature and degree of funds under management and control of the organization, and for which the broker makes a market. When the broker makes a market, high-pressure sales and improper qualification of the security can result in lawsuits by customers.

The underwriter distinguishes among the following:

- Institutional or retail customer market and commodities market
- Discount brokerage and retail securities brokerage
- Mutual fund complexes and brokers and dealers

Financial analyses, particularly analyses relating to services, vary greatly. Because brokers and dealers rely heavily on commissions and fees generated from the sale of securities, any significant changes in the economic environment or in the products environment in which they operate affect their financial results. Underwriters need to be aware of changes in regulations, laws, and the economy as they affect product mix and services.

EMPLOYEE THEFT/DISHONESTY EXPOSURES

Commercial crime and financial institution underwriting entails evaluating employee theft/dishonesty exposures. According to some reports, criminal activities, such as fraud, embezzlement, and employee theft, cost American businesses an estimated $400 billion annually. Outright employee theft costs U.S. companies $120 billion a year. Such thefts might be responsible for more than 30 percent of the nation's business failures.[5] A recent General Accounting Office report on IRS financial management practices revealed that IRS employees allegedly embezzled $5.3 million in taxpayer checks and cash from 1995 to 1997.[6]

Underwriters cannot know how quickly losses will be discovered, when they will occur, the amounts involved, or the employees who will perpetrate them. They can only identify the exposures and assess the applicant's commitment to preventing and reducing employee theft/dishonesty losses.

Exposures of Businesses Other Than Financial Institutions

The employee theft/dishonesty exposure of most businesses typically comes from trusted employees, including managers and supervisors. A trusted employee does not become an embezzler without opportunities and motivation. The following are some opportunities that can arise:

- The employer places too much trust in key employees.
- Employees get too close to suppliers, customers, and others outside the business.
- Employees' tenures in key positions become too long.
- Management keeps sloppy books and records.
- Management does not pay attention to details.

FOR FURTHER THOUGHT

Trusted Employees

Although companies must trust their top executives, even they should not be exempt from reasonable controls. Allowing one CFO freedom to act without controls cost his employer over $2 million. The CFO's responsibilities included complete discretion over company investments. Taking advantage of his position, he purchased 1,000 shares of preferred stock of an unknown company through a broker in a distant city. When asked about the investment, the CFO replied that he knew the company, and its preferred stock paid a 14 percent dividend. He had made good investments in the past, 14 percent was a good return, and as CFO he was above suspicion. The matter was dropped.

In reality, the shares were issued by a shell company without assets or operations that the CFO had set up several years before. He used the proceeds of the stock sale for personal investments.

> For a while, the stock paid its 14 percent dividend, but it was nothing more than a return of part of the purchase price of the stock. The CFO's personal investments were not profitable, and all of the funds were lost. When he could no longer pay the 14 percent dividend, the CFO was forced to confess.[7]

The list of motivations can be extensive. Mounting personal debts and losses or a feeling of being unappreciated are common motivators. Employees feel that the company (or society) owes them. The following are just some of the ways employees steal from their employers:

- Altering deposit slips to conceal money the culprit kept
- Removing from the bank statement checks the culprit negotiated for personal gain
- Having the bank statement mailed directly to the culprit's attention without the insured's knowledge
- Splitting cash and check deposits to hide the cash pocketed
- Writing checks on the employer's account to pay personal bills
- "Lapping," or using the proceeds from future customers to cover the payments from previous customers that the employee has used for personal gain
- Accepting kickbacks from suppliers

Financial Institution Exposures

In financial institutions, employee dishonesty losses generally take longer to discover. As with other businesses, the trusted employee is the most common culprit. Positions often associated with major frauds are presidents, vice presidents, treasurers, accountants/bookkeepers, tellers/cashiers, credit managers/loan officers, and branch/assistant managers.[8] Executive or senior officers can generally conceal their frauds longer than middle managers. Cashiers, tellers, accountants, and bookkeepers hold the positions in which fraud is most frequently committed. The severity of losses by cashiers and tellers, however, is lower than losses by accountants and bookkeepers because losses caused by cashiers and tellers are detected earlier. The financial institution's internal control mechanisms influence how much embezzlers take and how quickly the institution catches them.

> **FOR FURTHER THOUGHT**
>
> ### Finding on Frauds Committed by Supervisors and Managers
>
> The number and size of frauds carried out by employees at the supervisory level and higher are notable. Nearly half of the frauds and the largest dollar amounts involved people in positions of responsibility. Because people in such positions make up far less than half of the total work force, this finding suggests that they are more likely than low-level employees to defraud their employers. High-level employees are not necessarily less honest, but they are subject to fewer controls and are often in a position to override controls that do exist.[9]

Submitting false documents is the most common way embezzlers conceal fraud. They usually alter loan documents, including loan applications, credit reports, loan approval forms, authorizations for disbursement of funds, contracts, or loan security documents. Other documents include purchase invoices, disbursement checks, deposit and withdrawal slips, food stamp applications, customers' checks, deposit slips, cash-over or cash-short reports, cash receipts, shipping documents, and payroll documents.

EMPLOYEE THEFT/DISHONESTY LOSS CONTROL

What applicants do to reduce moral hazards and eliminate opportunities for theft and embezzlement is the best measure of their commitment to preventing employee theft/dishonesty losses. Applicants that exercise good human resource and internal control procedures have made the commitment.

Human Resource Procedures

Good human resource procedures are crucial to maintaining a well-functioning organization. The human resource department's role does not stop after an employee is hired. Human resource departments help management train new hires, monitor performance and salaries, and manage turnover and termination.

Hiring Practices

The human resource department's first responsibility is screening job applicants. Applicants might have walked in off the street or might have learned about the position from advertisements, recruiters, job postings, or an employee's recommendation. Underwriters are concerned with how thoroughly job applicants are screened. As much as legally allowed, human resource staff should verify a job applicant's work and personal history, including debt history, employment history, progression in job responsibilities, history of substance abuse or prior crimes, motor vehicle records, hobbies and activities, and educational qualifications for the job. Underwriters who are concerned about an insurance applicant can obtain information about hiring practices from the human resource department.

Debt History

Looking into job applicants' debt histories helps employers decide whether applicants can meet their current financial obligations on the salaries the employer offers. Employees with large debts might be tempted to steal from their employers. Underwriters are wary of businesses or financial institutions that have employees who are heavily in debt.

Employment History

Human resource staff might review job applicants' employment histories and obtain explanations for gaps. Valid reasons exist for employment gaps and a gap does not necessarily mean the applicant is an unsuitable candidate.

However, careful investigating could uncover adverse employment experiences that the applicant might not have voluntarily revealed.

Progression of Responsibility

Job applicants' work experiences should reflect a reasonable progression to higher responsibility and improved skills. The human resource staff might therefore investigate an applicant's rapid advancement to a higher responsibility level or job position. Unreasonably fast promotions might have been a reward for colluding with a manager in dishonest activities.

FOR FURTHER THOUGHT

Investigating Red Flags

Because of the endless possibilities for employees to steal from their employers, underwriters might become cynical. Remember that valid explanations might exist for almost any underwriting "red flag." Good underwriters recognize the possibilities, investigate to determine the facts, and base their underwriting decision on those facts.

Substance Abuse or Crime History

Generally, underwriters view substance-abuse screening programs favorably. Substance dependency can create an embezzlement potential, contribute to poor work performance, and increase medical claims. The presence of supervisors and managers who are trained to detect employees' substance abuse is a positive underwriting factor. Such training should be an integral part of a risk management program.

Screening employees who have committed a crime is a sensitive area. When a business or financial institution reveals to the underwriter that one of its employees has a criminal record, the underwriter must carefully examine the circumstances. The applicant should furnish all the facts to the insurer. Usually, insurers exclude employees who have committed crimes. However, in some cases, an applicant might ask the underwriter to make an exception. A senior underwriting manager can provide advice in this situation. If the employee has exhibited many years of employment stability and honesty, the underwriter might cover him or her. If, however, the employee is on parole from a burglary conviction, it is highly unlikely the insurer will agree to grant coverage.

Motor Vehicle Records

Good driving records can indicate a responsible employee. A history of flagrant disregard for driving regulations or consistent careless driving might suggest that the employee is not a good candidate for employee dishonesty coverage. Human resource staff might verify driving records and investigate irregularities before hiring the applicant.

Hobbies and Activities

A job applicant's hobbies and activities might reveal inconsistencies between the applicant's lifestyle and the job he or she is seeking. An underwriter should be concerned if a business has a pattern of hiring employees who engage in expensive hobbies or activities that exceed their expected income.

Educational Qualifications

Human resource departments might confirm job applicants' educational backgrounds to verify that they honestly represented their qualifications and to be sure applicants meet the standards set for the job. Every job category should have a description, education requirement, classification, and salary range. If the human resource department is not properly matching applicants to job classifications, underwriters should be concerned about potential moral hazards and management problems.

Personnel Training

A business or financial institution communicates its policies and procedures to employees through training. Training does not just teach employees how to do their jobs. It familiarizes them with the business's security, products, organizational structure, corporate policies, employee benefits, supervisory procedures, and opportunities for cross-training. Training should also teach employees the business's moral standards. Underwriters expect crime insurance applicants to clearly state a code of ethics and a conflict-of-interest policy and to train employees on these issues.

Personnel Evaluation and Salary Administration

Personnel evaluation and salary administration are two separate functions. Some businesses have a policy against awarding salary increases during a personnel evaluation. Nevertheless, the two activities are related. Well-managed organizations have regularly scheduled personnel evaluations. Underwriters look for human resource departments that enforce such policies.

Applicants should be sure their employees' salaries are commensurate with the salaries of competitors' employees doing the same functions in the same geographical locations. Besides deterring employee dishonesty, salary reviews and appropriate adjustments keep turnover caused by low salaries to a minimum. Embezzlers often justify their crime with the excuse that their employer does not pay them their worth. Underwriters might review how often applicants' human resource departments monitor employees' salaries.

Employee Turnover and Termination

High employee turnover reflects poorly on the management in any business, but underwriters are especially interested in turnover rates for financial institutions. High turnover in supervisory or management positions has serious operational exposure implications. Underwriters commonly ask applicants to supply a list of employees' names, positions, and hire dates. By reviewing such a list, underwriters can detect any turnover patterns in key positions. Underwriters pay more attention to training standards and hiring practices in businesses with high turnover.

Applicant businesses should have clearly defined termination procedures. For example, when applicants fire their employees, they should immediately eliminate employees' password access to computers and remove their names from the payroll. Terminated employees should be required to turn in all keys, access cards, and company equipment issued to them. Underwriters expect human resource, payroll, and security staffs to work closely to properly handle termination procedures.

Control Procedures

Interviews with convicted burglars, robbers, embezzlers, and forgers reveal that the primary contributor to their crimes was opportunity. Although employees usually commit fraud alone, businesses and financial institutions should take precautions to prevent collusion among employees. Underwriters should work with producers and applicants to reduce opportunity. Underwriters cannot prevent a loss, but they can reduce its likelihood by helping applicants identify and implement internal loss prevention and reduction techniques that limit opportunities to steal. Common ways businesses and financial institutions discover fraud include the following:

- Management inquiries
- Audits
- Customer complaints
- Informants' tips
- Discoveries made when the defrauder is not at work
- Voluntary confessions

Some ways of detecting fraud are out of management's control, but management can use deterrent procedures, such as external and internal audits and other controls, that can reduce the applicant's loss exposure

External Audits

A qualified CPA should formally examine the applicant's accounts and verify their correctness at least annually. An underwriter should be concerned if an applicant's external audits occur less often. Where the CPA sends the audit report is also important. Copies should not go exclusively to the person responsible for the applicant's financial records.

Because employee theft/dishonesty coverage excludes owners, partners, and nonemployed directors, underwriters want external audits sent directly to these persons and to the chairperson of the audit committee. Had the CPA in the above example sent the audit to such people, the culprit's scheme would not have succeeded.

As stated earlier, the CPA's report should verify the correctness of the accounts. Reports that use the words "compile" or "review" are not sufficient information for an underwriter.

> **FOR FURTHER THOUGHT**
>
> **Claim Illustration**
>
> An insured's CPA sent all twelve copies of an annual audit to the insured's treasurer. The treasurer spent several hours correcting the numbers to match the set of books the treasurer maintained at the office. After finishing the alterations, the treasurer forwarded the altered copies of the audit to the board of directors. The board was so pleased with the doctored numbers that it gave the treasurer a raise.

Internal Audits

Businesses that conduct internal audits reflect to the underwriter that management is committed to exercising strong internal controls. The quality of internal auditing depends on the qualifications and motivation of the personnel and the standards the department sets. Audit staff should be organizationally independent of the departments they audit. An internal audit function is effective only if top management supports its activities and if the auditors have direct access to the top managers and the board of directors.[10]

> **FOR FURTHER THOUGHT**
>
> **Lack of Internal Controls at a Hospital**
>
> A hospital with revenues of over $200 million per year could have afforded to develop good internal controls but did not do so. When the accounting office issued checks, the first two checks placed into the printer were used only to start the runs. They were blank when they came out of the printer. The accounting manager took those two checks, typed his name as payee, wrote the checks for several thousand dollars, and deposited the checks into his personal account. He then ran the checks through the check-signing machine, which would place one officer's name on the checks. The amounts were small enough that two signatures were not required. The accounting manager voided the check numbers in the accounts payable check log.
>
> The manager was also in charge of reconciling the hospital's bank statement. He could remove the canceled checks, discard them, and make journal entries to cover the amount of the checks and the reconciliation balance to the general ledger. The amounts were small compared to the hospital's revenues to make it unlikely that an audit could trace the money. This continued for nine years with the loss exceeding $200,000.[11]

Underwriters should investigate the internal audit department's expertise. They can do so by reviewing the number of certified personnel participating in audits and checking their training and experience to be sure they are qualified in their specialty, especially in electronic data processing audits. They can also analyze turnover in the department, hoping it is small, because auditors need time to familiarize themselves with the departments they review. Underwriters study the auditor's report and management's response to it. They also examine the quality of the auditor's work papers and the auditor's thoroughness in reviewing high-risk areas.

Internal auditors should have access to top management but should not report to operational management. For example, audit departments in financial institutions generally report to an audit committee of the board containing highly qualified personnel familiar with operations and internal control processes.

Underwriters evaluate whether the internal audit department has time to investigate special projects such as embezzlements, mergers, acquisitions, or follow-up reviews of departments with previously unsatisfactory audits. The time, budget, and scope of audits should be sufficient to evaluate internal control procedures properly.

Internal auditors might obtain support from external auditors. Underwriters examine the working relationship between internal and external auditors. Executive and operating management's willingness to respond to an audit comment is also significant. The audit committee's role is to ensure that management responds appropriately to the internal audit. Underwriters prefer that management cooperate with auditors and respond to auditors' comments.

Separation of Duties

No single employee should have sole responsibility for all the steps in any business operation that could be vulnerable to loss. For example, no single employee should be responsible for receiving cash and recording collections in the accounts receivable records. Applicants should clearly define the duties of officers and employees, including their authority and responsibility. No fewer than two people should handle and record each transaction.[12] Separation of duties is one of the "Golden Rules of Internal Control." If employers observed this rule, employee fraud would decrease dramatically. Employers could prevent or catch losses easily. Proper separation along natural lines makes separation of duties practical for even a small business. Underwriters should not accept applicants that do not practice separation of duties.[13]

Key duties that any business or financial institution should keep separate are:

- Authorizing transactions
- Collecting or paying cash
- Maintaining records of accountability

The asset most vulnerable to fraud is cash, and access is usually direct. The most commonly used fraud technique-unrecorded sales-requires no concealment, at least not in the form of falsified records. When an embezzler attempts to falsify records, the records most often tampered with are those involving receivables, payables, loans, and payroll.[14] Exhibit 4-6 lists specific functions that banking and lending institutions should keep separate.[15]

> **EXHIBIT 4-6**
>
> ## Duties That Should Be Separated in Financial Institutions
>
> ### Banking Operations
>
> Tellers and proof-transit employees should not perform functions in other departments. An employee, independent of the teller operations, should issue new account documents and assign account numbers.
>
> Employees with physical custody of cash should not post accounting transactions or reconcile account balances.
>
> Officers' and employees' accounts should use separate series of account numbers and should be reviewed periodically for unusual activity.
>
> Transactions to dormant accounts should be reported separately and reviewed periodically by employees independent of the teller or bookkeeper functions.
>
> Account statements should be mailed to customers on a regular basis. All customer inquiries should be handled by employees independent of the teller and accounting functions.
>
> Responsibility for originating, processing, and reconciling wire transfers should be segregated.
>
> Proof-transit responsibility for batch control processing, transaction encoding, and reconciling control totals should be segregated.
>
> Responsibility for initiating administrative expenditures, preparing negotiable instruments, and reconciling transactions should be segregated.
>
> Administrative expenditures should be disbursed from a separate operating account and segregated from normal bank transactions.
>
> ### Lending Operations
>
> The functions that should be performed by individuals independent of the lending function are:
>
> - Credit reviews
> - Property appraisals
> - Disbursements of loan proceeds
> - Processing of loan payments
> - Preparing delinquent loan lists
> - Disposals of repossessed collateral
> - Adjustments to employee loans
>
> An independent loan officer should review adjustments, renewals, and extensions to the loan application.
>
> The completeness of loan files should be reviewed by an independent person before disbursing loan proceeds.
>
> Lending officers should not have access to accounting records or be allowed to post entries without appropriate officer approval.

> Loans that have been charged-off should be segregated and maintained under separate accounting control.
>
> Detailed statements of the loan balances, including charge-offs and pledged collateral, should be mailed at least annually. Exceptions to those balances must be resolved by employees outside the lending functions.

Dual Control

Dual control requires two people to perform certain operations. Underwriters of even the smallest businesses should insist that more than one person sign checks, make deposits and withdrawals, and reconcile bank accounts. Businesses writing large volumes of checks should require a countersignature on checks exceeding a specified amount. The amount is usually related to the average amount of checks the business issues on a regular basis. If the business is too small to assign employees for dual control, owners, partners, directors, or outside accountants (persons excluded from employee theft/dishonesty coverage) can serve as the second party. Two effective safeguards are to have an outside accountant reconcile the bank account monthly or have an excluded person, such as the owner, reconcile the account on a regular or unannounced basis. Businesses with valuable assets or inventory should also have a dual control system in place.

Besides the dual controls described above, financial institutions should have at least two people control the following:

- Vault cash
- Investment securities
- Negotiable collateral
- Trusts and securities
- Unissued stock certificates
- The reserve supply of official checks and drafts
- Dormant accounts of depositors
- Unissued Series E bonds
- Unissued travelers' checks
- Safe-deposit spare keys and locks
- Spare keys to tellers' cash drawers
- Night depository safes

> **FOR FURTHER THOUGHT**
>
> ### Dual Controls Must Be Enforced
>
> A twenty-year hospital employee stole $140,000 over two years by creating false accounts payable checks to fictitious hospital patients. She created fictitious patient names for accounts payable forms for patient refunds. She requested that the checks be brought back to her. She forged the patients' names on the back of the check, signed her own name, and deposited the checks in a bank account. The investigation found that a supervisor reviewed the checks. Some of the checks were initialed by the supervisor, but the supervisor never questioned the employee, who was well liked in the hospital's accounting and finance office.[16]

Rotation of Duties

Rotating duties helps prevent or reduce loss caused by an employee acting alone. Employees should rotate responsibilities long enough for a manager to discover irregularities. An added benefit of rotating duties is that cross-trained employees can substitute for each other in emergencies.

Mandatory Vacations

Mandatory vacations serve a similar control purpose as rotation of duties. Many embezzlers can only succeed if they adjust records on a daily basis. If they cannot access books and records, even for a brief time, a substitute will detect their scheme. Applicants should require all officers and employees to take annual vacations of at least five consecutive business days. Some underwriters prefer ten consecutive business days. If the insurance application does not show the business has such a policy, the underwriter should investigate further. Some flexibility might be necessary with small- to medium-sized commercial businesses that cannot afford to allow personnel to take extended vacations.

FOR FURTHER THOUGHT

A Case for Mandatory Vacations

One employee successfully "lapped" cash receipts for twenty-nine years at a cost of over $100,000. Extending over the employee's entire career with the company, the scheme was discovered only when the employee retired. The employee had access both to cash receipts and to the records establishing accountability for the receipts. The employee withheld checks from accounts receivable collections. He then took cash from later collections and covered the theft by crediting the previously withheld checks to the accounts of the customers who had paid cash. Later receipts were credited to the accounts of the customers who had sent in the first batch of checks, and so on.

Lapping requires continuous close attention. If misapplied receipts are not covered quickly, the customer receives a past-due notice and complains, and the scheme is undone. The thief must keep track of normal delinquencies and be prepared to deal with plant closings, strikes, market problems, and business disruptions of all kinds. This trusted employee was noted for his diligence. He never required help and never took a long vacation.[17]

Direct Verifications

Financial institutions commonly use direct verifications to deter losses. **Direct verifications** confirm transactions or balances directly with the bank customers. Employees who know that the bank will confirm transactions with customers are less likely to embezzle customers' funds. A systematic verification plan also enables financial institutions to detect honest errors and employee fraud sooner than if no system were in effect.

Though direct verifications are associated mostly with financial institutions, retail operations have a similar system when customers return goods. Retailers require employees who refund money to have customers complete a form asking for the customer's address and phone number. Later the retailer can directly verify the refund with the customer, if necessary.

Employee Monitoring and Surveillance

Employee monitoring and surveillance can be a useful control measure. Surveillance can detect employees stealing inventory and cash. Underwriters should expect applicants to use some of the following procedures:[18]

- Check employees who arrive early or stay late when there is no need to do so.
- Permit no employees to make sales to themselves.
- Restrict all employees to a single exit, if possible.
- Use care about allowing employees free access to storerooms.
- Monitor employee packages and require they be opened and checked when removed from the premises.
- Make all deliveries through the store.
- Investigate all inventory shortages carefully; prove even minor losses.
- Inventory all supplies, equipment, and merchandise systematically.
- Use surveillance cameras that monitor traffic at hidden doorways.

> **FOR FURTHER THOUGHT**
>
> **Surveillance Cameras at the IRS**
>
> At four Internal Revenue Service (IRS) centers, the General Accounting Office (GAO) found that employees could bring their personal belongings into areas where mail was sorted and opened. IRS records showed that nine theft cases from January 1995 to July 1997 involved employees who had put stolen checks and cash into duffel bags, purses, or lunch boxes.
>
> The GAO recommended that the IRS consider installing surveillance cameras to monitor staff when they are sorting and opening mail and when they are processing checks and cash sent in by taxpayers. The GAO also suggested that the agency provide lockers for employees so they can store personal items outside processing areas.[19]

SUMMARY

Underwriters refer to many sources of information to evaluate applicants. The application provides information for selecting appropriate coverages and ratings. Supplemental information appears on additional questionnaires. Financial reports, agents and brokers, and other documents are sources to complete the information underwriters need to properly evaluate applicants.

After gathering the information, underwriters analyze the information to determine the organization's overall health and identify crime exposures that can be addressed through loss control. The organization's overall health varies by ownership, organizational structure, growth, the economic environment, business plan, management, board of directors, and financial strength. Crime exposures for commercial organizations and financial institutions can be controlled through human resource and control procedures. Human resource procedures include the following:

- Hiring practices
- Personnel evaluation and salary administration
- Personnel training
- Employee turnover and termination

Control procedures include the following:

- External audits
- Internal audits
- Segregation of duties
- Dual control
- Rotation of duties
- Mandatory vacations
- Direct verifications
- Employee monitoring and surveillance

CHAPTER NOTES

1. ACORD forms are modified whenever necessary to meet the requirements of regulators and the insurance business. The most recent edition of any ACORD form should always be used.
2. A source for additional information on forms of business organizations is *West's Business Law*, 6th ed., Kenneth W. Clarkson, Roger LeRoy Miller, Gaylord H. Jentz, and Frank B. Cross (St. Paul, Minn.: West Publishing Company, 1995).
3. More information about call reports can be found on the Internet at www.ffiec.gov.
4. The X-17A-5 reports, which are the annual audit of the business might be available from the Public Reference Room, Mail Stop 0102, Washington, D.C. 20549-0102.
5. Josh Martin, "Dissecting the Books," *Management Review*, June 1998, pp. 47–51.
6. Stephen Barr, "Audit of IRS Finds Fraud by Workers: GAO Report Details System Inefficiencies," *The Washington Post*, November 16, 1998, p. A23.
7. Ernst & Young, *White Collar Crime Loss Prevention Through Internal Control* (Warren, N.J.: Chubb & Son, Inc., 1989), p. 27.
8. Wilfred Harold Silvester, "Analysis of Fraud Cases—Aids to the Auditor" (Ph.D. diss., University of Missouri, 1978), pp. 4, 7, and 9.
9. Ernst & Young, p. 10.
10. Ernst & Young, p. 31.
11. R.W. Deckert, *Stopping Employee Theft* (Columbia, Md.: Diverse Assets Creations, Inc., 1998), pp. 115–116.
12. U.S. Congress. House Committee on Banking. *Report on Crimes Against Banking Institutions*. 80th Cong., 1964. H. Rept. 1147, p. 23.
13. Ernst & Young, pp. 28–29.

14. Ernst & Young, p. 9.
15. The Fidelity and Deposit Companies, *Embezzlement Controls and Other Safeguards for Financial Institutions* (Baltimore, Md.: The Fidelity and Deposit Company of Maryland, 1990), pp. 6–7, 9.
16. Deckert, pp. 120–121.
17. Ernst & Young, pp. 24–25.
18. American Mutual Insurance Alliance, *Judging the Crime Risk* (Chicago: Alliance of American Insurers, 1970), p. 207.
19. Barr, p. A23.

Chapter 5

Underwriting and Loss Control, Part II

Chapter 4 discussed sources of underwriting information, general underwriting considerations, and employee theft/dishonesty exposures and loss control. This chapter examines loss control measures for crime exposures other than employee theft/dishonesty. For those exposures, underwriters evaluate applicants' physical security and security procedures for their effectiveness in reducing losses. Because of their unique characteristics, computer fraud and extortion loss exposures require special underwriting attention. Underwriters gather supplemental information about those exposures and evaluate unique loss control measures. The chapter concludes by explaining the factors insurers consider when calculating a final premium.

PHYSICAL SECURITY CONSIDERATIONS

Providing adequate physical security for businesses and financial institutions is a delicate balancing act because the goals for effective security and for sales often conflict. For example, bulletproof glass separating bank tellers from customers is unattractive from a sales and service perspective but effective for security. When underwriters review applicants' physical security procedures, they balance their need for ideal security measures with the applicant's need to provide a favorable business environment.

Building Security

Businesses can frequently reduce crime losses at little cost by using common-sense steps to protect the property. Building security can be enhanced through the techniques described in Exhibit 5-1.[1]

> **EXHIBIT 5-1**
>
> ### Building Security Techniques
>
> Doors and Windows
>
> - Properly maintain all doors and windows to prevent easy entrance.
> - Always lock rear and side doors that are not used for public access. Use panic door hardware or an approved equivalent so that required exit doors conform to building codes.
> - Avoid window displays or signs that obstruct the view into the building.
> - Remove expensive, easily carried merchandise from show windows every day at closing time.
>
> Lighting
>
> - Illuminate all entry points with bright automatic lights.
> - Maintain a night light inside the building, especially near a safe that is visible to passersby outside the building.
>
> Housekeeping
>
> - Keep the area around the building free of high grass, weeds, or shrubs that could provide cover for burglars.
> - Keep fences in good repair and keep the fence area clear of debris and boxes.
> - Lock up all ladders.
> - Make sure fire escapes and exits provide for quick exit but difficult entry.
> - Keep power sources hidden and protected. Check and test them regularly.
> - Leave the cash register open and empty at night to prevent unnecessary damage.
> - Establish a nightly final inspection routine to ensure that all physical security systems are functioning properly and to prevent someone from hiding inside the building.

The procedures in Exhibit 5-1 might be enough protection when the applicant and underwriter expect the probability and severity of loss to be low. However, businesses in high crime areas or with merchandise that is attractive to thieves should strengthen their physical security. Exhibit 5-2 lists additional physical security measures that such businesses should consider.[2]

Safes, Money Chests, and Vaults

Burglars or embezzlers prefer stealing cash to stealing other kinds of property. Money, therefore, requires a high degree of protection. However, many businesses use safes and vaults that do not meet their needs. Most safes are fire-resistive but not burglar-resistive, and businesses do not understand the difference. A fire-resistive safe protects its contents against fires, but it does

> **EXHIBIT 5-2**
>
> **Physical Security Measures for High-Risk Businesses**
>
> Exterior Doors
>
> - Doors should be of substantial construction. Security experts recommend that they be a minimum of 1.5 inches thick made of solid wood, wood core with 16 gauge metal facing inside, or solid metal.
> - Windows in the doors should be force-resistant glazing or protected by metal grillwork.
> - Doors should be well secured to the structure.
> - Locks should be heavy deadbolt with a bolt that extends at least one inch into the bolt receptacle.
>
> Windows
>
> - Protect windows easily reached from the ground and not fronting on main roads and windows on upper stories that are accessible from nearby structures. Protection should be either bars or screens, depending on local building and fire codes.
> - Glass store display windows, vulnerable to "smash and grab" attacks, should be made of force-resistant glazing if the merchandise displayed is high-value, such as jewelry, furs, or televisions.
>
> Exterior Lighting
>
> - Mount lights on the roof or poles so intruders cannot attack them easily.
> - If the area is fenced, light an area of ten feet on either side of the fence.
> - Light yard storage areas well.
>
> Fences or Barriers
>
> - Fences should be flush with the ground and a minimum of seven feet in height, with barbed wire at the top tilted toward the outside of the protected area.
> - Barriers include walls, barbed tape, or concertina (coiled barbed wire).
>
> Protection Against Other Tenants and Visitors
>
> - Cutoffs between tenants should be of solid masonry construction, from the floor to the underside of the roof.
> - Openings should be locked with suitable hardware.
> - Other tenants should not have free access to the insured's property.
> - Visitors should be supervised.

not protect them against someone who knows how to manipulate the dial mechanism to open the safe. No safe or vault can be totally "burglarproof," but certain types and models provide greater protection than others. Underwriters Laboratories Inc. (UL) rates safes for their fire resistance and tests burglar-resistive safes against simulated burglary attacks. It classifies their resistance against various burglary attack tools, ranging from common hand tools to explosives. The insurance application, whether an ACORD or company form, requires prospective insureds to provide specific information about their safes and vaults. Insureds might use the terms "safe" and "vault" interchangeably. If there is any doubt as to the correct term, underwriters should ask for clarification.

Classification of Safes and Money Chests

A safe's classification as fire-resistive or burglar-resistive affects an underwriter's decision about whether to accept a risk and how much premium to charge. However, increasing premiums cannot compensate for a deficient safe. Some safes are designed to be both fire- and burglar-resistive.

According to the ISO definition, **fire-resistive safes** have a metal shell filled with a fire-resistive insulation. Their purpose is to protect paper records by retarding the penetration of heat from a fire. Such safes might be mounted on wheels. They provide minimal burglar protection. Underwriters treat safes designed to protect records as "no safe" when they underwrite and price money and securities coverages because fire-resistive safes do not provide adequate burglar protection. If the applicant has a fire-resistive safe, the underwriter might insist that the applicant keep only petty cash in the safe overnight. Otherwise, the underwriter might attach an endorsement limiting the insurer's liability if a loss occurs while the business is closed.

Burglar-resistive safes are made of laminated or solid steel with a door at least one inch thick and a body at least one-half inch thick. They have sophisticated locking and relocking devices. (A relocking device locks the bolt mechanism when a thief attacks the lock.) They should be well anchored to prevent burglars from removing them from the premises. Burglar-resistive safes protect valuable commodities from theft. Their designers did not intend for the safes to protect paper from fire. **Burglar-resistive money chests** have a round door and are encased in concrete or are inside a fire-resistive safe.[3]

UL tests safes against various methods of burglary and assigns letters and numbers to indicate how burglar-resistive they are. Safes that have been tested bear a label on the inside of the door indicating the degree or level of protection they provide. Applicants can probably provide the safe or vault manufacturer's name. An insured who has had a safe for many years, however, might not know the name of the manufacturer. An old safe may bear a label from either UL or the Safe Manufacturers National Association (SMNA), which no longer exists. Most underwriters treat an unlabeled safe as a non-burglar-resistive safe for underwriting and rating purposes.

The letter abbreviations and numbers used on UL labels are described as follows:

- TL = Tool-resistive
- TR = Torch-resistive
- TX = Torch- and explosive-resistive
- Number = Minimum working time the safe resisted attack

The numbers following the letters, usually "15," "30," or "60," indicate the net number of minutes UL test engineers attacked the safes before they could gain entry. Those numbers are important to underwriters because they indicate how much time the police or central station personnel have to reach the premises before the burglar escapes with the safe's contents. A safe with the number "30" on the UL label means that police or security personnel have thirty minutes to respond to the applicant's alarm. Many newer safes' labels show combinations of the above letters, such as "TXTL," meaning torch-, explosive-, and tool-resistive. A TXTL-60X6 safe is the highest UL rating. Such a safe will resist attacks on all six sides by tools, torches, and explosives for 60 minutes. Exhibit 5-3 summarizes the UL tests and requirements for burglar-resistive safes.

EXHIBIT 5-3

Underwriters Laboratory (UL) Tests and Requirements for Burglar-Resistive Safes

Burglary Classification	Resistive to Tools
TL-15	Common hand tools, picking tools, portable mechanical and electric tools, grinding points, high-speed and carbide drills not exceeding ½ inch diameter, and pressure-applying devices or mechanisms
TL-30 TL-15X6 TL-30X6	Same as TL-15 and abrasive cutting wheels and power saws
TRTL-30	Same as TL-30 and a cutting torch
TRTL-15X6 TRTL-30X6 TRTL-60X6	Same as TRTL-30 and impact tools
TXTL-60X6	Same as TRTL-15X6 and nitroglycerine or other high explosives

Adapted from material by Underwriters Laboratories Inc.

Although the presence of a safe does not eliminate the possibility of a burglary loss, it does reduce its likelihood, depending on the safe's burglar-resistiveness and the thief's skill.

Exhibit 5-4 lists ISO's mercantile safe and vault classifications of burglar-resistive safes and chests and shows the rating classification of each. The safe classification (first column) determines the rate the insurer will charge for the limit of insurance the applicant selects. A burglar-resistive safe with a C classification costs more to insure than a safe with a K classification. The higher the letter designation, the more secure the safe is and the lower the rate will be.

EXHIBIT 5-4

Safe and Vault Classification

Safe, Chest, Cabinet or Vault Classification	CONSTRUCTION		
	Doors	**Walls — Safe, Chest or Cabinet**	**Walls — Vault**
B (Fire-resistive)	Steel less than 1" thick, or iron	Body of steel less than ½" thick, or iron	Brick, concrete, stone, tile, iron or steel
	Any iron or steel safe or chest having a slot through which money can be deposited		Not Applicable
C (Burglar-resistive)	Steel at least 1" thick	Body of steel at least ½" thick	Steel at least ½" thick; or reinforced concrete or stone at least 9" thick, or non-reinforced concrete or stone at least 12" thick
	Safe or chest bearing label: "Underwriters Laboratories Inc. Inspected Keylocked Safe KL Burglary"		Not Applicable
E (Burglar-resistive)	Steel at least 1½" thick	Body of steel at least 1" thick	Same as for C
ER (Burglar-resistive)	Safe or chest bearing label: "Underwriters Laboratories Inc. Inspected Tool Resisting Safe TL-15 Burglary"		Not Applicable
F (Burglar-resistive)	Safe or chest bearing one of the following labels: 1. Underwriters Laboratories Inc. Inspected Tool Resisting Safe TL-30 Burglary 2. Underwriters Laboratories Inc. Inspected Torch Resisting Safe TR-30 Burglary 3. Underwriters Laboratories Inc. Inspected Explosive Resisting Safe with Relocking Device X-60 Burglary		Not Applicable
G (Burglar-resistive)	One or more steel doors (one in front of the other) each at least 1½" thick and aggregating at least 3" thickness	Not Applicable	Steel at least ½" thick; or reinforced concrete or stone at least 12" thick; or non-reinforced concrete or stone at least 18" thick
H (Burglar-resistive)	Safe or chest bearing one of the following labels: 1. Underwriters Laboratories Inc. Inspected Torch and Explosive Resisting Safe TX-60 Burglary 2. Underwriters Laboratories Inc. Inspected Torch Resisting Safe TR-60 Burglary 3. Underwriters Laboratories Inc. Inspected Torch and Tool Resisting Safe TRTL-30 Burglary		Not Applicable
I (Burglar-resistive)	Safe or chest bearing one of the following labels: 1. Underwriters Laboratories Inc. Inspected Torch and Tool Resisting Safe TRTL-60 Burglary 2. Underwriters Laboratories Inc. Inspected Torch, Explosive and Tool Resisting Safe TXTL-60 Burglary		Not Applicable

Safe, Chest, Cabinet or Vault Classification	CONSTRUCTION		
	Doors	Walls	
		Safe, Chest or Cabinet	Vault
J (Burglar-resistive)	Safe or chest bearing the following label: Underwriters Laboratories Inc. Inspected Torch and Tool Resisting Safe TRTL-30X6 Burglary		Not Applicable
K (Burglar-resistive)	Safe or chest bearing one of the following labels: 1. Underwriters Laboratories Inc. Inspected Torch and Tool Resisting Safe TRTL-60 Burglary 2. Underwriters Laboratories Inc. Inspected Torch Explosive and Tool Resisting Safe TXTL-60 Burglary		Not Applicable
Vaults meeting these specifications or better	Steel at least 3½" thick		Steel at least 1" thick or 18" of reinforced concrete or 36" of non-reinforced concrete

Used with permission of Insurance Services Office.

Classification Of Vaults[4]

Vaults are complete enclosures designed for the safe storage of valuable commodities. They are usually constructed at the building site as permanently affixed, integral parts of the building.

Like safes' ratings, vaults' ratings reflect their ability to resist penetration or attack. The thickness of the walls, ceilings, and floors, and the materials and type of reinforcement used in their construction influence their rating. The thickness of the solid steel used for the door and the design of the locking and relocking mechanisms also determine the vault's rating. The entire vault structure is rated as a single unit. If any component carries a lower classification, the entire unit receives that lower classification.

Vaults can be built of "generic construction" at the site with no testing laboratory rating. The thicker the concrete in the walls, floors, and ceilings, and the more steel reinforcements, the better the classification. Vaults may also be constructed of modular panels and assembled at the site. Tested panels will bear a UL Burglary Resistant Vault Panel label identifying their degree of burglar-resistiveness. Vault doors are constructed of intrusion-resistant materials with a burglar-resistant lock and relocking device. Tested doors will bear a separate UL Burglary Resistant Vault Door label. Vault classifications range from 1 to 10R. The 10R rating is the most burglar-resistive and receives the lowest insurance rate.

Alarm Systems

Unlike some physical protection devices, such as fences or barriers, alarm systems do not prevent a burglar from entering a premises. They can sometimes serve as a deterrent, but their primary function is to indicate when an intruder has entered the premises. If the communications are fast enough, the burglar may be captured or at least interrupted before escaping with many of the insured's goods.

Some alarm systems use electrical circuits that sound an alarm when the circuits connect or disconnect, depending on the system. Others use more sophisticated electronic devices that activate when a foreign object, such as a burglar, is within the premises. The most sophisticated systems use invisible light rays that give off a signal when broken. Sensing devices for protecting the perimeter or the interior are usually connected to either local or central station alarms. Finally, banks and stores often have holdup buttons or foot pedals that the bank teller or store clerk can trigger silently while a robbery is going on. The alarm, which is silent at the location being robbed, goes directly to a central station company or the police station. Such alarms protect employees who might be harmed by the robber if the alarm were audible.

Perimeter Protection Devices

Perimeter protection devices detect attempts to enter the building through doors, windows, walls, roofs, or other openings. Most perimeter alarm systems consist of electrical contacts or metal tapes on doors or windows. Metal tapes or foil can also be used on walls, ceilings, and floors. Light beams also provide perimeter protection. A light source and a receiver sound an alarm when someone or something obstructs the beam. Intruders activate these devices when they go through an opening in the premises. Sonic and vibration detectors can be attached to walls, ceilings, or windows to detect attempts to penetrate a surface. They respond to a specific sound or vibration that intruders cause when they attack the surface the device is protecting. Their sensitivity to sounds or vibrations is specialized; for example, a detector designed for glass would not be suitable for a metal wall.[5] Exhibit 5-5 illustrates common perimeter protection devices.

EXHIBIT 5-5

Perimeter Protection Devices

Door Switches (Contacts) These devices are usually magnet-operated switches. They are affixed to a door or window in such a way that opening the door or window removes the magnetic field. This activates the switch causing an alarm. These devices may be surfacemounted or recessed, exposed or concealed. A variety of switches exists for every kind of door or window and for all levels of security.

Metallic Foil (Window Tape) Metallic foil is the traditional means for detecting glass-breakage. Strips of thin foil are affixed to a glass surface. Breaking glass ruptures the foil and interrupts the detection circuit to signal an alarm. Thin foil, however, is easily damaged by people or objects accidentally touching the glass surface.

Also, bonds at the corners and between multiple-foil strips deteriorate with time. Metallic foil, therefore, requires frequent maintenance, especially on glass doors.

Wooden Screens Openings such as air-duct passages and skylights can provide paths for an intruder. These can be secured by a cage-like frame of wooden rods. An intruder breaks the wire embedded within the frame, which triggers an alarm.

Wood screens are custom-built for each application. They can be mounted permanently or removed when the alarm system is turned off. Wooden screens require little maintenance. They are suitable for protecting openings where aesthetics are not important.

Lacing (Paneling) Lacing can protect walls, doors, and safes against penetration. Lacing is a closely woven pattern of metallic foil or fine brittle wire on the surface of the protected area. An intruder can enter only by breaking the foil or wire. This activates the alarm. A panel over the lacing protects it from accidental damage.

Continued on next page.

> **Photoelectric Devices (Eyes, Beams)** Photoelectric devices transmit a beam across a protected area. When an intruder interrupts this beam, the photoelectric circuit is disrupted. This starts the alarm.
>
> Modern photoelectric devices are a great improvement over their predecessors. Today's photoelectric devices use diodes that emit infrared light. These make the beam invisible to the naked eye. The beam usually pulses rapidly to prevent compromise by substitution.
>
> Photoelectric devices are effective and reliable. Some have ranges of more than 1,000 feet for large buildings and hallways. These devices provide excellent protection for relatively low-risk areas.

Area Protection Devices

Area protection devices detect burglars after they are inside the premises. Most detect motion and some detect noise. Common motion detectors are ultrasonic, infrared, or microwave. Ultrasonic motion detectors emit high-frequency tones.

The alarm starts when the intruder disrupts the wave pattern of these tones. Infrared detectors scan the protected area with receptors sensitive to the intruder's body heat. Microwave detectors sense the intruder's movement with high-frequency radio waves. Sound detectors respond to noises the intruder makes. Exhibit 5-6 summarizes how area protection devices operate.

Object Protection Devices

Object protection devices provide direct security for specific property. They are the final stage of an in-depth protection system after the insured has installed perimeter- and area-protection devices. Insureds attach these devices to safes, filing cabinets, display cabinets, models, works of art, and expensive equipment. Proximity detectors turn the protected object into an antenna, electronically linked to the alarm control. Intruders trigger the alarm when they enter the electrostatic field or touch the object. Vibration detectors use highly sensitive crystals or microphones to detect sounds intruders make when they try to break into objects. These devices can be adjusted to sense heavy sledgehammers or delicate cutting tools. Exhibit 5-7 describes this category of protection.

> **EXHIBIT 5-6**
>
> ### Area Protection Devices
>
> **Ultrasonic Detectors** These devices sense movement. Ultrasonic means "above the range of hearing." An intruder disrupting the ultrasonic wave pattern initiates the alarm. 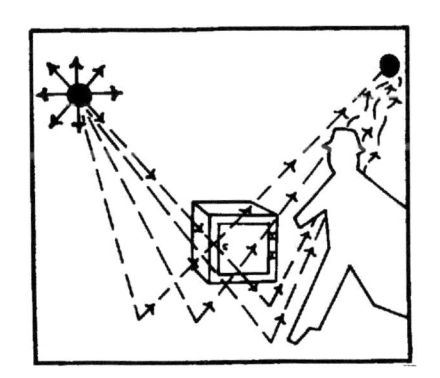
>
> Ultrasonic devices can be mounted on the ceiling or wall. They protect three-dimensional areas with an invisible pattern. However, they are prone to false alarms because of excessive air currents or ultrasonic noises from mechanical equipment. Again, proper application is important.
>
> **Infrared Detectors** These devices are part of the motion-detection group. They sense the body heat of an intruder as he or she passes through the protected area. A change from the area's normal heat profile triggers the alarm. Infrared detectors are relatively free of false alarms. They provide relatively inexpensive protection for confined areas.
>
> **Microwave Detectors** This kind of motion detector uses high-frequency radio waves, or microwaves, to detect movement. Microwave devices have greater range than ultrasonic. Since microwave devices do not use sound or air, they are not prone to false alarms from air currents. However, they can cause false alarms because they penetrate materials such as glass and because metal objects reflect them. This means microwaves can detect motion outside the protected area if the detectors are not properly installed.

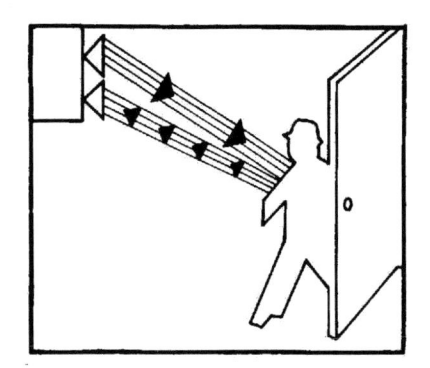

Local Alarms

Many simple alarm systems connect to an interior gong or alarm and to a gong on the premises' exterior. Some also turn on electric lights to illuminate the protected area, or set off flashing lights. An interior alarm system may be effective in a business with 24-hour security personnel who can respond quickly. An outside alarm is only effective if someone is in the area. It is

> **EXHIBIT 5-7**
>
> **Object Protection Devices**
>
> **Object Protection** Object protection provides direct security for individual items. It often is the final stage of an in-depth protection system with perimeter and area protection devices. The objects most frequently protected are safes, filing cabinets, display cabinets, models, and expensive equipment.
>
> **Proximity Detectors (Capacitance or Electrostatic)** With this system, the object itself becomes an antenna, electronically linked to the alarm control. When a person approaches or touches the object, its electrostatic field becomes unbalanced. This initiates the alarm. Only metal objects isolated from the ground can be protected this way. 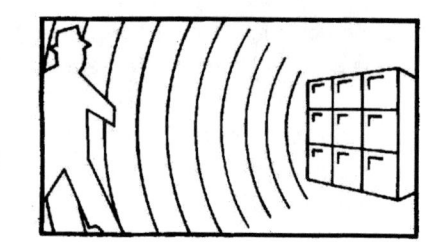
>
> **Vibration Detectors (Seismic)** These sensing devices use a highly sensitive piezoelectric crystal or microphone to detect the sound pattern that a hammerlike impact on a rigid surface would generate. These devices are attached directly to safes and filing cabinets or walls and floors. 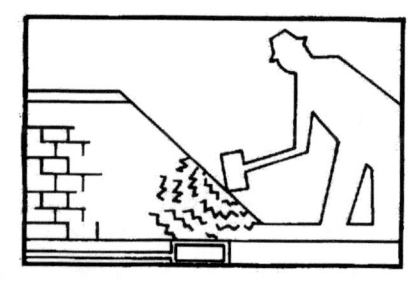
>
> The devices instantly detect a vibration an intruder makes. Some vibration detectors are adjustable. They can be adjusted to detect a sledgehammer attack on concrete or the delicate penetration of a glass surface. This kind of protection generally is for securing the perimeter surfaces of a vault. The correct number, spacing, and location of these sensors are important for suitable detection.

essentially useless in an industrial or mercantile district where few people are around at night. Local alarms often ring for hours before anyone pays attention to them. By the time police receive the alarm, the burglar and the goods axe long gone. Local alarms are considered the least effective system. Many underwriters insist on improvements before insuring an applicant that is protecting valuable goods with only a local alarm system.

Central Station Alarms

A more effective type of alarm system is one connected directly to a commercial alarm company's central station. Staff at the alarm company monitors the central station continuously. The central station company sells or leases its service to a client and installs, maintains, and responds to alarms. When intruders enter the subscriber's property, they trigger the alarm and a signal goes directly to the company. The alarm system guard contacts the police via a direct line to the police station and then goes to the premises. The system's disadvantage is the time delay between when the operator receives the alarm and when the police receive the message.

Alarms With Direct Lines to Police

Alarms with direct lines to police use automatic sensors or manual switches connected by a telephone line to a signal board or indicator at the police station. Their advantage over central station alarms is immediate notification to the police. If the burglar tampers with the alarm line, a local alarm sounds, providing an alternative alarm if the primary alarm becomes inoperative.

Alarms Unique to Financial Institutions

Silent alarms are particularly common in financial institutions. They alert police or security personnel when a burglary is happening, without the perpetrator knowing an alarm has gone off. Staff use manual buttons, foot pedals, or other trigger mechanisms to set off the alarm. The most sophisticated systems use motion, vibration, sound, or pressure as triggers. Many banks also install semiautomatic alarm systems, such as money traps. Money traps in cash drawers trigger an alarm when money (often bait money, described later) separating two contact points is pulled from a clip.

Evaluating Alarm Systems

Alarm systems vary widely. Underwriters need to understand the types of systems applicants have and their quality. Insurance rate manuals generally give credits only for UL-listed alarm systems. UL-listed alarm systems are ones installed by UL-listed burglar alarm installation companies. UL alarm certificates show the grade, type, and extent of the alarm system. Underwriters consider these certificates when they grant insurance rate credits. Applicants need to know that no matter how expensive their alarm system is, they may not receive a premium reduction if their system does not have a UL certificate. A sample UL certificate appears in Exhibit 5-8.

Alarm systems are, at best, deterrents to crime and are primarily loss reduction devices. No alarm system is foolproof and skilled burglars can find ways around the system. In addition, response time is crucial. A robbery or burglary can take only two or three minutes. Insurance applicants must make every effort to be sure authorities can respond quickly to an alarm, and they should have a plan for decreasing the likelihood of hostage-taking.

Mirrors and Cameras

Mirrors and cameras are two effective and relatively inexpensive ways to reduce losses. Retail stores, particularly convenience stores with only one or two employees on the premises, install mirrors in strategic locations to discourage shoplifting. With mirrors, a cashier can watch customers who ordinarily would be out of the cashier's range of sight.

How well cameras deter crime is uncertain, but they are good for identifying thieves. Surveillance cameras are usually video, though some systems use still or motion picture film cameras. They usually operate in two modes: suspect or continuous. A suspect mode camera operates only when someone activates it or trips an alarm. A continuous-mode camera monitors the premises constantly and does not rely on an alarm or tripping device to start it. Applicants place cameras at strategic points to cover at-risk areas. For example, banks install cameras to cover entrances, teller areas, vaults, and safes. Most bank-automated teller machines have video cameras monitoring transactions continuously.

Some surveillance cameras transmit to monitors at a guard station, where guards or security personnel scan the monitors continuously. Other systems record on videotape, and security personnel view the tapes periodically. Surveillance cameras are not used just to catch outside thieves. Securities firms use video cameras to review cage activity,[6] and manufacturers install them in areas with valuable inventory to guard against employee theft.

Underwriters review whether applicants maintain and upgrade their surveillance systems. Financial institutions commonly have maintenance agreements that provide for routine, uniform updates of all their equipment. Underwriters value insureds that avoid mixing older models with newer models of equipment. Mixed equipment not only increases maintenance costs but also makes a uniform standard for security equipment impossible.

Tear Gas, Dye Packages, Fog, and Inventory Tags

Financial institutions are the most frequent users of tear gas or dye packages to deter and disrupt robbery attempts. Packages are bundled in the money the burglar takes off the premises. After an appropriate delay, the package explodes. Tear gas packages disable thieves enough to impede their fast escape. Dye packages mark the criminal for easy identification.

Fog is another deterrent to theft in retail operations. When a robber enters the premises and triggers the device, a nontoxic fog engulfs the area and obscures the thief's sight. A large golf-equipment retailer installed such a system to reduce losses from titanium golf club thefts.

Retailers have a choice of several types of inventory tags to prevent shoplifting. The oldest is the beige-colored, bulky, plastic tag that clothing stores attach to merchandise. If the shoplifter leaves the store with the tag still attached, an alarm goes off. Electronic equipment and computer retail stores use another kind of tag. It is a three-dimensional inventory piece glued to the

EXHIBIT 5-8

UL Burglar Alarm System Description

Underwriters Laboratories Inc.®
Northbrook, IL   Santa Clara, CA
Melville, NY   Research Triangle Park, NC
A not-for-profit organization dedicated to public safety and committed to quality service

File No: BP9999   CCN: CPVX
Service Center No: 1
Expires: 1-JAN-2000
Issued: 1-JAN-1997
Entry No: 1119977   Version: 6

CENTRAL STATION
BURGLAR ALARM SYSTEM DESCRIPTION
For Certificate Serial No: BC72101499

Protected Property:
A RETAIL STORE
123 N MAIN ST
NORTHBROOK, IL 60062
Request signed on 14-DEC-1996 by:
JOHN SMITH

Alarm Service Company:
AN ALARM SERVICE CO
333 PFINGSTEN RD
NORTHBROOK, IL 60062
Request signed on 13-DEC-1996 by:
JOHN DOE

Comments and Clarifications: None

System Description:
  System 1 Type: Premises   Extent of Protection: 3
  System 2 Type: Stockroom   Extent of Protection: 3
  System 3 Type: Safe   Extent of Protection: Complete   Quantity: 2
  System 4 Type: Vault   Extent of Protection: Complete   Quantity: 3

Area Covered: Implied - Entire premise

Remote Monitoring:
AN ALARM SERVICE CO
333 PFINGSTEN RD
NORTHBROOK, IL 60062
  File No: BP9999 Service Center No: 1

Alarm Transmission Method:
Multiplex

Line Security: Standard

Alarm Sounding Device: Inside and Outside

Alarm Investigator Response: 20 minutes, One Runner without Keys, Law Enforcement.

Control and Transmitter Units (Mfgs. & Models):
  A CONTROL UNIT MADE BY A MANUFACTURER

© 1996 UL   This form is to accompany the Certificate

Used with permission of Underwriters Laboratories Inc.

merchandise, which sales clerks must neutralize with an anti-magnetic tool before the customer leaves. Like the clothing tag, anyone who attempts to walk out with the tag attached will set off an alarm. The effectiveness of both of these alarms depends on how quickly store personnel respond to the alarm. A third type of tag does not set off alarms or require quick security response but it does damage goods. The tag is attached to clothing and has an ink cartridge inside. If a sales clerk does not remove it with the proper tool, the ink capsule ruptures and dyes the clothing, leaving such an obvious stain that the thief cannot wear the clothing without someone noticing. To reduce unnecessarily damaged merchandise, users of this third type of tag must train their sales personnel to remove the tags after making a sale.

Watchpersons and Guards

Instead of central station alarm systems, some businesses use watchpersons. Watchpersons periodically patrol the applicant's property (typically hourly), sometimes accompanied by a dog. Many businesses require their watchpersons to carry a special clock that records their visits to stations throughout the premises. Each location has a key that, when inserted into the watchdock, records the time the watchperson visited that particular station. The employer knows whether the watchperson completed his or her rounds by checking the records in the watchdock. The system's weakness is that if an intruder overpowers the watchperson during the night, no one knows about it until the premises reopen the next morning.

Under another watchperson system the patrolling watchperson periodically reports back to a fixed, central location, which staff or a central station company continuously monitors. If the watchperson does not report when expected, a guard investigates immediately. Because robbers might force a watchperson to continue making rounds while a theft is in progress, most applicants set up signaling systems so that the watchperson can secretly signal for help without the robber knowing.

Ideally, watchpersons patrol frequently but irregularly to prevent thieves from predicting their schedules. The effectiveness of a watchperson security system depends on the quality of the personnel and how often they make their rounds. Whether the applicant hires its own watchpersons or leases a watchperson service, underwriters might investigate how thoroughly the employer of these watchpersons checks their backgrounds and how well they train them.

Some financial institutions and retail operations with expensive goods employ armed guards or contract for guard services. Guards are usually present when the business opens and closes. Sometimes they are on the floor throughout the day. Some businesses use roving security guards who go from location to location at unspecified times throughout the day. Guards often monitor video and alarm systems. They may also escort employees when they deliver deposits to banks. Some guards do not carry weapons but their presence deters crime. As with watchpersons, underwriters should investigate how guards are hired and trained.

Messenger Protection

If the applicant wants messenger coverage, the underwriter will ask how the applicant protects its messengers. Applicants with multiple locations may use more than one bank messenger. The number of guards, armed or unarmed, accompanying the messenger is important if the messenger is carrying a significant amount of money to the bank. It is also significant if the messenger picks up money from several locations and accumulates the money from all the stops before making a single deposit to the bank. A guard can either be with the messenger or act as a "trailer," which means the guard follows the messenger at a discreet distance or in a separate vehicle. Off-duty police often serve as messengers.

Underwriters also need to know how messengers convey the deposits. Robbers are less likely to go after messengers who use a private conveyance, usually a car, than messengers who travel on foot. Applicants should inform the underwriter if they use armored motor vehicle carrier services. Some insurers also ask about safety satchels. An applicant's bank may provide a bank deposit bag with a key lock, but unless it is a UL-listed bank satchel, underwriters will not give a premium credit to insureds who use them.

Cash-Handling Procedures

Underwriters expect financial institutions to exercise specific cash-handling procedures. Most financial institutions designate a vault teller who has general control over cash. The vault teller's cash is usually kept in a secured compartment or safe-deposit box in the vault. Floor tellers go to the vault teller to request additional cash. Floor tellers usually do not have direct access to the vault cash. A key-locked day gate shields vaults during business hours. Some institutions keep reserve cash inside a safe with a delayed locking device that allows access only at certain times during the day. Some safes open only when a certain amount of time has passed after someone dials the combination. At night, time locks keep the vaults locked until a specified time during the next business day. Incoming cash should only be received after the vault time locks have expired so that the cash can be immediately stored in the vault.

Floor tellers keep two drawers of cash. One, called the working drawer, contains a nominal amount of cash. The other, called the reserve cash drawer, holds a larger amount of cash and has a separate lock and key. When their accumulated cash exceeds a specified level, floor tellers must report to the vault teller and place excess cash in the vault. Other loss control procedures for floor tellers include locking cash drawers at the counter whenever they leave the counter unattended and counting cash in a secure area under lock and key and out of sight of customers.

Financial institutions should exercise dual control when staff opens night depositories. Two people should count the receipts away from public sight and access. The same procedure applies to cash when an armored car or courier service delivers it. Two people should take the cash into a secure area, count it, and put it into the vault immediately.

Retail businesses use similar cash-handling procedures. Most businesses limit the amount of money cashiers keep in their drawers and designate employees and escorts to pick up excess cash from cashiers on a random basis. Some businesses install pneumatic tube systems at the cashier stations. Cashiers send excess cash directly to a central office using the tubes. Cashiers either lock their till or remove the cash drawer when they leave their station and count their money out of customers' sight.

Signals

Most financial institution theft losses occur at opening and closing times. For that reason, financial institutions commonly designate authorized persons to post an all-clear signal to the security office or central station company when they open and close the business. If the security office does not receive the signal, a security person alerts the police.

Bait Money

Financial institutions that hold large reserves of cash in the teller areas often use bait or decoy money. Bait money is unmarked bills with serial numbers the institution has recorded and filed with the police and the FBI. In a robbery, the teller gives the robber the bait money. As the robber uses the bait money, banks receiving the money with the recorded serial numbers alert the police. Using bait money leads to earlier identification, apprehension, and conviction of a robber than using unmarked money does. Underwriters might verify that financial institutions using bait money update and record it regularly.

COMPUTER FRAUD CONSIDERATIONS

Employees commit most computer fraud, but computer fraud caused by outsiders is increasing. Although most reported computer-related losses are money thefts, perpetrators of computer fraud can also steal securities and other property. For example, computerized inventory records and warehouse orders can be manipulated to steal property. Thus, underwriters are concerned with many aspects of computer security.

Most computer fraud insurers have created supplemental questionnaires. Exhibit 5-9 lists questions typically found in insurers' computer fraud supplemental questionnaires. These questions reflect control procedures that most applicants should follow.

Because computer systems are always changing and a thief's ingenuity is inexhaustible, controls cannot cover all possibilities. However, careful management can reduce the risk of computer fraud.

Hiring and Personnel Management

Human resource staff should use recruiters and interviewers who understand computer systems and can ask appropriate questions to screen out unqualified or suspicious job applicants. Some recruiters are trained to interpret "body

EXHIBIT 5-9

Sample Computer Fraud Supplemental Questionnaire

Organization and Operation

1. Are EDP personnel prohibited from performing the following functions:
   a. Initiation or authorization of transactions, including master file changes?
   b. Initial entry of transactions?
   c. Initiation of error corrections except for the errors originating within the EDP department?
   d. Maintaining custody of assets (including negotiable instruments) other than computer supplies and equipment?
2. Does the EDP department report to an officer who is both a senior executive and who does not represent substantial user functions within the institution?
3. Does an internal audit function perform regular reviews of:
   a. EDP department activities to determine their compliance with established policies and procedures?
   b. New systems under development for adequacy of controls, auditability, and proper implementation?
   c. Existing systems on an ongoing basis?

Systems Development and Maintenance

1. Are there comprehensive written standards established governing the development or acquisition of application software, and are these standards enforced?
2. Are program changes and their effective dates recorded in a manner that preserves a complete and accurate chronological record of program status?
3. Are there separate production and test libraries for:
   a. Source programs?
   b. Executable programs?
   c. Job control statements?
4. Is the work of independent software contractors (including contract programmers) subject to effective review for propriety?

Hardware and System Software

1. Are security and control features in the operating system and related system software (including new releases) reviewed by EDP management before acceptance and installation, and are all control features tested?
2. Are changes to the operating system and related system software subjected to effective control standards and procedures similar to those applied to application programs?

Continued on next page.

Physical Security

1. Is access to the EDP department effectively restricted to authorized personnel through use of locks on all access points, security guards, and/or electronic entry control procedures such as magnetic cards?
2. Are combinations or security codes that are used in connection with access control devices changed when EDP employees are terminated, and periodically otherwise?
3. Is there a separate file librarian function?
4. Do internal audit personnel periodically attempt to penetrate the physical and logical security features of the EDP system?

Communications and Related Software

1. Are authorized users of online applications provided with secret passwords?
2. Does the system detect and report repeated unsuccessful sign-on attempts?
3. Does your communications network use encryption techniques?
4. Is the responsibility for following up on security violations clearly established?

Data and Procedural

1. Is a control and balancing function performed for all production processing by a separate group within the EDP department or by appropriate user departments?
2. Is there effective control over rejected transactions, including:
   a. Positive identification of rejected record?
   b. Review for the cause of rejection?
   c. Correction of each rejected record?
   d. Prompt re-entry of the correction into the system whereby it is subjected to the same controls as original data?
3. Are master file changes documented in writing and do changes to critical fields require supervisory approval?

language" to analyze an applicant's honesty. Human resource staff should also thoroughly check job candidates' backgrounds.

Other management procedures include the following:

- Training backup personnel for every procedure
- Removing a terminated person from the work area immediately
- Preventing a single person from having access to and control over computer systems
- Regularly monitoring salary administration and employee satisfaction

Some businesses use outside service companies to maintain computer equipment or to create software. They should investigate the integrity of these service companies and their staff. The service company should be bonded and carry liability and workers compensation insurance on their employees. Underwriters want to ensure that crime exposures from such outside service companies are minimized.

Internal and External Auditing

The information systems department should undergo periodic internal and external audits just as any other department handling money or valuable inventory. Computer-proficient auditors should conduct both unannounced and regularly scheduled audits. The audits review how the department carries out procedures, backs up its systems, implements program changes, tests programs, and follows up on reported errors. The information in computer fraud supplemental questionnaires might be the basis for such audits.

System Procedures

Information systems departments should have clearly defined operations procedures. An example of such a procedure is allowing staff to initiate new programs or alter existing ones only after they have received authorized orders. Management should clearly define staffs roles and responsibility. Only an authorized supervisor, manager, or executive can override controls in a program, and a written report must go to upper management to confirm the override order. Crucial programs should be identified and the responsibility for maintaining them should be divided. When possible, departments should use "threat-monitoring" programs that disconnect the computer and report attempts at irregular usage. For example, a computer might reject further attempts to log on after three unsuccessful attempts. The department should conduct frequent checks and cross-checks of its procedures and be independently audited. Finally, the department should have a specific plan for emergencies. Ideally, someone outside the department would design the plan to prevent an insider, or someone who knows the system, from simulating an emergency that allows system overrides and thus the opportunity to commit fraud.

Data Control

Information systems departments must provide secure storage for data disks and tapes and carefully monitor inventory. The department should have a well-protected library that stores all disks and tapes in a safe or vault when employees are not using them. The library staff should be independent of the information systems personnel and keep written records of who uses the tapes and disks, where they are used, and when they are used. The department should periodically audit and inventory the storage area and audit its record keeping. The information systems department should sequentially number the financial instruments it prints, such as checks, purchase orders, or invoices. It should also record destroyed or voided instruments. The department should run daily totals of the number of instruments processed and cross-check the totals. The totals and cross-checks should be performed by separate staff.

Data Communication Security

An applicant's security measures must prevent unauthorized access to the systems. At a minimum, only persons who have special identity cards should enter the computer area. Some facilities use technical recognition systems, such as machines that read fingerprints, handprints, or voices. Every user must have an identifying password or security code. These passwords or security codes should change frequently and unpredictably. Only one person should be responsible for deciding when and how passwords change. Some applicants use machine-readable cards instead of passwords. A machine can read the magnetic code on the card but people cannot. Thus, an unauthorized person must steal the card to obtain access. The computer systems should be programmed to report efforts to use obsolete passwords, codes, or cards and to disconnect the terminal on which the unauthorized user is attempting to log on. Highly sensitive operations should have additional passwords that only a select group of people knows. Applicants should build scramblers or cryptographs into any transmission devices that send data via the telephone or microwave relays.

Software Security

Businesses must ensure that programming installed on the system is legitimate and that the information systems department safely stores the backup programs. The department should keep a system activity log of programming inputs and changes. Supervisors should review records daily. As few persons as possible should have access to programs and program documents. Program designers should build validating tests into all programs. The department should periodically check programs, including those that erase or delete files, to verify that they are operating properly. Remote terminals should not be allowed to input or print out any programs. Finally, the department should keep all backup files and data documents in a separate facility.

Physical Security

Just as businesses keep cash secure from the public, they should keep their computer equipment inaccessible to outsiders. The equipment should be located away from windows and as far from street entrances as possible. Rooms where computer equipment is stored should be protected by an alarm that alerts security personnel when an intruder attempts to enter. Security personnel might guard the area and insist on proper identification before admitting anyone to the computer area. Appropriate personnel should escort visitors. In-house security or someone from the staff should accompany outside service company personnel even if they are regular visitors. Contractual agreements with outside service companies should state that nothing is to be removed from the premises and that analyses must be conducted on the premises.

EXTORTION CONSIDERATIONS

For most insurance applicants, chances are small that an insured will be an extortionist's target. However, underwriters prefer that applicants create a written extortion contingency plan to avoid confusion and mistakes if someone threatens the insured. Although the details of the plan should not be public, key employees should understand it.

No single plan meets every insured's needs. Details vary by type and size of business, centralization or decentralization of operations, number of employees, and the prominence of owners or officers. A good plan defines who should be in charge, who is responsible for taking particular actions, how decisions will be made, and how to communicate clearly and efficiently. Insureds should designate a coordinator and an alternate who are responsible for designing and carrying out the plan. The coordinator is not always the person who first receives the threat, so the plan should outline what the employee who receives the threat should do. Exhibit 5-10 is an example of instructions that could be incorporated into an extortion contingency plan.

EXHIBIT 5-10

Guidelines for an Extortion Contingency Plan

Actions to Ensure Personal Safety

Recommendations should address the employees' activities while:

- At home
- At work
- On business travel
- On vacation
- Driving
- Walking

Actions the Coordinator or Alternate Should Take After Being Notified of a Threat

Notify the following authorities:

- FBI: (telephone number)
- State police: (telephone number)
- Local police: (telephone number)

Carry out the authorities' specific instructions.

Immediately after calling the authorities, call one or more of the persons named below, who can authorize payment of the ransom demands. Notify the insurer.

Name	Office Telephone	Home Telephone	Pager
(Person #1)			
(Person #2)			
(Person #3)			

If payment to the extortionist is authorized, record the serial numbers of the currency or securities. If payment is to be made with property other than money or securities, obtain photographs of the property, describe it in detail, and record identification numbers.

Continued on next page.

Actions the Receiver of the Extortion Threat Should Take

If the extortionist telephones:

Alert someone nearby by note or gesture that a threatening call is in progress.

Have the alerted person call the telephone company and ask the company to trace the call.

Have the alerted person call the threat coordinator or alternate.

Name	Office Telephone	Home Telephone	Pager
(Coordinator)			
(Alternate)			
(Alternate #2)			

Make no promises.

Write down anything that might help authorities:

- Time of call
- Exact words of the threat
- Tone of voice
- Unique or identifiable speech characteristics
- Background noises
- Accent
- Gender of caller
- Use of unusual or colloquial expressions

Keep the caller on the phone as long as possible by asking questions.

Sample questions:

Who is this?

Where are you calling from?

May I speak with [the kidnapped person]? (If the caller refuses, ask for a description of the victim, e.g., height, weight, color of hair and eyes, birth date, and clothing.)

What do you want? How much?

Exactly where should the payment be delivered?

When should it be delivered?

How will I recognize the person who will collect the payment?

How will that person recognize me?

When will I know the kidnapped person is safe?

When will you release the kidnapped person after the payment?

Will you call me again? When?

If the extortionist sends a written threat, call the extortion threat coordinator immediately.

Each business should design a plan that best suits its operations. Trade organizations might have established extortion guidelines. The FBI and state and local police might review the plan and recommend improvements. Businesses that have extortion insurance should keep that fact confidential and tell only key personnel. Insureds should keep the following information about personnel who are potential extortion targets in a file accessible to the extortion threats coordinator and alternate:

- Recent photographs
- Fingerprints
- Written descriptions
- Date of birth, sex, height, and weight (updated annually)

PRICING

After considering the loss exposures and how those exposures might be modified through loss control, underwriters determine a price for the requested coverage. Pricing is affected by loss costs, the insurer's multiplier, limits and deductibles, and the insured's loss experience. Rating crime coverage varies by the type of crime insurance.

Loss Costs

In the past, many insurers depended on advisory organizations, sometimes called rating bureaus, to calculate rates, prepare rate filings, submit the rate filings to state regulatory authorities, and obtain approval of the filings. However, advisory organizations have discontinued the calculations of rates in most states and calculate and file prospective loss costs instead. **Prospective loss costs** are loss data that have been modified by loss development, trending, and credibility processes, not including expenses. Prospective loss costs consider such items as location, type of business, and type of coverage.

The advisory organizations calculate the advisory loss costs, prepare the necessary filings, and submit them to the state insurance departments as required. Each insurer that is a member of or subscriber to the advisory organization can use the advisory prospective loss costs by adding its own expense loading, based either on its own expense data or on industry data.

Loss costs vary by class of business. The advisory organization that compiles the loss cost rate manual assigns a class code to each class of business. Each class code is assigned a loss cost. The higher the exposure to losses, the higher the loss cost factor. For example, a business with a relatively low risk of loss might have a loss cost factor of $0.75 per exposure unit. A high-risk business might have a loss cost factor of $1.49 per exposure unit. The **exposure unit**, or standard unit used in insurance rating, in employee theft or dishonesty insurance is the number of insured employees.

Insurer Multipliers

Insurers consider expenses and reasonable profits in final rates by developing a multiplier of the loss costs. Insurers use different multipliers because insurers' expenses and expected profits differ. The multiplier takes into account the insurer's commission expenses, acquisition expenses, underwriting expenses, loss adjusting expenses, general administrative expenses, premium taxes, and allowances for contingencies and profit. This multiplier is affected by the need to stay competitive in the market and often by state regulation.

Limits and Deductibles

Insureds might assume that only small losses will occur. This fact and the insured's desire to reduce premiums might lead to low policy limits. Because crime forms do not contain a coinsurance clause, insureds are not penalized for having inadequate limits. However, losses may exceed the policy limits. Underwriters might write low policy limits if they believe that higher limits would create a moral hazard. Another reason for writing low limits might be inferior security protection compared to the amount of exposure.

The insured is responsible for losses lower than the deductible. Deductibles encourage loss control because the insured has a financial interest in every loss. Sophisticated insureds recognize the value of retaining small, frequent losses that they can readily contain through loss control techniques or finance without undue strain on their cash flow. The higher the deductible, the lower the insured's final premium.

Experience Rating

Experience rating modifies the premium rate based on a particular risk's loss experience. The underwriter increases or decreases the insured's rate based on how the insured's previous loss experience deviates from the average experience of other businesses in its class. Experience rating is an incentive for insureds to exercise effective loss prevention and control measures.

Underwriters use experience rating for insureds who generate large enough premiums to be credible. The underwriter compares the insured's losses during an experience period (usually three years) to the expected losses for the insured's class and modifies any differences by a credibility factor. The credibility factor reflects how confident the underwriter is that the insured's past experience will predict its future experience. The result is a debit or credit to the class-rated premium.

Rating

Each crime coverage agreement is rated separately. Insurance Services Office and the Surety Association of America publish rules and loss costs for rating the coverages available in their respective forms. The following sections describe rating considerations for selected crime coverages and financial institution bonds.

Employee Theft

When coverage is written on a blanket basis, the insurer should know the number of employees having an opportunity to cause a loss. Such "ratable" employees are identified through a list of positions generally associated with the handling of money or valuable property, such as accountants, auditors, paymasters, and stock clerks. The premium for blanket employee theft coverage is taken from a rate table containing base premiums that vary according to the number of ratable employees. Basic charges for both scheduled and blanket employee theft coverage are modified by a factor that varies by type of business organization.

Rating employee theft coverage written on a scheduled basis is governed by the number of individual employees or positions to be covered and the amount of coverage applicable to each. A basic charge applies to each of the first five employees covered for a particular amount, and a significantly lower charge applies to any additional employees covered for the same amount.

Forgery or Alteration

Premiums for forgery or alteration coverage are determined in a manner similar to that used for blanket employee theft coverage. The basic premium is determined by the limit of insurance and is modified by a significant discount factor. A discount factor is used because the forgery or alteration loss exposure is not as great as the employee theft exposure.

Inside the Premises—Theft of Money and Securities and Inside the Premises—Robbery or Safe Burglary of Other Property

Inside the Premises—Theft of Money and Securities and Inside the Premises—Robbery or Safe Burglary of Other Property uses three factors in calculating the premium:

1. Type of business conducted by the insured
2. Fire resistance and crime resistance of the safe or vault used to store cash, checks, securities, and other covered property
3. Location of the covered premises

Premium discounts are available for coverage inside the premises if

- The insured has an approved alarm system.
- Security guards are on the premises when the business is closed.
- The business is open twenty-four hours a day.

Outside the Premises

The basic premium that applies to coverage for a messenger outside the premises is determined by the type of business conducted by the insured, the location of the covered premises, and the number of guards accompanying the messenger. To this basic premium are added separate rates for each category of property that can be covered.

Computer Fraud

Rates for computer fraud coverage are based on:

- The insured's business classification
- The amount of insurance required
- The number of exposure units, which is based on the number of employees as well as directors, trustees, and officers

The premium varies with the deductible selected. Crime and Fidelity Experience and Schedule Rating Plans may be applied.

Money Orders and Counterfeit Paper Currency

The premium for Money Orders and Counterfeit Paper Currency coverage is determined by the rate for each $1,000 of insurance written.

Financial Institution Bonds

The rates for financial institution bonds reflect such factors as the average amount of assets, audit procedures, internal controls, management and personnel qualifications and procedures, and unique or unusual exposures. Rates are discounted or increased based on the underwriter's evaluation of those factors.

SUMMARY

For crime coverages other than employee theft, underwriters consider the applicant's physical security features and procedures. Building security includes simple, inexpensive measures to reduce opportunities for thieves to gain entrance to the building. Safe, vault, and money chest security depends on the device's design. Underwriters Laboratories Inc. rates safes and vaults for their ability to resist unauthorized entry. Other physical security procedures include the following:

- Alarm systems
- Mirrors and cameras
- Tear gas, dye packages, fog, and inventory tags
- Watchpersons and guards
- Messenger protection
- Cash-handling procedures
- Signals
- Bait money

Computer fraud and extortion loss exposures have unique characteristics. Underwriters often request that applicants complete supplemental questionnaires to gather more information on these loss exposures. Supplemental questionnaires vary by insurer but often contain similar questions regarding security procedures and emergency plans.

Crime insurance prices are determined from loss costs, insurer multipliers, limits and deductibles, and experience rating. Loss costs are developed by advisory organizations and represent the premium necessary to cover claims. Insurer multipliers represent expenses, contingencies, and profit allowances. Limits and deductibles affect the rates charged because they reflect the amount the insurer might be called upon to pay for claims. Experience rating reflects the insured's loss experience and encourages effective loss control measures to reduce future losses. The considerations for rating crime coverage and financial institution bonds vary to reflect the type of coverage provided.

CHAPTER NOTES

1. American Mutual Insurance Alliance, *Judging the Crime Risk* (Chicago: Alliance of American Insurers, 1970), pp. 188–189.
2. American Mutual Insurance Alliance, *Burglary and Theft* (Norwood, Mass.: Factory Mutual Engineering Corporation, 1988), p. 211.
3. *Burglary and Theft*, p. 204.
4. *Burglary and Theft*, p. 220.
5. *Burglary and Theft*, p. 214.
6. U.S. Congress, House Committee on Banking, *Report on Crimes Against Banking Institutions*, 80th Cong., 1964, H. Rept. 1147, pp. 19–20.

Chapter 6

Claim Handling

No matter how carefully crime insurance or fidelity bonds are underwritten, claims inevitably occur. Effective claim management allows an insurer to balance its obligations to policyholders and claimants while complying with policy provisions.

The policyholder is responsible for proving the validity and the amount of the claim. The claim process allows the policyholder to do so while giving the insurer the opportunity to investigate the loss, ensure that the policyholder has complied with the terms and conditions of the policy, and protect the insurer's rights of recovery if a payment is made.

The first step for the policyholder is to submit a notice of loss to the insurer. The policy specifies how and when this is to be done. Upon receipt of a notice of loss, the insurer verifies coverage and begins its investigation. The policyholder completes a proof of loss and furnishes evidence to prove the loss. Although the policyholder must prove that a loss is covered under a policy, the claim representative reviews and analyzes the evidence provided and brings any deficiencies to the policyholder's attention.

After investigating the claim, the claim representative evaluates and settles the claim. If a policyholder sues the insurer, the claim representative is responsible for litigation management. Claim representatives work closely with lawyers and others throughout the dispute resolution process. Throughout the claim management process, the claim representative works to identify and protect any potential sources of recovery available to the insurer.

Although this chapter focuses on the handling of employee theft/dishonesty claims, it describes a process that can be used in handling all types of crime insurance claims.

CLAIM MANAGEMENT

Claim management's general objectives provide a basis for the claim department's actions. Claim representatives gather relevant information, control loss and loss adjustment expenses, and ensure that policy provisions are followed. The goal is to meet policyholder obligations promptly, in compliance with legislation, and in a financially responsible manner. Claim representatives should prepare well-organized and documented claim files and comply with unfair claim settlement practices acts.

General Objectives

Three general objectives of claim management are:

- To investigate the claim and fulfill the insurer's obligation to the policyholder promptly and fairly
- To control loss and loss adjustment expenses, including recovering losses and expenses from third parties when possible
- To protect the insured's and the insurer's interests by applying policy terms, conditions, limits, and defenses appropriately

The insurer does not have any duty to prove losses or find culprits. The claim process involves gathering facts by which the insured intends to support the insured's claim, examining and evaluating those facts, and testing the credibility of those facts. These objectives are described in more detail later in this chapter as the claim process is discussed.

Claim Files

Each insurer sets its own standards for file organization and maintenance. The goal is to present all relevant coverage and claim details thoroughly and clearly. A complete claim file includes the following information:

- Identification of the parties involved in the claim
- A description or copy of the policyholder's coverage
- Details of the claim investigation
- An evaluation of the claim
- Settlement details and recovery information

Choosing What To Record

A claim file documents the investigation, evaluation, and resolution of a claim. Maintaining a detailed, current file helps to structure a claim representative's analysis and documents the rationale for the final decision or settlement. The facts of the claim are clearly documented to support the final outcome.

It is seldom possible to record every detail but claim representatives should ensure that all vital information is documented. In addition, discretion is essential because files might be subpoenaed by third parties. For that reason, claim representatives should document facts rather than conjecture.

Organizing Files

Many claims are resolved quickly and easily; however, some are complex. A complex claim generates large volumes of documentation and requires an efficient system for classifying, cross-referencing, and retrieving information. Many insurers rely on computers for information management or document storage through the use of scanning technology. However, paper files are still common. To ensure easy access to the information they contain, files must be organized. An efficient way to organize paper files is to separate documents into categories such as the following:

- Policy and underwriting documents
- Correspondence
- Litigation papers, such as pleadings, briefs, and depositions
- Documentary evidence (organized by transaction type—such as loans)
- Reports
- Interview statements
- Accounting statements
- Audits, including regulatory examinations
- Indexes, charts, and graphs of file data

Sometimes lawsuits related to fidelity claims occur, but the fidelity insurer is not directly involved. For example, the insured's directors and officers might be sued because of their participation in the loss relating to the fidelity claim. In this case, the claim representative includes a separate section in the claim file containing information about the lawsuit.

UNFAIR CLAIM SETTLEMENT PRACTICES ACTS

All states have laws designed to prohibit unfair trade practices. States have also enacted consumer protection legislation that prohibits unfair claim settlement practices. These laws are called **unfair claim settlement practices acts**. Although laws vary by state, they define what regulators consider to be unfair practices, commonly including the following:

- Knowingly misrepresenting to claimants and policyholders facts or policy provisions relating to coverage
- Failing to acknowledge and act promptly on communication
- Failing to set and meet reasonable standards for the prompt investigation and settlement of claims
- Not attempting to settle claims in good faith, promptly, fairly, and equitably when liability has become reasonably clear
- Compelling policyholders to sue by offering substantially less than the amounts ultimately awarded to them by the court
- Refusing to pay claims without conducting a reasonable investigation
- Failing to confirm or deny coverage within a reasonable time after having completed an investigation
- Attempting to settle or settling claims for less than the amount a reasonable person would expect based on the insurer's advertising materials

State regulators monitor insurers' compliance with the legislation and, in cases of violation, can impose one or more of the following penalties:

- Fines
- Payment of interest on overdue claim settlements
- Payment of other fees and costs
- Injunctions or cease-and-desist orders
- Suspension of the claim representative's or company's license
- Revocation of the claim representative's or company's license

In some jurisdictions, surety claims are exempt from these laws because regulators recognize that suretyship is technically not insurance. Some of those states hold that suretyship does not involve a special relationship arising out of unequal bargaining power and thus is not insurance. Even in those jurisdictions, however, insurers must meet their statutory obligations to policyholders and claimants.

CLAIM PROCESS

The claim process can be described as follows:

1. Notice of loss
2. Coverage verification
3. Investigation
4. Evaluation
5. Settlement

At each step, claim representatives rely on their knowledge and experience to identify which information is relevant both to the policyholder's claim and to the insurer's subsequent chances of recovery. A thorough understanding of coverages and of the rights and obligations of the insured and the insurer forms the basis for their analysis. Familiarity with statutes, regulations, and court decisions pertaining to claims and salvage rights helps claim representatives to select and implement the best option for each claim situation.

Notice of Loss

Policies include requirements relating to the notice of loss, such as the following:

- Method of notice (how to notify the insurer of a loss)
- Source of notice (who notifies the insurer of a loss)
- Substance of notice (what information to include in a notice of loss)
- Time of notice (when to notify the insurer of a loss)

The insurer will verify that the policyholder has complied with these provisions. Legislation requires the insurer to promptly acknowledge receipt of a notice of loss. Sometimes the insurer needs to take action on a claim before having had the opportunity to verify that the policyholder has complied with the notice-of-loss provisions. In this case, the claim representative acknowledges receipt of the notice of loss and reserves any issue or potential issue relating to compliance with the notice-of-loss requirements.

Method of Notice

Policyholders are required to notify the agent or the insurer of a loss as soon as possible. Policyholders often report losses by telephone or the notice might be made in writing. Legislation requires the insurer to promptly acknowledge receipt of any notice of loss. The insurer promptly sends a written acknowledgement that includes the name of the person who reported the loss.

Source of Notice

Policies stipulate that the policyholder is expected to give notice of loss. However, sometimes other authorized parties, such as insurance agents or lawyers, can do so. An unauthorized notice might come from a variety of sources, such as a disgruntled former partner or co-owner or from an affiliated company that is not insured under the policy. A notice of loss received from an unauthorized source is not sufficient. A claim representative who receives such a notice of loss should verify it with the policyholder.

Substance of Notice

A loss is "discovered" when the policyholder first becomes aware of facts that would lead a reasonable person to assume that a loss covered by the policy has occurred. The policyholder must believe that a covered loss has occurred. Mere suspicion is not enough. Therefore, a notice of loss reporting that a policyholder is investigating the possibility of employee dishonesty is not sufficient.

The notice of loss should include information such as the following:

- Who the insured is and who sustained the loss
- When the events causing the loss occurred
- What events caused or contributed to the loss
- What events caused the loss to be discovered
- When the loss was discovered
- The amount of loss claimed to be caused by employee dishonesty
- What steps the insured has taken to reduce or recover the loss

When the notice of loss does not include these details, the claim representative investigates to resolve the data deficiencies, as described later in this chapter.

Time of Notice

Policies require the policyholder to give notice of loss "as soon as possible" and might further stipulate that it must be within thirty days after discovery of the loss. What constitutes notice "as soon as possible" depends on the circumstances of each loss. Some states might allow an insurer to deny the claim if the insurer's rights are prejudiced by a long delay in reporting the loss. Realistically, the insurer often does not know the date of discovery of the loss and is therefore unable to determine the timeliness of the notice.

Prompt notice of loss helps the insurer investigate and evaluate claims while information is current, memories are fresh, and documentation is readily available. It also helps the insurer to identify and preserve its right of recovery from the dishonest employee or other sources.

Although policyholders generally report losses under other forms of insurance, such as fire or auto insurance, immediately, that is not the case in fidelity claims. Fidelity claims might not be submitted until after the policyholder has completed an investigation and after the culprits have been fired.

Coverage Verification

After receipt of a notice of loss, the claim representative verifies that a policy is in force that provides coverage for the type of loss reported. The claim representative can usually verify coverage from the underwriting file by referring to the policy itself. Occasionally, policies insure against losses caused by individuals who are not the policyholder's employees, but independent contractors working for the policyholder. The Servicing Contractor's Rider is an example. In this case, the claim representative examines the contract between the policyholder and the contractor to determine the nature and scope of the contractor's duties and obligations and to assist in the verification of applicable coverage.

Insured

Some policies specify that the first named insured acts for all named insureds. When a policy names several insureds, some or all of whom have sustained a common loss, the insurer usually makes claim payments to only the first named insured. This allows the insurer to settle a claim without concern that other insureds will file competing claims.

Ownership of Property

Most policies apply to any of the following:

- Loss of property owned by the policyholder
- Loss of property held by the policyholder in any capacity
- Loss of property for which the insured is legally liable

However, this coverage is not intended to give rights to third parties, and some policies specifically state that the coverage is for the sole use and benefit of the named insureds. In addition, the courts do not recognize unnamed third parties as beneficiaries of the coverage unless the policy clearly expresses intent to do so.

Alter Ego or Sole Representative

In its legal sense, the expression "alter ego" refers to one person or entity that is the legal equivalent of another. In practical terms, an alter ego is a person who is in such complete control of an organization that the distinction between it and the individual blurs. For example, a person with the majority or total ownership of a company who exercises such command and influence that the board of directors has effectively no authority would be considered the company's alter ego.

A sole representative is similar to an alter ego in that the individual has exclusive authority to manage an organization's affairs. The difference between a sole representative and an alter ego is that a sole representative need not be a controlling owner.

Because alter egos and sole representatives are an inextricable part of the organizations they control, the law sees the individual and the organization as one and the same. Knowledge or actions of its alter ego or sole representative are attributed to the organization. Therefore, the policy provides no coverage for a loss that results from a dishonest act on the part of a policyholder's alter ego or sole representative.

The reasons for this lack of coverage are as follows:

- The dishonest act is attributed to the policyholder.
- Coverage for a wrongdoer terminates at the moment the policyholder becomes aware of the dishonest act.
- An alter ego or sole representative is not under the direction or control of the organization and so does not fall within the definition of employee.
- The wrongdoer rarely informs the insurer of the dishonest act, so the defenses of late notice, late filing of a proof of loss, and late filing of legal proceedings become available.

Underwriters scrutinize any potential alter ego or sole representative situation closely to evaluate and manage the exposure. Claim representatives thoroughly investigate any losses involving alter egos or sole representatives, and insurers have been successful in denying coverage in these situations.

Definition of "Employee"

As described in other chapters, policies vary in how they define the term "employee." A policy might be endorsed to include others (such as volunteers) as employees. In the case of a loss, the claim representative examines payroll records, time sheets, employment contracts, billing and payment records, or other documents to verify that the person accused of dishonesty is an employee within the terms of the policy. Information obtained from the policyholder's staff also assists the claim representative in confirming that the culprit is an employee.

Directors or Trustees Generally Excluded

Fidelity policies usually exclude the dishonest acts of directors or trustees because they are not employees. However, coverage might be available in the following situations:

- If a director or trustee commits a dishonest act while authorized by the policyholder to assume the duties of an "employee"
- If a director or trustee commits a dishonest act in his or her capacity as a committee member within the policyholder's organization

For example, a director acting as a member of a loan committee of a financial institution might be covered if he or she approved a loan dishonestly. In either case, the claim representative reviews the policy, endorsements, records, and documentation, such as payroll information or committee meeting minutes, to confirm the status of the director or trustee.

Other People Who Might Be Covered

Fidelity policies might expand the definition of employee to cover other people in specific situations, for example, "a guest student pursuing studies or duties" or "an attorney retained by the insured and an employee of such attorney while either is performing legal services for the insured." These and other individuals performing specific services for the policyholder might be covered as employees under the terms and provisions of the policy. The claim representative determines whether an individual comes within the definition based on the policy definition and evidence of the relationship provided by the policyholder.

Loss Caused by Dishonesty

Under employee dishonesty coverage, it is not sufficient to prove that the policyholder has incurred a loss and that an employee has been dishonest. Coverage applies only when the policyholder demonstrates that the loss was the direct result of the employee's dishonest act. This is referred to as proof of **causation** and is the basis of the insuring agreement. For example, a policyholder proves that it has an inventory shortage and that an inventory clerk is dishonest. However, this does not prove causation because the inventory shortage might have resulted from a record-keeping error in the accounting department. In each case, the claim representative reviews the evidence presented by the policyholder to evaluate whether or not causation has been established.

As described in Chapter 2, employee dishonesty policies are specific in their definitions of dishonesty. Most standard forms limit coverage to those losses for which the policyholder can demonstrate manifest intent on the part of the wrongdoer. Incompetence, negligence, misjudgment, or disobedience—intentional or not—do not constitute manifest intent.

Some policies limit coverage by stipulating that the financial benefit to the employee exceeds a certain amount or that other conditions must be met. For example, under Form No. 24 losses resulting directly or indirectly from loans must exceed $2,500 and the employee must have colluded with other parties to the transaction. Claim representatives must thoroughly review the policy provisions and apply them to the facts of the claim.

Time of Loss

As described in previous chapters, coverage can be written on a discovery basis or on a loss-sustained basis. The claim representative first determines the basis of the policyholder's coverage and any additional provisions. The next step is to establish when the loss occurred and when it was discovered and then determine whether coverage applies.

For example, to verify coverage under the Loss Sustained During Prior Insurance provision, the claim representative confirms the following:

- That there was no gap between the prior and current policies
- That the prior policy would have covered the loss
- That the loss occurred during the prior policy's coverage period
- That the discovery period of the prior policy had expired when the loss was discovered
- That the current policy would have covered the loss if it had been in force

Discovery of Loss

Coverage is based not only on when the loss occurred but also on the discovery of that loss. The discovery form and the loss sustained form cover losses discovered during the policy period under certain conditions as described in Chapter 2. Thus, establishing the date of discovery of a loss is an important part of a claim representative's investigation.

The date a loss is discovered affects more than the availability of coverage. Discovery also activates policyholder obligations to give notice of loss to the insurer, file a proof of loss, and file a legal action within a specified time period.

The claim representative reviews the policy to determine what constitutes actual discovery. Comparing policy provisions to the facts of the loss helps the claim representative to fix the date of discovery.

Exclusions

Claim representatives check policy exclusions to ensure that the loss is covered. Exclusions discussed earlier in this text eliminate coverage for acts of the named insured or partners; employees canceled under prior insurance; and inventory shortages.

The inventory shortages exclusion is important when an insured claims an employee theft or dishonesty loss because of an inventory shortage based on a physical inventory and profit-and-loss computation. Apparent inventory shortages can result from the causes listed in Exhibit 6-1. Such shortages exist because of inadequate record keeping rather than an actual inventory loss.

EXHIBIT 6-1

Causes of Apparent Inventory Shortages

- Errors in count when receiving, shipping, or transferring material or when taking a physical inventory
- Failure to adjust records to agree with the actual physical count of the previous inventory
- Failure to record material returned to vendors, shipped out for display, used as samples, or on consignment
- Failure to record material received, shipped, sold, or transferred to another location
- Errors or changes in pricing, such as markups and markdowns
- Incompetent or indifferent personnel
- Short-cutting or netting purchase bills against sales invoices to a customer who is also a supplier, resulting in transaction information that becomes lost or forgotten

Real inventory shortages occur for different reasons. Some causes of real inventory shortages are shown in Exhibit 6-2.

EXHIBIT 6-2

Causes of Real Inventory Shortages

- Shoplifting or theft by third parties, such as employees of an independently contracted guard service
- Damaged, spoiled, or destroyed material that is not properly accounted for
- Failure to open cartons and count the actual goods received
- Duplicate payments to vendors or payments to vendors for goods not received
- Duplication of deliveries to customers
- Shipments lost because of deliveries to wrong addresses or pilfering in transit
- Material incorrectly labeled
- Failure to include material packed and on the shipping dock in the current inventory account
- Failure to record material disposed of by gift
- Failure to record the difference in sales price and the cost price when material is disposed of at less than cost
- Scattered, misplaced, or forgotten merchandise

The existence of a shortage does not prove employee theft or dishonesty even when the loss is so large that bookkeeping errors are an unlikely cause. In addition, the theft of one or more items is not proof of the theft of many items. Actual evidence of employee theft or dishonesty is required to support a recoverable inventory shortage claim.

In inventory shortage losses, the claim representative reviews the policyholder's inventory practices. Examination of the procedures used to record, control, and measure inventory helps the claim representative evaluate the effectiveness of those procedures and the credibility of the policyholder's inventory records. The absence of deficiencies does not prove that the loss resulted from employee theft or dishonesty.

Despite an insurer's best efforts, the cause and amount of inventory shortage losses sometimes remain uncertain. Inventory records can be used as one piece of evidence to prove the amount of a loss. However, other records should support the claim and an accounting consultant might examine records to help determine the amount of the loss. If significant deficiencies exist in the policyholder's inventory practices, the insurer might choose to deny coverage. If the policyholder pursues an action against the insurer, detailed presentation of deficiencies might convince the court in the insurer's favor. Despite the inventory shortages exclusion, some courts have allowed inventory records into evidence in situations in which policyholders have proved employee theft or dishonesty. Thus, if evidence of employee theft or dishonesty exists, an insurer might negotiate a settlement with the policyholder, taking into account the inventory shortages exclusion.

Termination or Cancellation of Coverage

A claim representative confirms that coverage under the policy has not been terminated or canceled. Policies or coverages can terminate or cancel for a variety of reasons including the following:

- The policyholder canceled the policy.
- The policyholder requested the deletion of one or more named insureds.
- The policyholder deleted coverage for one or more employees.
- The policy expired.
- The insurer canceled the policy for underwriting reasons or nonpayment.
- Coverage for an employee automatically terminated when the insurer learned of a dishonest or fraudulent act committed by that employee.
- The policyholder was taken over by another institution; by a conservator, receiver, or other liquidator; or by state or federal officials.
- The policyholder failed to notify the insurer of a change in ownership.
- The insurer paid losses up to the aggregate limit of the policy.

The policy describes the requirements for cancellation or termination of coverage, and the claim representative confirms that the insurer and the policyholder have met the appropriate terms and conditions relating to cancellation or termination.

Right of Rescission

A claim representative's investigation might reveal that the policyholder materially misrepresented information to obtain the policy. The insurer might be entitled to rescind coverage because of a material misrepresentation on the part of the policyholder. The right of rescission exists under the following circumstances:

- When the insurer would not have issued the policy, renewed it, increased limits, or provided specific coverage knowing the true nature and extent of the loss exposure; and
- When the insurer can prove that the policyholder intentionally misrepresented the nature and extent of the loss exposure.

Proving misrepresentation on the part of a policyholder involves the following:

- Detailed investigation
- Careful consideration of the facts
- Close consultation with underwriting
- Reference to applicable law and precedent
- Review of any contract warranty or provision relating to misrepresentation

Such an investigation can strain the relationship between the insurer and the policyholder and, if the allegation proves incorrect, the claim representative might have difficulty settling the original claim. Even when a reasonable case can be made for rescission, courts might hesitate to find in the insurer's favor.

Reservation of Rights

Insurers are required to promptly acknowledge receipt of a notice of loss, usually before having had the opportunity to verify coverage or investigate. As a result, the insurer's acknowledgement includes a sentence or paragraph designed to protect the insurer's interests. This **reservation of rights** advises the policyholder that acknowledgement of the notice of loss or investigation of the claim does not constitute acceptance of liability or waiver of the insurer's right to deny the claim later based on the claim representative's investigation.

Insurers develop standard wordings for acknowledgements, reservations of rights, and other claim documents. Exhibit 6-3 is a typical acknowledgement letter. The insurer's broad reservation of rights is found in the last sentence.

During the course of an investigation, coverage questions can arise or the claim representative might require further evidence to support the policyholder's claim. Insurers develop and use reservation of rights letters to inform the policyholder of specific deficiencies in information, inconsistencies between the established facts and available coverage, and any limitation, exclusion, or defense that affects the policyholder's claim. Some issues commonly raised in reservation of rights letters include the following:

- Timely discovery of the loss
- Time of occurrence of the loss

EXHIBIT 6-3

Acknowledgement and Reservation of Rights

This will acknowledge receipt of your letter dated _____ , received in this office on _____ , wherein you state that _____ may have incurred a loss caused by employee dishonesty. In all future correspondence, please make reference to the above claim number.

In connection with that claim, enclosed are three (3) copies of <surety company name> Proof of Loss Under Fidelity Bond forms. These forms should be completed in as much detail as possible on the face of the form itself with documentation supporting your claim attached to each form. Also, please note that a statement of the manner in which the loss was sustained should be placed on the second page of each form. If the space provided on the second page is insufficient to completely relate the manner in which the loss was sustained, you should attach additional pages (as required) for your statement. I also call your attention to the additional instructions for making proof contained on the second page.

Upon completion of these forms and attachment of the requested documentation, these forms should be signed by an authorized representative of your company, notarized, and then two of these forms returned to me at the above address. The third form is for your own records.

In addition to the completion of the forms and the documentation supporting your loss, we would appreciate being provided with the following information on the employee or employees you state are involved in this matter:

1. The full name, address and telephone number of the employee or employees which you allege are responsible for the loss
2. A photocopy of the employee's or employees' withholding exemption certificate
3. A photocopy of the employee's or employees' application for employment
4. A photocopy of the police report, indictment, or other relevant information that you may be in possession of in connection with this matter
5. The exact date and circumstances under which you became aware of the alleged dishonest acts

Should you have any problems or questions concerning the completion of these forms, please contact me. Please note that these forms are provided without waiver of or prejudice to any of the rights and defenses, past or present, known or unknown which <surety company name> may have in connection with the above referenced Bond.

Very truly yours,

_____

Adapted from material provided by Fidelity and Deposit Company of Maryland.

- Timely filing of proof of loss forms
- Timely filing of legal proceedings
- Termination of coverage for a particular employee
- Relationship of the accused to the policyholder (such as alter ego or sole representative)
- Loss amount
- Loss causation

Proof of Loss Forms

Most policies require that the policyholder complete and submit detailed proof of loss. The policyholder is responsible for the information it contains. The insurer's acknowledgement of the policyholder's notice of loss might include a proof of loss form as in Exhibit 6-3. Other insurers might complete an initial investigation and verification of coverage before requesting proof of loss forms. Exhibit 6-4 illustrates a typical proof of loss form.

Essential Elements

The essential elements of a detailed proof of loss under a fidelity bond include the following:

- An assertion that a dishonest act was committed by an employee or other covered person
- An assertion that the dishonest act was the direct cause of a loss to the policyholder
- A description of the events leading to the loss
- A description of the items lost and their values

Proper Execution and Timely Filing

Policies require that proof of loss forms be completed and submitted properly. The claim representative reviews the forms to verify that the policyholder has met these requirements, including the following.

- That the proof of loss was completed by the policyholder or a properly appointed successor or assignee, such as a receiver
- That the proof of loss was filed within the period of time specified in the policy, usually 120 days from the date of discovery
- That the proof of loss has been sworn to, if required

Time Extensions for Proof of Loss Forms

Occasionally a policyholder is delayed in completing and submitting a proof of loss form and requests a time extension. In determining whether to grant an extension, the claim representative considers the following:

- Whether the insurer would be prejudiced in any way as a result of the delay
- Whether an insurer's prospective rights against others would be diminished or legally barred by time restrictions
- Whether the claim representative's opportunities to gather facts would be hampered or lost

EXHIBIT 6-4

Proof of Loss

Proof of Loss Under Fidelity Bond

_____ presents claim for loss under Bond
(Name of Claimant)

No. _____, issued on behalf of or covering _____

of _____ from and after the _____

day of _____ and in the amount of $_____ employed in the

position of _____ at _____

DETAILED STATEMENT OF CLAIM
(Attach original vouchers)

Date	Description of Item	Amount	Total

TOTAL LOSS

Credits
By salary or commission
Other credits (including securities, notes, offset, etc.)
TOTAL CREDITS
NET LOSS

State amount of the security, indemnity, or security against loss held in addition to aforementioned bond
_____.

I hereby certify the above statement is true and correct in every respect; that (I, we, or this company) _____ sustained a loss in the amount above stated through the dishonesty of _____ employed as _____; that (I, we, or this company) _____ has/have not accepted any security for or on account of same and that there are no counterclaims, offsets or credits of any nature whatsoever other than those appearing in the statements above; and that (I, we, or this company) _____ has/have fully complied with all the conditions of the aforementioned bond issued by (surety company name) _____.

Subscribed and sworn to before me this

_____ day of   _____
_____ Year   Official Capacity

_____
Notary Public

STATEMENT OF MANNER IN WHICH LOSS SUSTAINED

INSTRUCTIONS FOR MAKING PROOF

Statement of loss should be itemized, showing the names, dates, amounts, and descriptions of individual items of money, securities, or property, misappropriated, stolen, or embezzled, as nearly as can be ascertained, and if representing collections made, the dates, names, and addresses of the persons, firms, or corporations from which the collections were made.

Attach to proof all original vouchers, if possible, otherwise verified copies of same and any further evidence in explanation of support of the amount or amounts for which claim is made.

Adapted from material provided by Fidelity and Deposit Company of Maryland.

If the insurer agrees to grant a time extension, the claim representative makes specific reference to the overdue proof of loss forms in the reservation of rights letter and includes either the new deadline for submission of the forms or a provision for termination of the extension by the insurer. An approved delay in the submission of proof of loss forms does not relieve the policyholder of his or her duties to investigate the loss, to cooperate with the insurer, to protect his or her rights, and to pursue all appropriate methods of recovery. Granting the extension should not be construed as a waiver of the insurer's rights.

Investigation

The investigation focuses on establishing whether a claim is valid. The insured's duties following a loss aid in investigation. Although the policyholder must prove its right of recovery, the information the policyholder provides might be insufficient. Claim representatives can seek information from other sources, such as employees, former employees, bankers, legal or financial advisers, customers, or suppliers of the policyholder. Inquiries and requests are other methods for obtaining information.

Insured's Duties After Loss

In addition to notifying the insurer, insureds are required to do the following after a loss:

- Submit to an examination under oath
- Give the insurer a sworn proof of loss
- Produce all pertinent records
- Cooperate in all matters relating to the claim

These requirements stem from the fact that there is rarely an alternative source from which the insurer can obtain the information. Many documents relevant to the claim are in the policyholder's control. Cooperation is important because the circumstances surrounding employee theft or dishonesty can be disagreeable. The insured might not want to be involved in the investigation, especially if the suspected culprit was a trusted employee. However, policy provisions require that the insured cooperate in all matters relating to the claim. To satisfy its duties after a loss, the policyholder must identify the employee misconduct and present specific evidence compiled to demonstrate the following:

- That the claim comes within the coverage
- That the amount claimed is accurate and supported by appropriate documentation
- That the date of discovery or occurrence of the loss was within the required time period
- That the policyholder has complied with all policy requirements

Data Deficiencies

After receiving the proof of loss, the claim representative compares the policyholder's allegations with the evidence provided to identify deficiencies in the information presented. Resolving these deficiencies is one objective of the claim representative's investigation. Based on information presented in the proof of loss form, the claim representative might believe that no coverage exists or that there are coverage issues that the policyholder has not anticipated. In this case, the claim representative sends a reservation of rights letter and reviews the situation with the policyholder to determine whether information in the proof of loss requires correction or clarification.

Sufficiency of the information in the proof of loss varies based on the details of the loss. Proof of loss forms often contain insufficient information regarding the following:

- Specific details of the dishonest conduct
- Evidence on which the allegation of theft or dishonesty is based
- Evidence of manifest intent on the part of the alleged wrongdoer (if the policy covers employee dishonesty instead of employee theft)
- Proof of the amount of the loss
- Proof of causation between the dishonesty and the loss

For example, if a proof of loss fails to identify the thief, the proof of loss might be insufficient. Relying solely on accounting records to prove an inventory theft claim or providing only original receipts to prove the value of ten-year-old property could also be insufficient.

The claim representative advises the policyholder in writing of data deficiencies. This helps the policyholder determine what additional documentation to submit in support of the claim. For example, the policyholder might submit current appraisals of the property to supplement the original receipts and to support the amount of the loss.

Sources of Information

Four sources of information are people, documents, policies, and procedures. These sources of information help claim representatives gather the information needed to investigate the claim.

People

Individuals throughout the policyholder's organization can be excellent resources during the claim representative's investigation. Co-workers, supervisors, accounting staff, or others might provide valuable information or might have participated in the discovery of the loss. Others might have been unwittingly involved, such as a coworker who innocently processed a fraudulent loan approved by the wrongdoer. Individuals outside the organization, such as bankers, auditors, customers, or suppliers, can often shed light on the circumstances surrounding a loss.

The claim representative contacts the policyholder or other individuals by telephone, in person, or by correspondence. Telephone contacts are efficient for asking specific questions or providing simple explanations. When more detailed fact-finding or discussion is required, interviews or meetings are effective. To request large volumes of information that might take the policyholder some time to assemble, claim representatives generally send written inquiries. The claim representative documents each contact in the claim file by memo or by including a copy of follow-up correspondence. Follow-up correspondence records the issues discussed, the positions taken, agreements or disagreements between the policyholder and the insurer, action items, and an appropriate reservation of rights if necessary. In the planning, timing, and conduct of an interview, the claim representative is cautious not to appear to accept liability or to relieve the policyholder of its obligations to file a proof of loss, investigate, and prove the validity of its claim.

Although the policyholder must cooperate with the insurer, no other party is bound to provide evidence or to give information and often individuals are reluctant to do so. Tact and understanding help put others at ease. As a courtesy and to facilitate the meetings, the claim representative generally notifies the policyholder before meeting with others or with the employee or employees accused of dishonesty. Discretion is important, particularly when interviewing the alleged wrongdoer. The accused might sue the policyholder, the insurer, or both. To reduce the risk of the accused filing suit, the claim representative begins any interview with the accused wrongdoer by stating that the insurer has reached no conclusions and is simply gathering information. The following case illustrates how carefully losses under crime policies must be investigated to avoid lawsuits.

FOR FURTHER THOUGHT

Suspected Embezzlement

A general manager of a store was suspected of embezzling petty cash funds. Three company employees met with the general manager to investigate the incident. The general manager was fired because he failed to cooperate with the investigation. The three company investigators made statements about the fired general manager to several other employees during the course of the investigation. In addition, the new general manager made remarks about the situation to two applicants for job openings and to several friends of the fired general manager who called the store. The fired general manager sued the store for intentional infliction of emotional distress and several counts of defamation. The court granted the store's motion for summary judgment. On appeal, the court affirmed the summary judgment on the intentional infliction of emotional distress claim and one count of defamation. The remaining counts of defamation were reversed and remanded to the district court for additional proceedings.

Adapted from Starr v. Pearle Vision, Inc. 54 F. 3d 1548 (10th Cir. 1995).

Documents

The claim representative examines a wide variety of business documents provided by the policyholder to establish the validity of its claim and to prove the amount of the loss. Documents might be paper or electronic and could include the following:

- Reports
- Minutes
- Invoices
- Transaction records
- Memos
- Audits
- Financial statements
- Financial instruments
- Correspondence
- Accounts
- Inventory records
- Employment records

Policies

Most organizations have established policies that describe how business is conducted, how employees do their jobs, or the basis on which business decisions are made. Policies might be documented in policy manuals, directives, employment handbooks, job descriptions, or an organization's mission statement. For example, an employment handbook might require employees to decline gifts from customers. Policies help the claim representative identify the standard of behavior or performance required of the alleged wrongdoer. In the case of a policy covering employee dishonesty, this might help to establish whether the employee demonstrated manifest intent as required by the policy wording.

Procedures

Procedures describe how policies are implemented. For example, if company policy states that all customer orders are to be filled within twenty-four hours, the related procedure describes the actual steps involved in the order-filling process. An organization's procedures include processes for internal and accounting control. A review of the policyholder's procedures helps the claim representative identify the limits, restrictions, and authority within which the alleged wrongdoer worked.

Inquiries and Requests (I&Rs)

In addition to obtaining information through telephone or in person, the claim representative might send the policyholder formal, written requests for specific details. These letters are referred to as **inquiries and requests (I&Rs)**. The claim representative uses I&Rs to resolve data deficiencies in the policyholder's proof of loss, to request large volumes of information that might take the policyholder some time to assemble, or to clarify for the policyholder what evidence is required to establish the validity of a claim. I&Rs help establish and document claim issues that might have been lacking in the notice of loss or that have been raised through investigation.

Advantages

The advantages of I&Rs include the following:

- I&Rs help avoid potential inefficiencies, misunderstandings, and oversights that can result from oral communication.
- I&Rs provide a clear record of the course of an investigation, the information sought, and the evidence supplied.

- I&Rs help the claim representative complete an orderly, logical analysis of coverage, liability, and the details of the case.
- I&Rs guide the policyholder through the process of proving its loss.

Formation

The purpose of I&Rs is to establish and document evidence supporting a claim. Although some questions are common to many investigations, I&Rs are usually tailored to fit specific claim situations. The claim representative avoids using general questions or questions that allow for a "yes" or "no" response. This reduces the need for follow-up questions or the potential for misunderstanding. As information is developed, additional I&Rs might be required for clarification or to pursue a previously unrecognized aspect of a claim.

Precise, detailed questions generate information that is more complete and informative. Exhibit 6-5 lists examples of ineffective and effective questions.

EXHIBIT 6-5

Ineffective and Effective I&R Questions

Ineffective Question	Effective Question
How did you calculate the loss?	Provide the calculation that you used to determine your loss, including each credit and debit factor, the amount, and a description.
Who is (name of person)?	Explain (name of person's) participation in the events that brought about your loss.
Have you filed criminal charges?	What, if any, criminal charges have been filed against the employee, and where were they filed?

Evaluation

The claim representative reviews each claim to establish the amount of the loss that the policyholder has sustained. The loss is based on the evidence the policyholder provides. The portion of that loss that is collectible under the policy is based on the terms and conditions of the policy and the circumstances of the claim. Policy provisions can exclude losses or portions of losses for a variety of reasons, including the following:

- The loss sustained exceeds the limits of the policy, or a deductible applies.
- The loss was not sustained during the coverage period of the policy.
- The loss was not discovered during the required period.
- An excluded employee, alter ego, or sole representative caused the loss.
- The loss is not of the type intended to be covered—for example, lost profit on misappropriated assets.

- The policyholder did not comply with the terms and conditions of the policy relating to notice of loss, proof of loss, or other policyholder obligations.

In addition to clarifying whether a loss is collectible, policy provisions specify how the available coverage applies. For example, limits might apply per loss or per employee. The policy wording determines the portion, if any, of the loss sustained that represents a recoverable loss.

After a loss is discovered, the amount of the loss will not continue to grow. For example, a claim asserting that an employee has embezzled funds is based on past activities that cannot be changed. The insured has probably discharged the employee, and the amount of funds that the employee embezzled will not increase. However, the extent of the loss that has already occurred might not be fully known. For example, an insured might think the loss is $10,000 but find on further investigation that the loss is much larger.

Settlement

Claim representatives attempt to settle claims through negotiation. Settlements with other responsible parties might affect the final settlement. If negotiation is not successful, claims might be litigated.

Settlements Between Insureds and Others

If a policyholder has rights of recovery against another party and has reached a proposed settlement with that party, the insurer considers the proposed settlement before concluding the claim. The insurer might acquire the insured's recovery rights against the other party if the insurer makes a payment on the claim. Thus, the insurer wants to make sure that the proposed settlement is satisfactory. The insurer in this situation should verify that:

- The release does not release, waive, or diminish the insured's rights against any other parties from whom the insurer would have rights if it were to make a claim payment.
- The information in the settlement proposal has been verified and the information is accurate.
- The insured is satisfied that the proposal is the best settlement available.
- The settlement will reduce the insured's claim.
- The insured understands that the insurer's claim payment might be reduced because of the settlement.

Litigation Management

Despite an insurer's best efforts to settle, some claims result in litigation. The policyholder may sue the insurer as a result of disputes over coverage or the amount of the loss. If the claim cannot be resolved before trial, effective claim management improves the insurer's prospects of a successful defense and helps minimize the expenses associated with a suit. The claim representative continues to be responsible for management of the claim, working closely with lawyers, accountants, or other professionals; reviewing legal papers; discussing policy provisions or possible defenses with the lawyers; and maintaining a well-documented claim file.

Settlement Opportunities

Being sued by the policyholder does not preclude the claim representative from continuing attempts to settle. During the litigation process, the claim representative continues to watch for opportunities to reach agreement with the policyholder. In identifying potential settlement opportunities, the claim representative considers how settlement might affect factors such as the following:

- The insurer's subrogation rights
- Demands relating to the claim to which the insurer might become exposed
- Pending litigation in which the insurer is not involved, but which is related to the claim

Settlement Offer

If a policyholder agrees to settle rather than proceed to trial, the insurer makes a formal, written settlement offer through the policyholder's lawyer. The settlement offer sets out the terms of the agreement and the amount the insurer will pay to the policyholder. Any additional arrangements regarding salvage rights, related losses, or other matters are described in detail. To protect the insurer against further demands, and to ensure that settlement does not prevent the insurer from enforcing the terms and conditions of the policy in any subsequent loss or claim, the offer includes the following conditions:

- That the insurer reserves issues of fact, law, coverage, and liability
- That settlement does not relieve the policyholder from its obligation to prove a recoverable claim or the insurer's right to deny a claim
- That the policyholder cannot disclose the details of the offer except in legal proceedings between it and the insurer
- That acceptance of the settlement by the policyholder releases the insurer from any further claims or demands related to the loss in question
- That the policyholder will sign an appropriate release and not proceed with litigation against the insurer
- That the insurer is entitled to receive its share of recoveries
- That each party bears its own costs and expenses

RIGHTS OF RECOVERY

Generally, the law and policy provisions stipulate that when an insurer pays a claim, the policyholder's right of recovery from third parties passes to the insurer. This transfer of rights can result from subrogation or assignment. Subrogation and assignment allow the insurer to recover some or all of the amount paid and prevent policyholders from profiting from a loss. Some policies expressly provide for the allocation of recoveries between the insurer and the policyholder.

Subrogation

The policyholder has the right to recover from the dishonest employee, from any other person who collaborated with the employee, and occasionally from others. This recovery might take the form of payment or the acquisition of rights to property. As part of claim management, the claim representative identifies and investigates all avenues of recovery, deducts recoveries made by the policyholder from the loss settlement, and ensures that the insurer's recovery rights are protected. When an insurer pays a claim, it can reserve the right of subrogation according to the terms of the policy.

Assignment

Assignment is similar to subrogation in that the policyholder transfers its rights to the insurer when the insurer has paid a claim. Assignment is sometimes referred to as "contractual subrogation" because the policyholder's transfer of rights to the insurer is accomplished through a written agreement that specifies their respective rights to recovery. Assignment allows the insurer to recover payments made to the policyholder and prevents the policyholder from profiting from its loss by collecting from both the wrongdoer and the insurer.

Choosing a Course of Action for Recovery

After identifying potential sources of recovery, the claim representative evaluates the options available to determine the best course of action. Although recovery rights might exist, in some situations the insurer might elect not to pursue them. Considerations involved in choosing a course of action for recovery include the following:

- The financial position of the culprit. If the wrongdoer is bankrupt, the insurer might not recover any of the loss.
- The costs of pursuing a recovery. If the costs to pursue a recovery exceed the amount recovered, the insurer has little incentive for incurring expenses.
- The likelihood of successful recovery. If there is little chance of success, an insurer might choose not to pursue a course of recovery.
- The quality of evidence supporting a recovery. If evidence is sufficient to prove a loss but might not be sufficient to recover from a wrongdoer, the insurer might choose not to pursue a course of recovery.

Some avenues of recovery are subject to limitation periods. Policyholders might begin legal proceedings during the claim settlement process to avoid losing a recovery right. Cooperation between the insurer and the policyholder helps to ensure that the legal action does not hinder the insurer's subsequent ability to recover.

SUMMARY

Claim management's general objectives are:

1. To investigate the claim and fulfill the insurer's obligation to the policyholder promptly and fairly
2. To control loss and loss adjustment expenses, including recovering losses and expenses from third parties when possible
3. To protect the insured's and the insurer's interests by applying policy terms, conditions, limits, and defenses appropriately

Maintaining claim files and complying with unfair claim settlement practices acts are additional claim responsibilities.

Claims typically proceed through five phases:

- Notice of loss
- Coverage verification
- Investigation
- Evaluation
- Settlement

In the first phase, the policyholder submits a notice of loss to the insurer. Insurers are required to acknowledge receipt of notice of loss promptly. If the notice of loss meets the requirements in the policy, the insurer verifies coverage. The objective is to determine whether a policy is in force that provides coverage for the type of loss reported. Coverage verification confirms many facts relating to the policyholder, the employee who caused the loss, the time of the loss and its discovery, exclusions, termination or cancellation of coverage, rights of rescission, reservation of rights, and the proof of loss.

Investigation corrects data deficiencies. The claim representative interviews people, examines documents, and analyzes policies and procedures to evaluate whether the policyholder has proved the recoverability of its loss. I&Rs provide valuable information during investigation.

Claim representatives evaluate claims to determine the amount of the loss and the amount recoverable under the policy.

Despite an insurer's best efforts to settle, some claims result in litigation. In this case, the claim representative continues to manage the claim and attempts to settle with the policyholder.

After a claim is paid, the policyholder's rights of recovery from third parties are transferred to the insurer through subrogation or assignment. Throughout the claim process, the claim representative works to identify and protect potential avenues of recovery.

Index

Abbreviations
ERISA Employee Retirement Income Security Act of 1974
ISO Insurance Services Office, Inc.
SAA Surety Association of America
UL Underwriters Laboratories Inc.

Page references in boldface refer to definitions of key words or phrases.

A

ACORD Commercial Insurance Application, 4.3–4.4
ACORD Crime Section, 4.5–4.6
Agents, as source of underwriting information, 4.11
Alarm systems, 5.7–5.13, 5.15
   central station, 5.12
   with direct lines to police, 5.13
   evaluation of, 5.12
   local, 5.11, 5.12
   unique to financial institutions, 5.13
Alteration, 1.13–1.14
Application, crime insurance, 4.2–4.10
Area protection devices, **5.10**, 5.11
Asset quality ratio, 4.20, 4.23
Assignment, rights of recovery and, 6.23
Audit procedures and controls, application and, 4.9
Audits
   external, 4.31–4.32
   internal, 4.32–4.33
   underwriting computer fraud and, 5.21

B

Bait money, 6.18
Bankers Blanket Bond, **3.2**
Blanket coverage, employee theft, schedule coverage versus, 1.7
Board of directors, as additional underwriting consideration, 4.17
Bonds
   other financial institution bonds and policies, 3.13–3.15
   for other financial institutions, 3.9–3.13
   Standard Form No. 24, 3.2–3.9
Bond term, Standard Form No. 24 and, 3.8
Brokers, as source of underwriting information, 4.11
Building security, underwriting and, 5.1–5.2, 5.3
Burglar-resistive money chests, **5.4**
Burglar-resistive safes, **5.4**
Burglary, **2.7**
Business plan, as additional underwriting consideration, 4.16–4.17

C

Cameras, for security, 5.14
Cancellation of commercial crime insurance, 1.8–1.9
   as to any employee, 1.8–1.9
   automatic, 1.9
   by insurer, 1.9
Capital
   equity, **4.20**
   primary, **4.20**
Capital ratio
   equity, 4.19–4.20
   primary, 4.20
   underwriting and, 4.19–4.20
Cash-handling procedures, 5.17–5.18
Causation, **6.8**
Central station alarms, 5.12
Claim files, 6.2–6.3
Claim handling, 6.1–6.24
Claim management, 6.1–6.3
   claim files and, 6.2–6.3
   general objectives of, 6.2
Claim process, 6.4–6.22
Claims conditions, ISO crime forms, 2.17–2.19
Clients' property, optional ISO crime coverage of, 2.1–2.2
Combination Safe Depository Policy for Financial Institutions, **3.15**
Commercial crime insurance, 1.1–2.28
   limits of, 1.7–1.8
   overview of, 1.1–1.3
   special conditions of, 1.8–1.11
Computer Crime Policy for Financial Institutions, 3.13, **3.14**–3.15
Computer fraud, **1.20**–1.21
   crime exclusion of, 1.29
   rating and, 5.28
   underwriting considerations of, 5.18–5.22
Computer systems, Standard Form No. 24 and, 3.6
Consolidation—Merger condition, ISO crime forms, 2.16–2.17
Containers, damage to, Inside the Premises—Theft of Money and Securities, 1.15
Control procedures, employee/theft loss control and, 4.31–4.37
Corporation, as form of ownership, **4.13**–4.14
Counterfeit currency, Standard Form No. 24 and, 3.5
Coverage trigger, Standard Form No. 24 and, 3.8
Coverage verification, 6.6–6.16
   definition of "employee" and 6.7–6.8
   discovery of loss and, 6.9
   exclusions and, 6.9–6.11
   insured and, 6.6–6.7
   loss caused by dishonesty and, 6.8–6.9
   proof of loss forms and, 6.14–6.16
   reservation of rights and, **6.12**–6.14
   right of recision and, 6.12
   termination or cancellation of coverage and, 6.11
   time of loss and, 6.9
Coverages, application and, 4.2
Covered causes of loss
   employee theft and, 1.4–1.7
   under Inside the Premises — Robbery or Safe Burglary of Other Property, 1.16–1.18
Covered property, and employee theft, 1.7
   Money, **1.7**
   Other property, **1.7**
   Securities, **1.7**

Crime insuring agreements
   basic, 1.3–1.22
   exclusions, 1.22–1.29
   optional, 2.1–2.11
Crime policy conditions, 2.11–2.19
Crime risk control, 1.2
Criminal conviction, employee theft coverage and, 1.5
Custodian, robbery of, 1.16–1.18

D

Damage to premises, Inside the Premises—Theft of Money and Securities, 1.15
Data communication security, as computer fraud underwriting consideration, 5.22
Data control, as computer fraud underwriting consideration, 5.21
Deductibles
   application and, 4.2
   and ISO crime forms, 2.18
   Standard Form No. 24 and, 3.8
Direct verifications, **4.36**–4.37
Directors and officers, employee theft coverage of, 1.6–1.7
Discovery form, **2.11**, 2.14–2.16
   loss sustained form versus, 2.11–2.16
Dishonest act, 2.20–2.21
Door switches, **5.8**
Dual control, **4.35**
   enforcement of, 4.35
Duties in the event of loss, ISO crime claims condition and, 2.17
Dye packages, for security, 5.14

E

Economic environment, as additional underwriting consideration, 4.16
Employee, as defined in employee theft coverage, **1.5**
Employee benefit plans, employee theft coverage as part of, 1.10
Employee dishonesty coverage, **2.20**–2.23
   financial benefits, 2.21–2.22
Employee monitoring and surveillance, 4.37
Employee theft, and rating, 5.27
Employee Theft—Name or Position Schedule, optional ISO crime coverage of, 2.8–2.9

Employee theft coverage, **1.4**–1.12
   coverage territory, 1.11
   enhancements to, 1.11
   exclusions, 1.24–1.26
   persons excluded from, 1.6
Employee theft/dishonesty exposures, 4.26–4.28
Employee theft/dishonesty loss control, 4.28–4.37
Employee turnover and termination, 4.30–4.31
Endorsements, application and, 4.2
Equity capital, **4.20**
Equity ratios, **4.23**–4.24
ERISA fidelity bonding requirements, 1.12
Evaluation, claim, 6.20–6.21
Excess Bank Employee Dishonesty Bond, Form 28, **3.13**
Exclusions, to crime insuring agreements, 1.22–1.29
Experience rating, **5.26**
External auditing, as computer fraud underwriting consideration, 5.21
External audits, 4.31–4.32
Extortion, **2.4**–2.5
   optional ISO crime coverage of, 2.4
Extortion exclusion, Standard Form No. 24 and, 3.4
Extortion underwriting considerations, 5.22–5.25

F

Faithful performance of duty coverage, **2.19**
Fidelity, Standard Form No. 24 and, 3.3
Financial Institution Bond Form No. 25, **3.11**–3.12
Financial institution bonds, **3.1**–3.30
   rating and, 5.28
Financial institution liquidity ratios, 4.24
Financial reports, as source of underwriting information, 4.10–4.11
Financial strength, as additional underwriting consideration, 4.18–4.19
Fire-resistive safes, **5.4**
Fog, for security, 5.14
Foil, metallic, **5.9**
Forgery, **3.5**
Forgery or alteration
   insuring agreement for, 1.13–1.14
   rating and, 5.27
   Standard Form No. 24 and, 3.5

Form 14 for broker/dealers, **3.9**–3.11
   coverage for partners, 3.9–3.10
   insuring agreements of, 3.10
   other provisions of, 3.10–3.11
Form 15 for mortgage bankers and finance companies, **3.12**–3.13
Form 23 for credit unions, **3.13**
Form 28, Excess Bank Employee Dishonesty Bond, **3.13**
Fraud committed by supervisors or managers, 4.27–4.28
Funds transfer fraud, **2.4**
   optional ISO crime coverage of, 2.4

G

Guards, for security, 5.16
Guests' Property, optional ISO crime coverage of, 2.10–2.11

H

Hiring practices, 4.28–4.30
   as computer fraud underwriting consideration, 5.18, 5.20–5.21
   crime history, 4.29
   debt history, 4.28
   educational qualifications, 4.29
   employment history, 4.28–4.29
   hobbies and activities, 4.29
   motor vehicle records, 4.29
   progression of responsibility, 4.29
   substance abuse history, 4.29
Historical growth, as additional underwriting consideration, 4.16
Human resource procedures, employee/theft loss control and, 4.28–4.31

I

In transit coverage, Standard Form No. 24 and, 3.4
Indemnification condition, **2.19**
Infrared detectors, **5.11**
Inside the Premises—Robbery or Burglary of Other Property, optional ISO crime coverage of, 2.6–2.7
Inside the Premises—Robbery or Safe Burglary of Money and Securities, optional ISO crime coverage of, 2.7–2.8

Inside the Premises—Robbery or Safe Burglary of Other Property, **1.16**–1.19
    coverage extensions of, 1.18
    rating and, 5.27
    special limit of insurance for, 1.18
Inside the Premises—Theft of Money and Securities, **1.14**–1.16
    rating and, 5.27
Inside the Premises—Theft of Other Property, optional ISO crime coverage of, 2.5–2.6
Insurance company liquidity ratios, 4.24–4.25
Insurer multipliers, 5.26
Intent, manifest, 2.21
Interests insured, ISO crime forms, 2.16–2.17
Internal auditing, as computer fraud underwriting consideration, 5.21
Internal audits, 4.32–4.33
Inventory tags, for security, 5.14, 5.16
Investigation, claim, 6.16–6.20
    data deficiencies and, 6.16–6.17
    inquiries and requests (I&Rs) and, 6.19–6.20
    insured's duties after loss and, 6.16
    sources of information and, 6.17–6.19
ISO crime endorsements, 2.25–2.28
ISO crime forms and policies, 1.3
ISO safe and vault classification, 5.6–5.7

J

Joint Insured condition, ISO crime forms, 2.16
Joint venture, as form of ownership, **4.14**

K

Kidnap and ransom insurance, 2.5

L

Lacing, **5.9**
Lessees of Safe Deposit Boxes, optional ISO crime coverage of, 2.9–2.10
Limits and deductibles, 5.26

Limits of liability
    application and, 4.2
    Standard Form No. 24 and, 3.4
Liquidity ratios, **4.24**–4.25
Loan exclusion, Standard Form No. 24 and, 3.6
Loan-loss-reserve-to-nonperforming-assets ratio, **4.23**
Local alarms, 5.11, 5.12
Loss costs, 5.25
    prospective, **5.25**
Loss history, application and, 4.10
Loss sustained form, **2.11**, 2.12–2.14
    discovery form versus, 2.11–2.16

M

Management, as additional underwriting consideration, 4.17
Mandatory vacations, 4.36
Manifest intent, 2.21
Messenger protection, 5.17
Metallic foil, **5.9**
Microwave detectors, **5.11**
Mirrors, for security, 5.14
Money, as covered property, **1.7**
Money chests, 5.2–5.7
    burglar-resistive, **5.4**
Money orders and counterfeit paper currency, **1.21**–1.22
    rating and, 5.28

N

Name schedule, **2.8**
Named insured and location, application and, 4.2
Nonperforming-assets-to-total-assets ratio, **4.23**
Notice of loss
    claim process and, 6.4–6.6
    Standard Form No. 24 and, 3.8–3.9

O

Object protection devices, **5.10**, 5.12
On premises coverage, Standard Form No. 24 and, 3.3–3.4
Organizational structure, as underwriting consideration, 4.15
Other documents, as source of underwriting information, 4.11–4.12

Other Insurance condition, ISO crime forms, 2.19
Other organizational forms, 4.14
Other property, **1.7**
Outside the premises
    employee theft insuring agreement for, **1.19**–1.20
    rating and, 5.27
Ownership, as underwriting consideration, 4.12–4.15

P

Partnership, as form of ownership, **4.12**–4.13
"Per loss" versus "per employee" coverage, 1.8
Perimeter protection devices, **5.8**–5.10
Personnel evaluation and salary administration, 4.30
Personnel management, as computer fraud underwriting consideration, 5.18, 5.20–5.21
Personnel training, 4.30
Photoelectric devices, **5.10**
Physical security, as computer fraud underwriting consideration, 5.22
Physical security considerations, 5.1–5.18
Policy bridge endorsement, **2.15**–2.16
Position schedule, **2.8**
Pricing, 5.25–5.28
Primary capital, **4.20**
Property contained in customers' safe deposit boxes exclusion, Standard Form No. 24 and, 3.4
Prospective loss costs, **5.25**

R

Ratio
    asset quality, 4.20, 4.23
    equity, **4.23**–4.24
    equity capital, 4.19–4.20
    liquidity, **4.24**–4.25
    loan-loss-reserve-to-nonperforming-assets, **4.23**
    nonperforming-assets-to-total-assets, **4.23**
    primary capital, 4.20
Rating, pricing and, 5.26–5.28
Rating factors, application and, 4.8–4.9
Records condition, ISO crime forms, 2.17

Recoveries, ISO crime forms, 2.18
Red flags, investigating, 4.29
Riders for SAA financial institution bonds and policies, 3.17–3.30
Rights of recovery, 6.22–6.23
Robbery of a watchperson, 2.7
Rogue trading, 3.7
Rotation of duties, 4.36

S

SAA Crime Protection Policy, 2.20, 2.23
SAA financial institution forms, 3.2
Safe burglary, 1.18
Safe depository, optional ISO crime coverage of, 2.11
Safes, 5.2–5.7
    burglar-resistive, **5.4**
    fire-resistive, **5.4**
Schedule coverage, employee theft, blanket coverage versus, 1.7
Security
    data communication, 5.22
    physical, 5.22
    software, 5.22
Securities, **1.7**
    Standard Form No. 24 and, 3.5
Securities Deposited With Others, optional ISO crime coverage of, 2.10
Securities firm liquidity ratios, 4.25

Separation of duties, 4.33–4.35
Settlement, claim, 6.21–6.22
    between insureds and others, 6.21
    litigation management and, 6.21–6.22
Signals, for security, 5.18
Software security, as computer fraud underwriting consideration, 5.22
Sole proprietorship, as form of ownership, **4.12**–4.13
Standard Form No. 24, **3.2**–3.9
    exclusions to, 3.6–3.7
    insuring agreements for, 3.6
Subrogation
    ISO crime forms and, 2.19
    rights of recovery and, 6.23
Supplemental information, as source of underwriting information, 4.10
System procedures, as computer fraud underwriting consideration, 5.21

T

Tear gas, for security, 5.14
Temporary employees, employee theft coverage of, 1.5–1.6
Term management letter, **4.11**
Territory, employee theft, 1.10–1.11
Theft, **1.4**–1.5
Trading exclusion, Standard Form No. 24 and, 3.6
Trusted employees, 4.26–4.27

U

UL, 5.3–5.4
    labels of, 5.4–5.5
    tests and requirements of, 5.5
Ultrasonic detectors, **5.11**
Uncollected funds exclusions, Standard Form No. 24 and, 3.7
Underinsured employee theft losses, 1.12
Unfair claim settlement practices acts, **6.3**–6.4
Uninsured crime losses, 4.7
Underwriting considerations, 4.12–4.25
Underwriting information, sources of, 4.1–4.12
Underwriting and loss control, 4.1–5.29

V

Valuation—settlement, ISO crime forms and, 2.17
Vaults, 5.2–**5.7**
    classification of, 5.7

W

Watchpersons, for security, 5.16
Wooden screens, **5.9**